Men in German Uniform

Men in German Uniform
POWs in America during World War II

Antonio Thompson

LEGACIES OF WAR ⚬ G. KURT PIEHLER, SERIES EDITOR

The University of Tennessee Press • Knoxville

The Legacies of War series presents a variety of works—from scholarly monographs to memoirs—that examine the impact of war on society, both in the United States and globally. The wide scope of the series might include war's effects on civilian populations, its lingering consequences for veterans, and the role of individual nations and the international community in confronting genocide and other injustices born of war.

Copyright © 2010 by The University of Tennessee Press / Knoxville.
All Rights Reserved. Manufactured in the United States of America.
First Edition.

The paper in this book meets the requirements of American National Standards Institute / National Information Standards Organization specification Z39.48-1992 (Permanence of Paper). It contains 30 percent post-consumer waste and is certified by the Forest Stewardship Council.

Library of Congress Cataloging-in-Publication Data

Thompson, Antonio.
Men in German uniform: POWs in America during World War II / Antonio Thompson. — 1st ed.
    p. cm. — (Legacies of war)
Includes bibliographical references and index.
ISBN-13: 978-1-57233-728-2 (hardcover: alk. paper)
ISBN-10: 1-57233-728-1 (hardcover: alk. paper)

1. World War, 1939–1945—Prisoners and prisons, American.
2. Prisoners of war—United States—History—20th century.
3. Prisoners of war—Germany—History—20th century.
4. Soldiers—Germany—History—20th century.
5. Germans—United States—History—20th century.
6. World War, 1939–1945—Concentration camps—United States.
7. World War, 1939–1945—United States.
I. Title.

D805.U5T455 2010
940.54'727308931—dc22   2010019337

*This book is dedicated to my wife, Amy,
and my three children, Madeline, Julian, and Sophia.
My love for all of you is immeasurable.*

Contents

Foreword   ix
   G. Kurt Piehler, Series Editor
Preface   xi

1. Housing the Enemy: Prisoner of War Administration and Camp Construction   1
2. *Sprechen Sie Deutsch?* From Recruitment in the Third Reich to Incarceration in the United States   15
3. Igniting the Powder Keg: Nazi Influence within the Camps and the Last Acts of Defiance among POWs   37
4. Love Thy Enemy: Coddling, Segregating, and Fraternizing with German POWs   55
5. The Devil Is in the Details: German POW Labor and the American Home Front   77
6. Idle Hands: Recreation and Intellectual Diversion behind Barbed Wire   103
7. Exorcising the Beast: The Reeducation of German POWs in the United States   117
8. Leaving a Place Called Amerika   129

Notes   135
Bibliography   159
Index   175

Illustrations

Following page 71

Colonel George Chescheir, U.S. POW Camp Commander at Fort Benning, GA
Colonel George Chescheir and the POW School at Fort Benning, GA
POWs Boarding the Train at Fort Knox, KY
POW-Constructed Model Castle at Camp Ruston, LA
Examples of Barbed Wire Surrounding Camp
POW Buying Cigarettes at the Canteen at Fort Benning, GA
POW-Constructed Stadium Model, Camp Ruston, LA
Yugoslavian POWs Housed at Camp Ruston, LA
POWs Working in the Kitchen at Fort Knox, KY
POWs Carving Turkey at Fort Benning, GA
POWs Shopping at the Canteen at Fort Knox, KY

Foreword

World War II was a horrific war. Not only did millions die on the battlefield, but the regimes of Nazi Germany, Fascist Italy, and Imperial Japan also waged war on civilians. Germany engaged in a campaign of systematic genocide aimed at exterminating European Jewry and enslaving the Slavic populations of Eastern Europe. Soviet soldiers captured by the Germans were often summarily executed or faced brutal imprisonment in camps that provided little food or medical care. In turn, the Soviet Union reciprocated with similarly harsh treatment of German POWs. Most died in captivity, and those who survived would not see home until the mid-1950s. Japan never developed a systematic policy of genocide; yet it committed scores of atrocities against the occupied peoples of Asia, beginning with China. Historians have characterized the struggle in the Pacific as a war without mercy in which Japanese forces visited brutal treatment on American and other Allied prisoners of war. Forced marches, summary executions, starvation diets, forced labor, and inadequate medical care took a horrendous toll on those taken captive by the Japanese.

In a war marked by terror bombing of civilian populations, blockades that deprived belligerents of food, and death camps, there remained islands of humanity and places where the rule of law prevailed. International law developed after World War I prohibited the use of poison gas on the battlefield, and all belligerents in the war observed this prohibition with the exception of Japan in China. Despite the unspeakable cruelty of the Nazis toward the occupied peoples of Europe, they adhered to the Geneva Convention in their treatment of American and British Commonwealth prisoners of war. As a result, Americans held in German POW camps received regular inspections by the International Red Cross, lived in barracks that met basic standards for health and safety, and generally received regular (if spartan) food rations as well as the life-saving Red Cross packages containing food and medicine. Perhaps most important, they were allowed to correspond with families at home.

German adherence to the Geneva Convention was not a one-way street but mirrored the decision of the United States government to scrupulously follow international law in its treatment of captured German POWs. As Antonio Thompson's work demonstrates, providing for the transportation, housing, and feeding of approximately 371,000 German prisoners of war was a massive undertaking, especially considering that the regular American army numbered less than 200,000 in 1939. Thompson reveals in depth how the army built an elaborate system of prison camps across the United States, all while mobilizing for total war and putting millions of Americans in uniform. It conscientiously adhered to the letter and spirit of the Geneva Convention, which insisted that German POWs receive living quarters comparable to those of American GIs and rations equal to those of average soldiers. While German POWs were not pampered, they enjoyed a diet that allowed many to gain weight, and they were imprisoned in a part of the world safe from aerial attack.

The United States reaped benefits from treating German POWs humanely. Although captured officers could not be compelled to work, enlisted men provided much-needed labor on American farms, especially during harvests. There were a number of diehard Nazis who bristled at their imprisonment, and the military struggled to identify and isolate them, as well as protect German POWs who opposed National Socialism. But most POWs became complacent, and this is reflected in the relatively few attempts at escape or violent resistance to camp policies. As a result, German POWs working outside of prison camps could be lightly guarded, and soldiers assigned to watch them consisted of those too young, too old, or physically unfit to serve abroad. Moreover, the U.S. Army's reputation for good treatment of POWs encouraged many Germans to surrender, especially in the closing months of the war. Although systematic denazification efforts adopted in 1945 had, at best, marginal impact on changing the ideological leanings of the imprisoned, the overall policies of the army did influence the worldview of many German captives and certainly contributed to postwar reconciliation between West Germany and the United States.

The policies of the United States during World War II toward POWs remains a remarkable example of adherence to the rule of law and humanity in the midst of a horrendous war. Not only does Thompson's fine study serve to remind us of some of the good that occurred during this conflict, but it also will help inform current debates on how to treat enemy combatants captured in the struggle against terrorism that followed the attacks of September 11, 2001.

G. Kurt Piehler
The University of Tennessee

Preface

Only four works broadly examine the German POW topic. Judith M. Gansberg first covered it in her 1977 work *Stalag: U.S.A. The Remarkable Story of German POWs in America*. Although she examined the POW program in its entirety, the bulk of her research and the real value of her work concerned reeducation.[1] Arnold Krammer soon followed with *Nazi Prisoners of War in America* in 1979. Krammer drew together numerous primary and secondary sources to present a detailed overview of the program.[2] In 1981, Ronald H. Bailey released his book, *Prisoners of War*. Bailey's work, published by *Time-Life*, discussed the treatment of soldiers from all Axis and Allied nations captured during World War II, with one chapter on the Germans in America. Lewis H. Carlson published the most recent overview in 1997, titled *We Were Each Other's Prisoners: An Oral History of World War II American and German Prisoners of War*. Carlson allowed American and German POWs to tell their own captivity narratives and to "achieve a dignity and importance not found in traditional history books."[3] Using interviews, he followed thirty-four American and German POWs to contrast their experiences from the time of capture to eventual release.

Several other works address specific topics concerning the POW program or examine it at the regional, state, or local level. Some of the most important of these studies are Allen V. Koop's *Stark Decency: German Prisoners of War in a New England Village*, a 1988 examination of the Camp Stark, New Hampshire, POW camp; Allan Kent Powell's *Splinters of a Nation: German Prisoners of War in Utah*, published in 1989, which told of Utah's experience housing nearly eight thousand German POWs; and Robert D. Billinger Jr.'s *Hitler's Soldiers in the Sunshine State: German POWs in Florida*, published in 2000. Billinger's second work, *Nazi POWs in the Tar Heel State* (2008) is another example of a state-level study. I contributed a state-level study in 2008 with *German Jackboots on Kentucky Bluegrass: Housing German Prisoners of War in Kentucky, 1942–1946*. Two other noteworthy studies are John Hammond Moore's *The Faustball Tunnel: German POWs in America and Their Great Escape*, which appeared in 1978, and Ron Robin's *The Barbed-Wire College: Reeducating German POWs in the United States during World War II*, published in 1995.

Men in German Uniform: POWs in America during World War II relies heavily upon primary government documents. It also incorporates the existing secondary literature and oral history to provide a fresh and up-to-date look at the housing of German POWs within the United States during World War II.

This work makes two major arguments. I first argue that despite severe difficulties faced in every aspect of the prisoner of war program, and although exceptions existed, the United States adhered to and exceeded its obligations under the Geneva Convention of 1929 in handling its German prisoners of war. Each chapter demonstrates how the United States overcame major obstacles to create a program that set a national precedent and high international standards by providing treatment that met and even exceeded its Geneva Convention requirements. The United States struggled to maintain these principles even though success was not ensured. POWs in the United States had living facilities equivalent to those of U.S. soldiers, as required by the Geneva Convention. When such facilities were not available, both the POWs and the soldiers guarding them had to do without. The administrative system that handled the program, criticized for being a large and cumbersome bureaucratic network, performed as a system of checks and balances ensuring compliance with the Geneva Convention and War Department policy.

Even when problems of nationality or ideology erupted within the camps, the United States did not resort to force or violence to stifle them but took the more expensive path of screening and segregating the men. When difficulties arose in developing the labor programs, negotiating contracts, and dealing with recalcitrant POW laborers, officials worked to ensure an equitable and swift outcome. Although these solutions often went through several channels and revisions, the lessons learned could be applied to future difficulties. In fact, the recreation programs provide nearly irrefutable proof that U.S. officials went above and beyond the requirements of Geneva in its treatment of German POWs. The Geneva Convention contained few provisions regarding recreation and religious facilities, yet the War Department and its cooperating agencies provided, in many ways, more opportunities for these men behind barbed wire than existed in the Third Reich. One could ask, were these difficulties worth it? U.S. history and national pride demanded it, international law required it, and American POWs in German hands needed the nation to uphold these obligations. The positive treatment of POWs led some German soldiers to surrender to the United States and made more productive workers of them.

Another reason centered on the idea of reciprocity. A large number of American soldiers remained in German hands until the end of the war. While some may argue the contrary, and exceptions certainly exist, Germany attempted to maintain Geneva standards concerning its American prisoners. The Third Reich, however, kept tabs on the U.S. program and how its prisoners were being treated, as it did with all Allied programs, through Red Cross intermediaries. The United States was aware that any deviation from these standards could bring reciprocal action by the German government upon the Americans being held as POWs within the Reich.

The proper handling of Axis prisoners of war also held future foreign policy implications. Prior to the end of World War II, the United States realized the vital role that Germany and the other Axis nations would play in the postwar world. The United States hoped that imparting favorable impressions of America on the prisoners of war and their proper treatment in the United States, including a belated reeducation program, would pay dividends in the postwar world and the subsequent occupation of Germany.[4]

The secondary argument in this work is closely tied to its title, *Men in German Uniform*. The men captured in German uniform represented a conglomeration of many of the European and Asian peoples. Severe manpower shortages after the invasion of the Soviet Union and recruitment policies of both the Wehrmacht and the SS led to troops being recruited from Allied, neutral, and conquered nations alike. Additionally, as the war dragged on, the Germans began recruiting from among their own old, young, criminal, and politically undesirable elements. While the bulk of the forces captured were of German nationality, it was not uncommon to find Ukrainian, Romanian, or Mongolian prisoners side by side with Polish or French POWs, all wearing German uniforms and all in U.S.-operated prisoner of war camps. This often volatile mixture, noted by few at the time or since, created a second layer of difficulty in implementing and controlling the program.

This work collectively demonstrates the ability of a modern nation to provide exemplary treatment to bitter enemies in a time of national crisis and global war. While other belligerents, such as the Soviet Union or the Japanese, chose to treat their prisoners with brutality, resorting to the use of torture, starvation, and even murder, the United States chose the higher moral ground. It should be noted that the Geneva Convention bound only those who signed the treaty. Citizens of Axis nations living in the United States were subject to being interned but were not held in prisoner of war camps and, with perhaps a few exceptions, were not mixed with POWs. U.S. policy makers interpreted vague clauses of the Convention in a way that benefited the prisoners and never lost sight of the idea of reciprocity, future foreign policy concerns, and the basic concept of humane treatment for one's fellow man. Of course, it must be noted that, as with all policy, there was sometimes deviation between those creating it and those implementing it. Nevertheless, this timely study should serve as an example to future generations that, while difficult, it is possible for any nation to provide its captive enemy with humane treatment while maintaining security and mutual dignity for both the captive and the captor.

Chapter 1

Housing the Enemy: Prisoner of War Administration and Camp Construction

Between 1941 and 1945, about 425,000 Axis prisoners of war entered captivity in the United States. This large influx created huge demands for a nation already taxed with conducting a two-front war. The first POW entered the United States on December 7, 1941, and by the end of World War II, the country held more prisoners inside its own territory than it had or would in any conflict before or after.[1] This unprecedented feat is all the more remarkable considering that at the beginning of the war no facilities existed for housing POWs, and by its end, more than six hundred camps held captives. Prior to the arrival of the prisoners, an administrative system had to be created, communication networks between government agencies established, and the actual camps constructed. All this had to be done with little planning prior to 1942 and in light of the fact that POWs were entering U.S. custody in increasing numbers beginning that year. That the United States created this vast number of POW camps and the administrative apparatus for a successful POW program is a credit to American ingenuity, but difficulties arose nearly every step of the way.[2]

The United States relied on the untested Geneva Convention of 1929 to provide guidelines for POW care.[3] Several military and civilian agencies made up the administrative system that would implement these plans, which consisted of a mixture of prewar planning, continual modifications, cooperation, and compromise. The Military Police Corps (MPC), which had manned the POW camps in World War I (1914–1918), was disbanded and not reestablished until 1924. Their role in handling war prisoners was not defined until the publication of the 1937 military police basic manual by the War Department. The manual also planned for a new Office of the Provost Marshal General (PMGO), which had also disbanded at the end of World War I, and defined the roles of the War Department's Personnel Division (G-1) and the Adjutant General's Office.[4]

In the summer of 1941, with estimates that nearly 20,000 civilian enemy aliens would be interned if the United States entered the war, the military put the 1937 plans into effect. Major General Allen W. Guillion, judge advocate general, received a promotion to head the reestablished PMGO. The PMGO, with assistance from the MPC, the Office of the Judge Advocate General, and G-1, had responsibility for all interned civilian enemy aliens and POWs.[5]

Later that year the roles of these agencies became more defined. G-1 planned the enemy alien and prisoner of war internment policies and programs, and the PMGO created and implemented policy. The Department of Justice provided assistance, but mostly with the detention of civilians. This administrative organization seemed adequate to the task in 1941 and requested approval to construct the first three camps. The War Department, however, refused to begin construction because of "lack of funds."[6] On the morning of December 8, 1941, with the first POW in American hands and estimates that the United States would imprison thousands of the enemy, the nation entered the war without facilities or adequate plans to handle the flood of POWs that would soon arrive.

At the urging of Secretary of War Henry L. Stimson and Army Chief of Staff General George C. Marshall, the War Department underwent a complete reorganization the next year. The attack on Pearl Harbor and the realities of modern war forced the issue. By the spring of 1942, the War Department had created three new divisions: the Army Service Forces (ASF), Army Air Forces (AAF), and Army Ground Forces (AGF).

The ASF, headed by General Brehon B. Somervell, created a "unified supply and service command" that cooperated with civilian agencies to meet the supply, transportation, construction, and other needs of the War Department.[7] Once operational, the ASF had "duties in addition to its functions of procurement and supply," but "these duties were not precisely defined, several overlapped, and some were susceptible of elastic interpretation."[8] Included among these responsibilities were "the supervision and execution of War Department policies to make effective the provisions of the Geneva Conventions."[9] Essentially, this meant that the ASF now controlled all prisoner of war issues. Unfortunately, this wasn't made immediately clear to the other agencies involved in the POW program.

The War Department began attaching several existing departments to the ASF as well as creating new ones to be placed under it. This caused difficulties for Somervell, as "he simply received command authority over various agencies, each of which retained its separate identities and many of which retained a degree of autonomy."[10] Under the 1942 War Department Organization, nine service commands were created to replace the previous division of the United States into corps areas.[11] The service commands operated under the ASF and implemented policy formulated by the ASF, G-1, and the PMGO and also ensured that individual camp commanders within their jurisdiction understood this policy.[12] Throughout 1942, the ASF had to be continually restructured to clear up the jumble of conflicting, confusing, and overlapping authorities.

G-1, which was not subordinate to the ASF but cooperated with them, still had jurisdiction over much of what the ASF now controlled, and therefore plans and orders were often duplicated, changed, or canceled by accident and because of negligence. G-1 planned policy throughout the POW program, except for a brief period from March 1942 to April 1943 when reorganization caused confusion and G-1 allowed the PMGO to exercise this power.[13] While G-1's authority in some respects overlapped with the functions of both the ASF and the PMGO, it was nominally on an equal footing with the ASF. The PMGO, on the other hand, sought approval for policy formulation and implementation from both agencies. Despite this chain of command and frequent and close communications among these three departments, a great deal of confusion still existed in the administration and operation of the POW program.[14]

The PMGO also went through restructuring and, while now subordinate to the ASF rather than G-1, often acted independently and on equal footing with the ASF as a result of unclear lines of authority. Once placed under the ASF, the responsibilities of the PMGO grew, and the department expanded to include nine divisions and their constituent departments, furthering the mushrooming administrative structure. The PMGO's burgeoning responsibilities included formulating policy, implementing War Department policy regarding POWs, interacting with belligerent and protecting powers regarding POWs, and working with military and civilian agencies concerning the operation of the POW program.[15] The degree of the responsibility of the provost marshal general (PMG) over the prisoner of war program and his level of subordination and cooperation to the ASF and with G-1 varied throughout the war.

Several major changes implemented the next year streamlined the role of the PMGO. In 1943 the first large numbers of prisoners of war entered U.S. custody, and planners determined that regulations and facilities should separate enemy aliens and POWs. The Department of Justice, in an agreement with the War Department, assumed responsibility and jurisdiction for all civilian internees. The PMGO had been operating both the Prisoner of War Division and the Aliens Division and now could devote more of its focus to the POW operations. The PMG received assistance with his expanded responsibility through the appointment of Brigadier General Blackshear M. Bryan as assistant provost marshal general. Bryan headed both the Prisoner of War Division and the Military Police Division.[16] Bryan saw his own responsibility grow as more captured enemy soldiers entered the United States. The Prisoner of War Division expanded and reorganized on December 11, 1944, into the Prisoner of War Operations Division.[17]

Once the policies had been created, they were disseminated to the service commanders, who further ensured distribution and compliance among the individual POW camps. Two general guidelines issued in 1943 governed specifics of control and responsibility at the camp level. The first stated that "prisoner of war camps will be operated under the direction and supervision of the Commanding General of the appropriate Service Command in accordance with War Department regulations and directives."[18] The second stated that "the camp commander under the jurisdiction of the post commander, if any, will command the camp and be responsible for its operation, administration, management, and the control and treatment of the prisoners of war in his care."[19] Some POW camps existed as autonomous entities constructed for the sole purpose of housing prisoners of war. Others used space on existing military facilities.

Cooperating Administrative Systems

The War Department depended on several other agencies for assistance with the POW program, and they often provided a necessary check and balance to War Department planning and actions. The War Manpower Commission (WMC) and War Food Administration, for example, were instrumental in creating and facilitating the POW labor program. The Federal Bureau of Investigation (FBI) cooperated with state and local police forces in protecting the American people and home front facilities from harm by escaped POWs. Legal matters concerning prisoners of war, especially in the case of criminal activities, fell to the judge advocate general. Religious groups such as the Young Men's Christian Association (YMCA) and the Lutheran Commission played important roles in the spiritual lives of the POWs and in donating recreational equipment. Representatives from the Red Cross, the International Red Cross (IRC), and the Swiss Legation visited the camps.

The State Department, however, was the most important agency outside the War Department in the prisoner of war program. It monitored U.S. adherence to the Geneva Convention and acted as the liaison between the War

Department and foreign representatives concerning POW treatment. This responsibility forced the State Department to expand and create a branch devoted specifically to the POW program in 1942. A new Internees Section of the Special War Problems Division was responsible for U.S. soldiers and citizens held by the enemy and for enemy aliens and POWs in American hands.[20] Interestingly, it was headed for a time by Edmund Guillion, son of Allen W. Guillion, the provost marshal general.[21]

The Internees Section had several important responsibilities concerning POWs held by the United States. The Swiss served as the protecting power for the Germans, and Internees Section agents accompanied Swiss officials when they toured U.S. POW camps. POWs and elected spokespersons also spoke privately with Swiss agents, and a report of the findings of these meetings went to both the United States and Germany.

Members of the Internees Section also conducted individual tours of POW camps to ensure that the prisoners of war were "humanely treated and protected."[22] Graham H. Stuart, a State Department official, boasted that many of the camps operated by the United States "have received the highest commendation from the neutral representatives."[23] A typical report included "the adequacy of clothing, medical, and recreational facilities" and the "general conditions of the camp, [and] how these conditions meet the provisions of the Convention."[24]

Representatives of the Internees Section investigated all concerns and complaints of the agents of the protecting power and of the POWs. Complaints, investigations, and recommendations had to be forwarded to the U.S. State and War Departments and to the Swiss government. According to Internees Section member John Brown Mason, rather than complaining, the POWs more often were interested in "the so-called Afrika bonus, proxy marriages, divorces, acknowledgments of paternity, requests for validation of promotions on the battlefield just before capture, recognition as protected personnel, powers of attorney, wills, and other documents addressed to the German authorities."[25]

The completion of a working and cooperative administrative structure for the prisoner of war program was underscored by the pressing need to house POWs. While the administrative structure was being drawn up, reorganized, and completed, mostly through 1942, major U.S. military operations had not yet begun. The fact that the United States only captured one POW in 1941, Japanese mini-submarine pilot Kazuo Sakamaki, and by August of 1942 held a total of only sixty-five POWs (fifty-five German and ten Italian) led some officials to believe that camp construction was not pressing.[26] Yet the War Department had already issued orders that any future prisoners of war taken by U.S. forces would be transferred to U.S. territory, where they could be housed more affordably and efficiently under the Geneva guidelines. Another sudden change occurred in the fall of 1942 when the British asked if the United States would take an emergency shipment of as many as 175,000 of its prisoners of war over the next few months.[27] The British government was already strained providing for over 280,000 Axis POWs. The United States was at first inclined to accept only 50,000 but after much consideration agreed to the full number, provided they were divided into smaller groups and advance notice of no less than one month was given before these men were transferred.[28]

Organization and Dissemination of Policy Concerning the POW Program

Branches of the War Department, the State Department, civilian agencies, the IRC, and the Swiss government all communicated with one another through various forms of correspondence. Voluminous memorandums, ASF Circulars, War Department pamphlets and memos, Red Cross bulletins, Prisoner of War Circulars, and other paper trails notified government agencies and camp officials of program changes, provided clarifications of policies, and registered complaints and noncompliance.

The April 22, 1942, War Department manual, *Civilian Enemy Aliens and Prisoners of War,* set forth the first set of comprehensive guidelines for handling POWs. The manual, prepared at the request of Stimson and signed by Marshall, resulted from the collaboration of the War Department, the ASF, the PMGO, the Joint Chiefs of Staff, and the Joint Staff Planners.[29] It regulated the activities of the MPC in POW detention, handling, and housing, including matters related to clothing, food, bedding, medical care, morale, and religious and intellectual needs. The 1942 manual provided a blueprint for adhering to the 1929 Geneva Convention but could not anticipate all the problems that would be encountered. Although it set standards for handling POWs by providing for the most humane treatment possible, it relied mainly on the World War I experience of housing POWs in foreign territory. A clause that "considered portions of the alien and prisoner of war programs as being interchangeable" presented another shortcoming.[30] It also predated the first U.S. offensives and the arrival of the British POWs, and therefore its provisions remained untested. Continual program changes that dictated frequent updates of the 1942 manual further confused matters as a paper trail of overlapping, and often contradictory, regulations increased.[31]

The first update appeared on September 24, 1943. The War Department Prisoner of War Circular No. 1, "Regulations Governing Prisoners of War," provided only slight revisions with a decreased focus on enemy aliens. An entire series of Prisoner of War Circulars poured from the War Department over the next three years: ten in 1943, fifty-four in 1944, and fifteen in 1945.[32] Adding to this muddle of policy statements were numerous ASF Circulars, memos from the War Department, policy implementation questions and correspondence from service commanders and camp commanders, and queries and proposals from other agencies. New correspondence or policy often updated previous ones, but it was difficult to differentiate between new and outdated policies, as well as those that countermanded each other or new laws. Policy planning, implementation, and interpretation of the Geneva Convention often created mass confusion.

The War Department publication Technical Manual 19-500 in September 1944 solved many of these problems. It received regular updates "by the publication of change sheets or by the substitution of new pages. Therefore, there was no necessity for cross-referencing."[33] It represented the most successful attempt by the War Department to keep track of changes and combine them into one relatively current source. The constant contact and close cooperation among the ASF, G-1, and the PMGO helped prevent even more confusion at the upper echelons of the program. The PMGO took extra steps by conducting visits to service commanders and individual camps, and by holding conferences.[34]

Prisoner of War Camp Construction Program

At the beginning of U.S. involvement in World War II, no facilities existed for the housing of prisoners of war. Prewar plans approved by the secretary of war and attorney general on July 18, 1941, authorized the construction of three internment camps, with space for up to 3,000 enemy aliens. When the war began for the United States on December 7, 1941, work on these facilities continued. On December 8, 1941, the service commands received authorization and funds from the War Department to begin over a dozen more camps, primarily for the housing of enemy civilians.[35] Planning and construction proceeded rapidly during 1942, since existing facilities could house only 32,000 men and the War Department reserved these buildings solely for enemy aliens. Current production, even if hurried, would create only 22,500 more beds. These numbers fell far short of the proposed shipments from Britain, not to mention the modest number of enemy aliens and POWs already in U.S. custody. These numbers did not take into account future POWs and enemy aliens. The housing for both groups still fell under the purview of the ASF.³⁶

Continued pressure to provide housing in 1942 forced the War Department to work out an agreement with the Department of Justice to transfer responsibility for enemy civilians from the ASF to the Justice Department. This allowed the military to use some of the housing earmarked for enemy aliens for the 175,000 POWs transferred from Great Britain.³⁷ The release of camps designated for enemy aliens provided only temporary relief. Once the United States launched Operation Torch, the invasion of North Africa, in November 1942, the trickle of POWs entering the United States became a flood and the need for housing became top priority. The United States constructed new camps designed solely for housing POWs and converted space on existing military bases or other locations, most commonly defunct Civilian Conservation Corps (CCC) camps. Multiple restrictions hampered the pace at which new housing became available. These included strict standards set forth by the Geneva Convention and security concerns of the War Department. Additionally, sites required approval by the ASF, the PGMO, service commands, the Corps of Engineers, and the local community.³⁸

Article 9 of the Geneva Convention required that prisoners be kept safe from potential danger from the combat zones and from "unhealthful regions or where the climate is injurous."³⁹ Articles 10 and 11 stipulated that prisoners of war receive lodging and food and have access to hygienic facilities in the same "quantity and quality" as the holding power.⁴⁰ By September 1943, therefore, the United States dictated that "the type of construction of prisoner of war camps [be] equivalent to that provided for the United States troops at base camps."⁴¹ For example, if POWs lived in tent housing when permanent facilities became available, then the guards must live in similar facilities. Camps had to have "five barracks, a latrine containing showers and laundry tubs with unlimited hot and cold running water, a mess hall, and an administrative building for each company" and "a chapel, a station hospital, and large outdoor recreation areas for the use of all the prisoners at the camp. At some camps located on an Army post, certain wards of the post hospital are designated for the use of prisoners of war in lieu of a station hospital at the prisoner of war camp. In addition, the quarters for officers must provide 120 square feet per man, and those for other ranks 40 square feet per man."⁴²

These conditions were approximately the same whether the camps were newly constructed or converted from existing facilities. Other stipulations required ample recreation space and "sufficient heat and light for buildings or tents, adequate drainage, and a water supply."[43] Because of these demands, the military sought to use space on existing bases whenever possible. When this was not possible, CCC camps were converted, and at times, the United States temporarily housed POWs on old fairgrounds or in tent cities. They avoided new construction where possible because of restrictions placed not only on the facility but also on its location and on the cost. Prisoners often worked on new camps, but because of labor union protests, the United States used civilian labor when available.[44]

The War Department placed safety restrictions on potential sites for housing POWs. When planning for a POW camp, the military remained aware of the maxim that "it was the military duty of every German soldier, as well as the inherent desire of the Nazi, to procure his liberty, and, by fair means or foul, make his escape to the 'fatherland.'"[45] General restrictions prohibited POW camps from being built "within a radius of 40 miles of installations vital to the war effort."[46] In order to keep the camps in remote areas and away from large cities and populations, initial restrictions limited the "establishment of camps within the following states: Maine, New Hampshire, Vermont, Massachusetts, Connecticut, New York, Pennsylvania, New Jersey, Delaware, Maryland, Virginia, North Carolina, South Carolina, Georgia, Florida, and within certain areas of Washington, Oregon, and California."[47] Other broad restrictions prevented camps from being located within a "blackout area extending about 120 miles inland from both coasts, a 150 mile-wide 'zone sanitaire' along the Canadian and Mexican borders, or near shipyards, munitions plants, or vital industries."[48]

Finally, other requirements dictated that POW camps be located at least five hundred feet away from areas of civilian traffic or travel and have sufficient clearing to allow military patrols within and around the camps without hindrances.[49] Camps had to be surrounded by double chain-link fences no less than eight feet tall with room in between for guards and watchdog patrols. Guard towers stationed outside the fence and at least six feet above must have a clear line of sight for searchlights and line of fire for machine guns.[50]

Most POW camps were located in the South and West, although camps existed across the United States, since many of the remote locations satisfied the security concerns and these locations proved more cost effective. Initially, base camps constituted most of the housing for POWs. Base camps provided permanent or semipermanent housing for large numbers of POWs, typically ranging from 3,000 to 4,000 men each, but some camps held several thousand more men. Ideally, these camps were located where POW labor could most effectively be used. POWs replaced military personnel working on nonessential tasks, thus freeing manpower for the war effort, and could provide contract work in the community, thereby relieving some of the labor shortage, especially in agricultural markets. Yet the demands placed on the location and construction of camps often led to sites far from labor needs. In this trade-off between security and labor, security won. As the war progressed and the POWs demonstrated their relatively low security risk, the United States built more base camps near areas of large civilian labor demand. Branch camps, typically temporary structures that housed between 250 and 1,000 men, located POWs near seasonal labor and allowed these men to be quickly and affordably shifted to other areas as needed. Security remained paramount. All POW work details leaving camp were accompanied by guards, and these men had to return to camp each night.[51]

U.S. officials and camp guards received specific instructions outlined in the manual *Operation of an Eight Compound Enclosure*.[52] The manual included guard duties at each of the various posts within the camps: inter–sally port gate guards, compound gate guards, guard supervisors, and center tower lookout guards. The manual also listed prisoner of war rules of conduct, which included mandatory saluting of American officers and freedom to wear decorations but prohibited singing and organizing into groups unless approved by the compound commander.[53]

Officials also organized POWs within the camps. POW camps consisted of one or more compounds, each normally housing 1,000 men. Typically, they had one to four compounds separated by barbed wire. The men in each compound further divided into companies of 250. An average compound, therefore, had four companies. One American officer commanded each company with assistance from three sergeants: one duty, one mess, and one supply. Additionally, a corporal acting as clerk, a private, and one cook were attached to each group.[54] As time passed, the size of POW companies increased from 250 to 400 men and the number of support personnel per group decreased. The United States provided one military police escort company for each compound. Administrative officers and personnel varied, depending on the size, type, and location of the POW camp. The service commands usually provided twenty-two officers and seventy-three enlisted men for a 3,000-man compound, but actual numbers of guards and support personnel varied considerably, and guard escorts were drastically reduced after April 15, 1944.[55]

An administrative structure that the POWs themselves organized existed within the camps. The Geneva Convention encouraged such an organization, and the U.S. military supported it. The prisoners of war chose a spokesperson to represent them to the U.S. government and the protecting power. This allowed the POWs to communicate with representatives of the State and War Departments, camp commanders, members of the Swiss delegation (the neutral protecting power), the YMCA, the IRC, and the Lutheran Commission.[56]

Officers and enlisted men had separate spokesmen and U.S. camp officials approved both selections. These individuals could not be medical personnel or chaplains, because of their protected status. The highest ranking among the German POWs was usually their commanding officer, and he appointed a spokesperson for the POW officers, while the enlisted men elected one. Spokesmen also had the responsibility of ensuring the cleanliness of the POW compounds for periodic inspections.

POW officers enjoyed access to orderlies, "one for each general officer, one for each group of three field officers and one for each group of six company officers. In addition, cooks necessary for officers will be assigned from among enlisted prisoners."[57] This self-sufficiency of the POW compounds, however, led to problems among the prisoners concerning political ideology and national origin, and to violence within the camps, particularly concerning the issue of Nazi dominance.

Living Conditions

U.S. officials placed paramount concern on the living conditions of prisoners of war housed in the United States. The German government, through the Swiss government, became aware of any deviation from stated War Department policy and Geneva Convention standards. Violations typically resulted from lack of resources or knowledge on the part of local camp commanders. Since even the slightest violation resulted in complaint or reciprocal action by the German government toward American POWs in their custody, infractions by U.S. personnel received quick corrective action by their superiors. The housing situation at the Memphis ASF Depot in Tennessee provides just one of many such examples.

An inspection and subsequent complaint filed by Mr. Schneider from the IRC on September 2, 1944, demonstrated that at the Memphis depot "part of the prisoners are living in barracks, the remainder are living in tents.... There are no floors for the tents and the prisoners are somewhat discontented." [58] Additionally, the IRC representative found that a recent transfer of 250 POWs from Aliceville, Alabama, had been deprived of additional "clothes, soap, towels, or other toilet articles" that "should have been provided" for over a week.[59] Assistant PMG Brigadier General Blackshear M. Bryan recommended that if the POWs continued to live in tents, floors must be added.[60] A follow-up by

Major Howard W. Smith Jr., chief of the Camp Operations Branch in the Prisoner of War Division, stated that toilet articles must be provided to all POWs entering camps for the first time or being transferred from one camp to another. If POWs needed additional supplies, they must purchase such items for themselves from the camp canteens, using their canteen pay coupons earned from labor. Smith also ordered that he be apprised of the progress of constructing flooring in the tent camps so that he could inform the IRC.[61]

A second flurry of correspondence concerning the conditions at Memphis began on January 30, 1945, when the Swiss Legation again contacted U.S. prisoner of war officials, inquiring whether they had addressed the original complaint, as they received no reply.[62] This prompted the acting secretary of state to issue his own investigation into the matter by asking the War Department whether it had resolved the matter. He included the letter from the Swiss government as part of his investigation. He also stated that a previous assistant director of the Prisoner of War Division of the PMGO had assured him in November 1944 that the complaints emanating from Memphis would be investigated and resolved, but he had never received the report.[63] As early as September 14, 1944, however, an order by Colonel Stacy Knopf, director of the Security & Intelligence Division, directed that unused CCC buildings be transferred from Camp Tyson, Tennessee, to Memphis. Knopf also ensured that the POWs had access to toiletries either through military issue or from the canteen. The State Department and the IRC, however, had not been informed that these measures had been implemented.[64] It fell to Major Stephen M. Farrand, chief of the Legal Branch of the Prisoner of War Operations Division, to officially reply in February 1945 to the request of the acting secretary of state. Farrand gave a complete outline of all the POW housing at the Memphis. He stated that he had addressed the listed problems and that members of the International Red Cross Committee had again inspected the camp on January 20, 1945, and found the conditions satisfactory.[65]

Typical Construction Plans and Problems

Each newly constructed prisoner of war camp had facilities and layouts of a cookie-cutter type. Since all camps had the same amenities afforded U.S. personnel, there were few deviations, beyond differentiating between base and branch camps, in camp designs. The expense of construction was one of the most important factors after the site for a new camp was decided upon. An examination of the planning of two camps, Fort Devens, Massachusetts, and Camp Grant, Illinois, demonstrates the typical cost and construction considerations of POW camps. Two different plans for Fort Devens provide examples of the cost of building a 1,200-man compound and the addition of a 1,000-man compound to existing facilities.[66]

A military study conducted in December 1942 by the chief of engineers to determine the suitability of Camp Grant, Illinois, for the housing of 1,500 POWs found that the site met the security requirements set forth by the War Department, but as no facilities existed, they would have to be constructed.[67] The chief of the Sixth Service Command and the commander of Camp Grant both concurred with the chief of engineers and allowed for blueprints to be drawn up. Construction plans for the 1,500-man POW facility, constructed adjacent to the military base at Camp Grant, submitted on January 21, 1943, proposed that the POWs could occupy the camp "120 days after award of the contract, with final completion in 6 months. Additional time over the 120-day period is necessitated due to slow delivery of kitchen equipment and miscellaneous valves, etc."[68] Colonel C. Keller expressed concern in his preliminary report that the railroad track lay too close to the camp to be considered completely outside the 500-foot boundary from public thoroughfares.[69]

In April 1945, construction of the POW camp hit a snag as the result of a debate concerning the building of a POW hospital. POW camps had to have access to a military hospital or one within the enclosure. The Sixth Service Command informed Colonel R. G. Barrows of the Corps of Engineers that the existing hospital used by personnel at Camp Grant would be suitable for use by the POWs. Barrows informed the Sixth Service Command that POW hospital facilities, in a standard POW camp layout, were stand-alone facilities. The Sixth Service Commander, however, impressed upon Barrows the money and time that would be saved if the POW facility were constructed next to the current military hospital. Barrows forwarded the request to his superiors in Washington and included blueprints for both types of POW hospitals, one located entirely within the POW camp, and one attached to the existing military hospital.[70]

Lieutenant Colonel A. L. Tynes of the Medical Corps, in a letter to the provost marshal and the chief of engineers, objected to the POW hospital being built adjacent to the larger hospital at Camp Grant. He argued that since the POW hospital would be outside the actual compound, it increased the risk of POW escape and potential injury to civilians and it would require a larger guard detail than if the hospital remained entirely within the POW camp. In his opinion, these factors far offset any potential savings in time and money that would otherwise be gained. He also stated that if any POWs required extensive medical care, they could be transferred individually to the larger facility.⁷¹ Director of the Aliens Division (later assistant PMG) Brigadier General Blackshear M. Bryan concurred with Tynes's assessment but did not approve of the initial layout of the enclosed hospital, as "the north fence of the hospital enclosure is only two hundred eighty-five yards from the boundary line."⁷² Problems such as these continued to plague officials involved with the POW program.

Throughout the duration of World War II, the United States struggled with the handling, transfer, and housing of nearly 425,000 Axis POWs. Problems arose nearly every step of the way, and many solutions proved only temporary expedients. Continued administrative and policy changes tended to exacerbate the problem. Overcoming these challenges required a great amount of cooperation, ingenuity, and compromise on the part of U.S. agencies and officials. The arrival of hundreds of thousands of Nazi and other POWs from battlefields across the world soon tested the structure and patience of the U.S. prisoner of war program.

Chapter 2

Sprechen Sie Deutsch? From Recruitment in the Third Reich to Incarceration in the United States

> Many of the prisoners were convicts, social rejects, hoodlums, psychopaths. Many were not even Germans, either, but foreign conscripts who ... had been impressed ... a catch-all, as the failing Reich, scouring its jails for military manpower, drafted common criminals and political prisoners alike—an unholy and explosive mix.
>
> —Wilma Parnell

The heterogeneous group of "German" men who filled the POW camps in the United States joined the Third Reich at various stages of the war and as need demanded. Their differences further compounded problems already being experienced by U.S. officials. As the well-oiled Wehrmacht war machine that pounded Europe from 1939 to 1942 deteriorated under material and man power demands, German replacements began to include the morally questionable and the physically fatigued, plus many anti-Nazi Germans. Convicts and non-German recruits joined draftees and the aged, drawn from all over Europe, in a futile attempt to stave off defeat. An astounding 371,683 German POWs had entered prison camps in the continental United States by the end of May 1945. American GIs knew Italian soldiers from those in German uniforms but made few other distinctions and, overwhelmed by the hundreds of thousands of POWs captured between 1943 and 1945, barely processed these men. Although accustomed to a degree of interservice rivalry in the U.S. armed forces, the GIs had no idea how deep these fissures ran across the Third Reich's military. American captors could not conceive of how Germany's long-standing multiparty political system affected the degree to which these German POWs clung to the old tradition. Removing their captives from the battlefront was their primary goal, and given the urgency of the situation, processing the POWs in the field often only involved disarming them. Little thought was given to the differences between the men in German uniform. Besides, what would it matter if Fritz or Hans came from Austria or Poland or was a Democratic Socialist or National Socialist? They were still German, still the enemy, and all Nazis. Aryan mythology aside, the prisoners came from across Europe and Asia. Brown-skinned and brown-eyed soldiers of every conceivable age mingled with the "Teutonic" blond-haired, blue-eyed "German" youth. Germans and non-Germans and Nazis and non-Nazis mixed with the ideologically unsuitable, socially undesirable, and physically and emotionally unreliable. Some of these warriors used to feed the Nazi war machine had little or no grasp of the German language. While the Americans considered the German soldiers a homogenous group, the men in German uniform always remained conscious of the distinctions.

The decision to put these men in German uniforms and integrate them into existing units, born of military necessity, dealt an ideological blow to many in the Third Reich who never truly approved of or accepted this dilution of the "master race." After the British transfer of 175,000 men, the POWs entered the United States in three broad waves, the first from North Africa and southern Italy in 1943, the second from northern France after D-day in 1944, and the last from the winter of 1944 through the defeat of Germany in May 1945.[1] POWs in each of these groups represented distinct variations in the moral, ideological, and national mixture of German military manpower. Despite these glaring differences, it took months for the United States to develop a screening process that went beyond differentiating among German, Italian, and Japanese. In late 1944, U.S. planners discovered variations among the German POWs, but attempts to segregate POWs based on nationality and ideology were slow. The following discussion demonstrates how this broad mixture of soldiers became members of the German army and later German POWs.

The German army that invaded Poland in 1939 consisted of the best men the nation had to offer, full of élan, highly trained and disciplined, and heavily indoctrinated with Nazi ideology. The baptism by fire during the blitzkrieg years of 1939 to 1941 strengthened this tight integration. These quick battles gained the soldiers military prestige and experience at the cost of relatively low casualties. Rapid expansion on the eve of the invasion of the Soviet Union in the summer of 1941, however, forced a change in the recruitment policies of a Wehrmacht already burdened with the war in North Africa and garrisoning units in occupied Europe. The war against the Soviet Union turned into a quagmire. Successes created larger front lines that needed to be manned, while reverses cost lives. A second seemingly subsidiary decision added to the toll, when on December 11, 1941, Germany declared war on the United States in support of its Japanese ally. The Germans kept up these various demands, fielding over four million men for their 1942 campaign in the Soviet Union, but replacements came at the price of substituting quantity for quality.

Sheer numbers of men, even when available, could not replace the experienced units decimated on the Eastern Front. Of the dwindling first-rate troops, "only a few elite units were kept well supplied with modern fighting machines, but they were no longer able fundamentally to change the overall situation."[2] Continually shifting troops from one front to the other, coupled with this recruitment policy, directly affected the demographics of the prisoners of war captured by the United States.

Early military success coupled with Nazi pressure enticed many Europeans to ally with Germany. The largest number of foreign recruits heralded from Austria, which became officially annexed to Germany after the Anschluss of 1938. The Austrians were ethnically German and spoke German, making distinction between the two groups difficult for American screening personnel. The profound differences in nationality and religion between predominately Catholic Austria and Protestant Germany led to numerous problems between these nations and played a key role in Austria's being left out of German Unification in 1871, even though a large portion of southern Germany remained Catholic. Behind barbed wire, these differences created extraordinary tensions.

The conquered nations of Western Europe provided Germany with laborers and soldiers. Nazi parties in occupied nations beat the drum of National Socialism and served as the focal points for the SS and regular military recruitment. Norway provided two SS brigades and a 1,200-man legion.[3] Denmark supplied thousands of workers. Those more adventurous preferred military service, and about 250 joined the Waffen SS and the Danish Frikorps.[4] Regiment Westland and SS Regiment Nordwest came from the Low Countries. Although Germany initially barred the Flemish from recruitment on racial grounds, a Flanders Legion of 900 men eventually formed, albeit with German officers, who resented "being put into a non-German unit" plagued by "morale problems."[5] Hitler even begrudgingly accepted the French so-called Anti-Bolshevik Legion. Heightened racial and physical requirements, however, led to fewer than 3,000 Frenchmen from a pool of as many as 15,000 being accepted.[6] Even the Italians requested SS training, and between September 1943 and May 1945 about 15,000 Italians served on German rosters.[7]

Recruits also came from foreign fascist parties and countries with similar political leanings that were not occupied by or officially allied to Germany, such as Spain. The Spanish government, under its caudillo, Francisco Franco, encouraged recruitment for what became the Division Espanola de Voluntarios, or DEV (Spanish Division of Volunteers). The DEV, also known as the Spanish Blue Division, started with about 18,000 men.[8] It joined the German roster as the 250th Infantry Division and marched from Poland to the Soviet front in August 1941. Spanish spirits seemed relatively high. One Spanish soldier, Ismael Garcia Romero, wrote home on January 27, 1942, that "I haven't received a letter from you in a long time and I'm so angry because of no letters that I ate my cigar, two hot peppers, a pencil and a piece of cheese. . . . I can't wait to eat the good home made meals we used to have. Here we don't even have time to sleep, so I'm writing you so I don't lose my writing skills. Please answer me and don't be lazy. Love and kisses."[9] The number of Spanish volunteers swelled to as high as 47,000, and these men fought with great determination against better-equipped Soviet divisions. One battalion refused the order to return to Spain in 1944 and remained with the Wehrmacht.[10]

Germany also drew upon the large number of German immigrants in the United States. The Nazis even temporarily supported an American Nazi Party. When Hitler called upon all those of German descent to return to the fatherland, hundreds of American-born or naturalized German immigrants responded. Some served in German uniform and eventually spent time in U.S.-operated POW camps.[11]

Swedish volunteers joined the Death's Head and Viking SS divisions, and Swiss volunteers joined the Wehrmacht and other SS divisions. Even Liechtenstein provided eighty-five volunteers, more than any other ally "proportionate to its population. Forty of those 85 men were killed or went missing in action."[12]

Nearly every nation in Western and Northern Europe thus provided manpower for the Third Reich. The number of nationalities and non-Germans recruited in the West, however, paled in comparison to the manpower Germany recruited from the East.

German recruitment among Allied and occupied Europe produced a small but steady stream of manpower that boosted German morale and demonstrated a general European hatred of Communism, or at least confidence in the capability of German arms. Once the war in the East commenced, thousands of fresh volunteers poured in from German's Baltic and Balkan allies and from Eastern Europe and other territories controlled by the Soviet Union.

Occupied Czechoslovakia and Poland faced the same conscription regulations practiced within Germany. The Slovakians offered troops to Germany as early as the Polish invasion of 1939. When Germany marched into the Soviet Union, it did so with allied contingents from Finland, Romania, Hungary, Croatia, Slovakia, and Italy. These allies were given various levels of autonomy, but as the months dragged on, the Germans assumed greater control over the allied armies, integrating Romanian, Slovakian, and Hungarian troops into the Wehrmacht. The war of liberation also led to numerous Estonians, Latvians, and Lithuanians, citizens of countries with large Germanic populations, joining the Germans to help liberate their homelands.[13]

Many Soviet citizens even volunteered for the German war effort in some capacity. Thousands signed up for the Hilfswillige, or "Hiwis." The Hiwis, literally translated as "those willing to help," were a catchall group of volunteer men and women, many former Soviet soldiers or prisoners of war. They played various roles in support of the occupying German armies, acting as scouts, informants, and workers. Many assisted in concentration camps and eventually figured prominently in manpower considerations.[14] The Germans deployed entire Hiwi anti-partisan units.[15] Captured Soviet soldiers and officers who traded their loyalty for service in the Wehrmacht provided another large source of manpower. They committed treason against the Soviet Union and willingly accompanied German command, if not out of loyalty, then out of fear of execution if they fell into the hands of their former comrades. These shifting patterns account for the large number of Soviets serving the Wehrmacht who ended up in POW camps in the United States.

Thousands of those suffering under the Soviet yoke joined the various Eastern legions established by the Wehrmacht.[16] The men who made up these units represented nearly every ethnic group within the Soviet Union. According to one estimate, "nearly 20 percent of 'German' manpower on the Eastern Front in 1944 consisted of volunteers from the Soviet Union."[17]

The Reich also dredged manpower from its own prisons and concentration camps. Socialists, communists, deserters, and convicts served the fatherland. Discipline among these groups waned and demoralization was widespread. Max Seydewitz, former Reichstag member, commented that "in the first years of the war, soldiers were shot out of hand for offenses which in any other army would have been punished with a term in jail at most" and that "at a later stage, the growing manpower shortage brought about a certain lessening of the death sentences meted out" since "the military situation did not allow such squandering of valuable manpower." He added that "the men thus saved from execution, however, were nothing but 'dead men on leave.'"[18]

Hitler's skepticism about recruiting from among Germany's convicts led to the implementation of various rules governing the qualifications and use of these new soldiers. Specifically, he desired to test the feasibility by recruiting a "trial" division. Normal age and physical requirements for military service remained in effect, but the other variables made what became the 999th Penal Division truly unique. Germany gave preference to prisoners who had military experience and barred hard-core criminals, those guilty of treason, and homosexuals. As far as the Reich was concerned, the barrel had been turned upside down and what fell out became the penal divisions. The Reich demonstrated its disdain for these men by utilizing them to clear mines and perform other suicidal tasks. Still, the Nazis gathered all their political enemies together and placed them in the service of the German war effort, sometimes under the command of a professional officer. The anti-Nazi members of these less than effective units gave "lip service to Prussian discipline," but the plans that they formulated "seldom included dying for Adolph Hitler."[19]

Attempts to recruit prisoners of war resulted in more psychological benefit than material gain. Irish collaborators attempted to convince Irish POWs to defect from British allegiance and join an Irish Legion of the Wehrmacht. The incentives of "free booze and prostitutes" persuaded only a few, despite the promises of "a beating" for holdouts.[20] German recruiters found Indian soldiers serving under the Union Jack more easily persuaded, and about 2,000 left prison and joined the German-created Indian Legion.[21] Smaller numbers of Americans and Englishmen betrayed their homelands to join the SS American Free Corps and British Free Corps.[22]

Falling into American Hands

German forces engaged by the Western Allies were typically numerically inferior, and at times qualitatively inferior, to those deployed in the Soviet Union. A comparison of raw numbers demonstrates that in June 1942, during the North African campaign, the Western Allies faced three Axis divisions, the Soviets 182. In December 1944, during the German Ardennes Offensive, the Western Allies fought 93 divisions, the largest number that they faced during the entire war, while the Soviets still bore the brunt of 162 divisions.[23] The number of German units facing the Western Allies never came close to those in the Soviet Union.

Some divisions shifted between fronts. Other German units fled the Eastern Front to surrender to the Western Allies before a total military collapse forced them into Soviet POW camps. These troop movements led to the large numbers of Soviets and Eastern Europeans entering U.S. POW camps. The prisoners of war captured at each of these stages demonstrated the unique status of the German soldier.

1942–1944: Ardent Nazis, Kriegsmarine, and the Afrika Korps: North Africa, Sicily, and Italy

In November 1942, the Western Allies launched Operation Torch, the invasion of North Africa. The successful plan caught the Axis between the two Allies, the United States moving east from their staging grounds in Morocco and Algeria, and the British moving west from their Egyptian bases. The Allies had numerical superiority and a technological edge, but they faced the qualitatively superior Afrika Korps, under its extremely able commander General Erwin Rommel. An integration of German and Italian forces, the Korps continually faced overwhelming odds in North Africa. Although ultimately losing the war, it slowed the Allied victory and even inflicted reverses on the Allies, such as at the Kasserine Pass, the first major battle for U.S. troops. It finally collapsed on May 12, 1943, and over 230,000 Italian and German soldiers, most considered hard-core Nazis, Italian fascists, or ardent nationalists, became POWs. These men marched to the major holding camps established at Oran, Algeria, and Casablanca, Morocco.

The Allied invasion of Sicily, Operation Husky, launched on July 10, 1943, and the invasion of southern Italy, on September 9, 1943, followed the success of the North African campaign and netted thousands more Axis POWs. The men captured in Sicily and southern Italy joined their colleagues in POW enclosures in North Africa, awaiting transfer to the United States. Eventually, "the prisoner compounds swelled to the bursting point. By the late spring of 1944, the army found itself handling more German and Italian prisoners than there had been American soldiers in the entire prewar U.S. Army."[24]

Even at this early stage, not all POWs were German or Nazi. There were other political and national elements within the camps. Erwin Shulz, a member of the 999th penal battalion, recalled the treatment they received in North Africa: "Six or seven soldiers who had mentioned they wanted to be captured by the Canadians were arrested, court-martialed, and shot [most likely by their German officers or SS]. A group of Jehovah's Witnesses were also shot. As a warning, our company had to stand by and watch while they were murdered."[25]

1944: D-Day to Falaise: Declining Morale

The next large group of German prisoners was captured by U.S. and Allied forces after the June 6, 1944, invasion of Normandy, code named Operation Overlord. The Axis forces encountered in the D-Day landings were well supplied and well entrenched. This enabled them to fight effectively, but unlike the enemy forces encountered in North Africa, not all these troops were elite. In fact, with a few exceptions, such as the 352nd German Infantry Division, many were classified as second rate.[26] Most of the Axis forces were still deployed on the eastern front. The D-Day invasion succeeded, and the second front that the Soviets so desperately needed finally opened. The success of the attack can be measured by the concern of Hitler and the German high command in transferring many units to the West, including two SS panzer divisions.[27] This transfer of forces to the western front to bolster the "second-rate" and other Axis forces against the Allied invasion ensured that the United States would encounter a wide range of nationalities and political ideologies along the battlefields of Western Europe and Germany.

The Allies broke out of the Normandy beachheads near the end of the month. Operation Cobra, beginning on July 25, was the major thrust outward from the landing ground and into the French countryside. The decline in the quality and quantity of men available to the Third Reich became apparent to the Allies during the drive through France. Germany could still field large numbers of men, but many new recruits had substandard training or were "denied ... the most modern equipment."[28] In fact, many of the German divisions in the West suffered as "their best personnel [were] taken away in mass drafts to the Eastern Front, and replaced with newly called up 18-year-olds, men over 35, men with third-degree frostbite, and members of the *Ostbataillone*, formed from Red Army prisoners-of-war."[29] The number of prisoners captured in France increased drastically when many of the German forces were caught in the Falaise pocket encirclement, while others were captured during the invasion of southern France in August 1944, code named Operation Anvil.

Although German forces held out in Italy until the end of the war, the morale among some of the defenders sharply declined. Some, such as Karl-Heinz Hackbarth, captured in southern Italy on May 25, 1944, had good reason.

> We had about forty soldiers left in our Kampfgruppe, and I was the oldest. Most were still teenagers. On May 25, we were supposed to be protecting the rear of a tank regiment. We happened to notice the 999ers placing T-mines in back of us. Our unit was obviously considered expendable, and headquarters had not even told us about these mines. I thought to myself, "The hell with it all." We held a democratic discussion about what we were going to do when the Americans came. We agreed we would take our weapons apart, bury them, and surrender. We actually voted to do this.[30]

1945: The Ardennes to Berlin: The Collapse of the Wehrmacht

Prior to the launching of the Ardennes offensive in December 1944, Germany had already experienced years of military reversals. These steady losses on both fronts drained manpower and morale, and many of the men were already psychologically and physically defeated. The Ardennes Offensive drained the last lifeblood from the German war machine. In the last months of the war, the front lines of the German army were in constant flux and crowded by hundreds of soldiers making desperate attempts to escape the eastern front to surrender to the Western Allies. Commanders and soldiers alike realized that the war was all but over and appreciated the huge differences between Soviet and Western treatment of prisoners of war.

What began with so much promise in the East, utilizing the "most powerful striking force ever assembled in Europe" and the "resources of fifteen nations," turned into a shambles for the Germans.[31] The Soviets had not signed the Geneva Convention, and neither side afforded humane treatment to the other's prisoners. Soldiers became disheartened and troops that might never have seen combat on the Western Front desperately sought American lines. The mood of the soldiers on the Eastern Front changed in 1944 and 1945. *Soldat* Fritz Schmidt's letter of May 25, 1944, serves to illustrate the differences between the two fronts. "Within eight days there were six people dead and eight people severely injured from our Battery. This shows you how severe the battles are. The Russians have so many terrible heavy weapons. In the evening they tell us via loudspeakers that they will slay us one by one until summer. We may have to expect nothing good. I hope that the rain has come which you have been longing for. Good luck to you!"[32]

Siegfried Knappe, a former POW of the Soviet Union, further described the moral-decimating propaganda on the eastern front. "When we recaptured a city or town from the Russians, we usually discover that wanton murder and rape had been the norm while they had been there. German officers were simply shot and even enlisted men were shot just to get them out of the way. The rules of civilized warfare did not exist on the Eastern Front, and the Russians were made even more savage by the exhortation of the Russian journalist Ilya Ehrenburg to extract from the Germans 'two eyes for an eye' and a 'pool of blood for every drop of blood.'"[33]

The Western Allies, on the other hand, had signed the Geneva Convention, and Wehrmacht soldiers knew it. The Allies also dropped leaflets and broadcast messages promising fair treatment to the Germans and their allies if they surrendered. Further, the United States experimented in trial surrenders. They offered Germans the opportunity to surrender, and if they did not like it, they could return to their own lines. Many surrendered, further decreasing the morale of those who did not.

Colonel Hans von Luck, a panzer commander on the Eastern Front, attempted what many in the German Army did in the last days of the war to escape the clutches of the Soviets and surrender to the Americans. Luck took stock of his unit's situation during April 1945. Fighting near Baruth, they were pinned down by the Russians, nearly surrounded, with all hopes of escape likely to be cut off. Luck announced to his men that "we have been cut off in the rear. We are virtually out of ammunition, fuel is getting short. I hereby release every one of you from my command.... My thanks to you all. May God protect you." With those final words, Luck and his men desperately attempted to reach American lines. Of their fate Luck stated: "As I heard many years later, a few small groups did in fact succeed in reaching the Elbe and falling into American hands."[34] The Soviets captured many others, however, including Luck. Unfortunately for many Germans, because of an agreement between the Allies, many of those who served on the eastern front and escaped to British or U.S. custody were turned over to the Soviet Union.

Even after the failure of the Ardennes Offensive and the invasion of Germany from both the East and West in 1945, the Wehrmacht was made up of men with wide divergences in ideology and morale. At this late point some still believed that a German victory was possible or that Hitler had a "wonder" weapon ready to be unleashed. Many of these men, however, were resigned to defeat and eager to surrender to the West. Others clung to their beliefs in National Socialism and the might of German arms, and some still held an unswerving faith in Hitler. At a time when the very young, the very old, the physically and socially unfit, and the criminal element were taking up defensive positions, portions of the German army held on to this false faith. According to historian Omar Bartov, "increasingly during the last two years of the war, the troops at the front came to see themselves as the missionaries of the entire German nation, indeed of Western civilization as a whole." He concluded that "paradoxically, the soldiers' awareness of the regime's criminal actions (at least at the front) made them fight with even greater determination for its survival by intensifying their fear of the consequences of defeat."[35] Historian Stephen Fritz added that "for many, faith like this meant that no conditions were placed on their loyalty to Hitler."[36]

Processing in the Theater of Operations

Processing of prisoners of war in the theater of operations moved rapidly. Ideally, POW screening involved completing the basic personnel record with the soldier's name, serial number, and fingerprints; a list of items in his possession; and other identifying characteristics.[37] The fast pace of combat usually resulted in these men being disarmed and hurriedly moved to rear holding areas. Reportedly, at times only a few guards escorted hundreds of POWs. Lack of interpreters and personnel and the movement of POWs from rear areas to ships for transport often left the screening incomplete until POWs arrived in the United States.

Initial screening and segregation, especially prior to 1944, only separated German soldiers from Italians. The POWs captured in North Africa fit the image of German soldiers in American minds—strong, tough, brutal, and completely Nazified. With this prevailing notion, there seemed no need to further separate them once the Italians entered their own camps. These soldiers, however, should have been classified more carefully. This was also the first time American soldiers, reporters, and the public had seen enemy captives in large numbers. The only POWs behind U.S. barbed wire prior to this point were those taken from German ships and those transferred from the British.

The mood of POWs in North African holding camps could be summarized as astonishment at being defeated and dismay at the living conditions in the holding camps. One of the POWs captured in North Africa, Eberhard Ladwig, complained that the French guards on the transport train to Oran refused POW requests to use the latrine. The conditions at Oran were little better: "it was dirty and wet, and we were forced to sleep on the ground in the mud."[38] Werner Gilbert, a member of the Luftwaffe captured on May 11, 1943, in North Africa, thanked his British captors. Gilbert stated that a "group of Moroccan troops attempted to massacre us. Fortunately for us the British ... fired their weapons to disperse the angry crowd that had formed."[39] Friedrich Biallas remembered the suffering of the smokers among the POWs in the North African camps. Biallas recalled that "in order to satisfy their desire a good many did dry up tea leaves in the Winter sun, smoked them in pipes, or rolled cigarettes using newspaper. With this they did have bleu fume but no effect as from nicotine. Often they suffered minor illness. Non-smokers, like myself, were only able to wag their heads."[40] Once in Algeria, the POWs were transferred to American custody.

Georg Gaertner, captured in April 1943 in North Africa, was among the last of the Afrika Korps to be taken prisoner. He received processing and a serial number while in North Africa. He remembered the search and seizure that so many other POWs bitterly recalled: "We were searched for weapons and military papers, but not being officers we had neither. The fact never seemed to bother our captors who viewed us as a continual source of war souvenirs. At each stage of our shipment to the huge Allied holding pens at Oran we were searched repeatedly for any piece of Nazi equipment—medals, decorations, daggers, or Lugers—that might have escaped the notice of previous searchers."[41]

Gaertner offered some observations about the American military at the time of his capture. He thought that "everyone looked overweight and for a short time I even wondered if their weight was the reason they all rode in jeeps. Clearly they had only recently arrived in North Africa and did not yet have the 'dietary benefit' of several months on army rations in desert combat." His second observation startled him: "my next surprise was seeing black people. We did not have Negroes in Germany and as odd as it may seem today, I simply had never seen black people." He also observed the "astonishing amount of equipment" possessed by U.S. forces, "every imaginable type of vehicle and weapon. Yet, it was a small nagging detail that suddenly made me realize that I was looking at the victors of the war. It was the nonchalance with which they let their engines idle without any concern for a shortage of fuel."[42] After spending time in the holding camp at Oran, Gaertner received transfer to his first base camp in the United States, Camp McLean, Texas.

Reinhold Pabel, captured in Italy on October 14, 1943, recalled that just the night before his own capture he had held several GIs prisoner. He recalled telling his American captive that "I am just as much or as little a Nazi because I wear the German uniform as you are necessarily a Roosevelt man because you are wearing an American uniform."[43] Soon after this conversation, American forces surrounded Pabel's position. The Germans left their prisoners and attempted to escape the advancing Americans. Pabel was wounded in the failed attempt and became a prisoner.

Sent to a field hospital, Pabel recalled another encounter with racist and ideological stereotypes on November 10, 1943:

> There is a road-building company at work on the hospital grounds, an all-Negro outfit. I often join them when they have a break and talk to them. At first they were a little suspicious of me and openly surprised that I did not ignore them on account of their black skin. ... Now we have a lot of fun together. They all love good jokes and I enjoy watching their beautiful toothpaste-ad white teeth when they break out into those spells of roaring laughter. One of them

once remarked that I had been the only white that had given him a friendly word since he was taken into the Army, and he complained bitterly that the colored fellows had to do all the dirty work."[44]

After recovering from his wounds at a hospital in Bizerte, Tunisia, Pabel transferred to Casablanca. The train passed near neutral Spanish Morocco and the guards made frequent roll calls during the trip. Pabel recalled that "each time there was no response when a name was called we knew that another one had made a clean getaway, and each time that happened somebody from the crowd hollered, 'With advance unit to Germany!'"[45] During the transfer, sixteen of his fellow prisoners escaped.

Sailing for the New World

Earlier U.S. decisions to adhere to the Geneva Convention influenced the transfer of POWs from North Africa and Europe to America. This transfer offset the cost of POW care by locating POWs near areas in the United States that needed their labor. POWs were billeted on empty troop and supply ships and, when wounds or disease necessitated, on hospital ships. Regulations prohibited them from utilizing otherwise "vital" space, meaning that reserved for returning soldiers, the wounded, officers, nurses, or important cargo.[46] High-ranking officers and important enemy civilians received air evacuation and transport.[47] Transfer of POWs to the United States continued uninterrupted until Germany surrendered. Only two groups of POWs received transfer after V-E Day: those en route to the United States and past Gibraltar and approximately 100,000 additional POWs requested for labor in 1945.[48]

A convoy of ships sailed together to reduce the chances of U-boat attacks during the Atlantic crossing. These concerns made the journey longer than it may otherwise have been, but it allowed the POWs to reflect and get used to U.S. guards and personnel. Paul Mengelberg, a U-boat crewman, made the journey from England to Canada as a prisoner of war in early 1941. He recalled that being in the Allied convoy did little to distill the fears among the POWs of being torpedoed by one of their own submarines. He remembered it as "a scary trip, I know what torpedoes do to ships."[49] Yvonne Humphrey, a second lieutenant in the Army Nurse Corps, journeyed from North Africa to the United States onboard a converted coastal steamer along with German POWs. She found that other than having routine medical illnesses, the POWs were "polite, orderly, and cheerful."[50] Many of the POWs found the trip to the United States more comfortable than their stay in the makeshift camps in the North African desert. Ladwig recalled that "the food was wonderful" but added that he "was disgusted when some of our men ate everything they could get their hands on. Not even a wolf eats more than he can digest. One of our guys bragged that he had eaten thirty-six sausages at one meal. . . . Many of them naturally became seasick, although the seas were not rough."[51] When not getting seasick, the prisoners forgot about the war and their POW status, if just momentarily. According to Humphrey, they "were musically inclined. From somewhere or other we dug up a few instruments for them and every night they gave us a concert. They were quite good and it was pleasant to hear some of their fine old drinking songs and waltzes out in the middle of a war-infested ocean. It took our minds off the blackout, the threat of subs, and the general uncertainty of our trip home."[52]

Strict discipline and labor details onboard the ships snapped the POWs back to reality. Regulations were maintained despite captivity, and "if a soldier failed to salute a superior officer with sufficient snap, he would be seriously reprimanded or perhaps confined to quarters."[53] Humphrey mentioned to a German officer the work ethic of the POWs as they conducted routine work details. He replied matter-of-factly, "But of course, *Fraulein,* everyone in Germany works. We are trained to work and fight. There is no time for pleasures. And so we shall win this war."[54]

A few German POWs avoided the potentially deadly but usually humdrum Atlantic crossing by getting air transport to the United States. Jim Stiles, a Navy aviation mechanic and sometimes pilot, spent the war on anti-submarine patrol in Brazil. He recalled that his squad sank seven U-boats. A ship rescued the survivors and brought them to shore, where the Naval Air Transport Service whisked them to the United States for interrogation and processing. Stiles recalled his posting as "an unusual location to be during the war." While there, they had to contend not only with some of the local German immigrant population but also with ships landing potential saboteurs, and "German sympathizers" in Brazil and neighboring Argentina. Stiles remembered that according to the agreement with the Brazilian government, they could not engage a submarine unless it was at least five miles out to sea, but "of course, if the Germans made it within three miles then they [the Brazilian government] would take their submarine or ship and keep it."[55]

For most of the POWs the trip to the United States proved safe and uneventful, if necessarily long. Former POW Howard Tromp recalled the numerous detours between the temporary holding camp at Oran and ultimate arrival in New York: "the liberty ship took us to Glasgow, Scotland, we thought we would stay there, but in a few weeks . . . we were put on a French luxury liner." The

Louis Pasteur transported Tromp and his POW colleagues to Halifax, Canada, "where we lay in port for a couple of days, but they had no room for us . . . they . . . did not make arrangements for us. Then all of a sudden the ship took off again and we went to New York. And we got out in New York and they were watching the first Nazi prisoners of war arriving in the United States. That was a big thing in those days."[56]

Processing in the United States

The POWs disembarked at one of two major induction centers: Camp Shanks, New York, or Norfolk, Virginia. Once they arrived, they completed the screening process. They then had their belongings disinfected and searched. Officials confiscated weapons and items of intelligence and placed currency with the Enemy Prisoner of War Information Bureau to be returned after repatriation.[57] German soldiers carried *Soldbücher*, which included military and personnel identification. Many of these books, however, had been lost, stolen, or destroyed at some point between capture and disembarkation in the United States. Many soldiers had no proof of their status. Proving rank held great importance, because officers could be exempt from working. They also enjoyed privileges based on rank, including pay. Switzerland, as the protecting power, verified many of the claims of soldiers who lost their *Soldbücher*, but this sometimes took months. POWs complained bitterly about the illegal searches and seizures in the weeks from capture to camp and the loss of precious heirlooms such as watches, wallets, and medals. Former POW Paul Lohmann recalled that the American soldiers "searched us very thoroughly . . . our weapons were taken, they took everything. Letters, wallets, pass papers, photos, all that we had left after their search was the clothing that we were wearing. A few American soldiers took the wrist watch's [*sic*] that we were wearing. Some of the soldiers showed us the wrist watches that they had been taking from German Prisoners, they had wrist watch's [*sic*] on both arms up to their armpits."[58]

Former POW Helmut Hörner remembered the Americans searching him and his colleagues and "the entire contents of our pockets, including our wallets, fly before our feet. Before our eyes strange, dirty fingers sort through our possessions and take all money and photographs with military objects from our wallets. Bitterly I see the picture of my wife disappear into the pocket of a dirty thief."[59]

Oskar Schmoling, another former POW, also recalled that "one American was so proud that he had seven or eight of our watches on his arm."[60] The problem became so extensive that the ASF issued regulations requiring that all "effects and objects of personnel use, identification documents, insignia of rank, and decorations will not be taken from prisoners of war" but instead sent to the "Property Section, Prisoner of War Information Bureau, PMGO, Fort George G. Meade, Maryland. Any foreign currency withdrawn . . . will be forwarded to the . . . Finance Section, PMGO."[61] Not all German POWs experienced the same treatment from American GIs. Ernst W. Floeter remembered being searched and the GI throwing away his good-luck piece. Floeter communicated in French to the GI, asking if "I might keep it. He picked it up and gave it back to me, and I still have it."[62]

The final step of processing involved issuing a serial number. Some of the POWs received them in the theater, but many received them at the point of disembarkation. The first two numbers indicated the place of capture, such as North Africa or France, and the third entry designated the nationality with either an *I* for Italian, *J* for Japanese, or *G* for German. A dash separated these first three characters from the rest of the four-digit serial numbers given consecutively to the POWs.[63]

POWs who did not receive a serial number in the theater received one from their permanent camps in the United States. These numbers indicated what service command the POW had been transferred to, ranging from 1 to 9, followed by a *W* for the War Department. The third character again denoted nationality—Italian, German, or Japanese. A consecutively assigned serial number, separated by a dash, followed these three characters.[64] Prisoners captured by the U.S. Navy received slightly different serial numbers indicating the naval district that processed each individual.

POW Reactions to the United States

The POWs expressed varied reactions upon their arrival. Some "were amazed to find American sea-coast cities still standing, having been told that they were long since leveled by aerial attacks. They finally concluded that we rebuilt faster than Germany tears down."[65] Others, like Heinz Richter, expressed sheer incredulity: "Suddenly we saw the Statue of Liberty stretching powerfully to the sky. How many thousands of immigrants from all countries had she greeted. I was struck by both confidence and fear. America—who would have thought that I would see the country of which so much was told. And now I was to live here, not as a free man, to be sure, but as a P.O.W. What would the future be like? It is hard to describe the impression which the gigantic skyscrapers made on me."[66]

As trains transported the POWs through the U.S. countryside, they expressed similar amazement. Richter exclaimed that "we traveled for days through huge areas, incredible distances for a German. Our Germany is not much larger than one of the American states."[67] Others remarked upon American culture and lifestyle. One German housed at Camp Shelby, Mississippi, wrote in the diary that he later left behind:

> The disappointment about scenery which races by is pretty great. There is nothing to be seen but woodland and again forest and in between townships here and there. Most of the homes there are wooden structures in the style of our weekend houses (toy box construction). Much furniture or household articles could not be inside of them. Half of their lives is apparently taking place on those very huge porches. Almost nowhere is there a rocking chair missing. The medium-sized country towns consist most at all, at least in this cotton (region), of a spinning and weaving mill, a few stores along the road and furthermore of the already mentioned more or less pretty wooden houses. The cottage may be about to collapse, [but] an automobile is most surely parked in front of it. For hours and hours you pass by ever uniform scenery. Corn and cotton fields alternate with forests in between. There are no high mountains. The heat which we would have been glad to leave behind in Africa, accompanies us here too, to our sorrow. In case the train stops for a while, the temperature in the car becomes almost unbearable. Because the windows may be opened only four inches wide, it is naturally not much better while traveling.[68]

Reinhold Pabel whiled away his time onboard a transport train en route to Camp Grant, Illinois, engaging in mischief with the guards. He "deftly questioned the guard on my end of the car for our destination, and then, on my next washroom trip, casually told the other guard where we were going." He also remarked of the American home front that "the first impression we had was the abundance of automobiles everywhere. On the other hand, we discovered a sharp contrast to the obvious wealth in the poor construction and preservation of the numerous frame houses, especially in Kentucky."[69]

The new arrivals found that the POW camps in the United States operated along more efficient lines than those in the theater. Many expressed surprise at their welcome at permanent camps. Heinz Richter, also stationed at Camp Grant, explained the normal routine:

> Upon entering the camp, we reported to clerks who filled out forms with our personal data and took our fingerprints. We

had to take off our uniforms. Everything, including shoes and underwear, was thrown away. I was allowed to keep my wedding ring, a picture of my dear wife, and my belt, which I still wear to work today. We received new underwear, new socks, new shirts, and new green uniforms like those the Americans wore. The only difference was that a large PW was printed on every sleeve and pant leg and on the back of shirts and jackets. The hats also had PW printed in white. Now we all looked like P.O.W.'s. It was a bit painful, but we were amazed that everything we got was new and also that it fit well. Even the shoes were new and of the proper size. We also got toothpaste, a toothbrush, soap, towels, and even a handkerchief. We were all quite excited.[70]

Howard Tromp recalled that, to his amazement, "they gave us fresh underwear, three sets of shorts and three sets of t-shirts. Brand new. I mean . . . we had not washed clothes in months . . . and that day we also got . . . delousing."[71]

Another POW, captured in North Africa and transferred from Great Britain to the United States, expressed similar sentiments: "In 1943 I was sent here to Fort Carson. Of course that was much better than being in the German Air Force. We ate better, we slept better, we were housed properly. Our standard of living was the highest that any PW could hope to have."[72]

The majority of prisoners captured during the first two years of the war came from fighting in North Africa, Sicily, or southern Italy or were captured aboard naval vessels or transferred from the British. These men were predominantly German or Austrian and typically heavily indoctrinated with Nazi ideology. Many felt that their stay in the United States would be brief and would end when the United States either surrendered or Germany conquered them. These men entered U.S.-operated prisoner of war camps, and the highest-ranking officer still controlled the lives of the soldiers he commanded. This included electing the camp spokesperson and imposing disciplinary measures on the POWs. These men's authority within the camps simply continued the routine for many Afrika Korps members. They willingly followed the strict discipline and Nazi principles practiced within the camps. These similarities among the POWs were the main reason that Nazis and non-Nazis, Germans and non-Germans, were not separated. There seemed to be little difference.

The second and third large waves of prisoners, those captured after D-Day, were of all the nationalities represented by the Wehrmacht and held various political ideologies. They were typically of lower morale, less German, and less indoctrinated. By simply relating their tales of capture, which often included comments on Allied material supremacy and German setbacks, they could be labeled defeatists within the camp. These men learned, through punishment and observation, the harsh reality that the POW camps could be a microcosm of Nazi Germany.

One POW, a submariner captured near Spain at about the time of D-Day, was sent to a holding camp in Cherbourg, France. He recalled the living conditions in the camp: "For a whole week it was raining, always raining! No tents, no nothing. You slept just like you were out on the ground. A lot of guys made suicide attempts." The number of men probably exacerbated the conditions. "They couldn't make the barbed wire up fast enough for so many they caught. There were thousands of them."[73]

Captured on August 8, 1944, in Plougastel, France, Paul Lohmann's feelings toward his captors' search and seizure changed once he witnessed the looting of dead German soldiers by French civilians, who carried out this morbid task with "lots of screaming and yelling. With much effort they tore the shoes and boots from the feet of our dead comrades. To us it was . . . dreadful." While witnessing that gruesome sight, the POWs were questioned by "an American Major who knew a little German" and quickly ordered his men "to stop the French from stripping the bodies. That order to the GIs for us represented that we would get decent treatment from the Americans."[74]

Oskar Schmoling had a harrowing experience after his capture in France. He marched to the Normandy front at the age of sixteen and his group deployed just before D-Day. He joined the large group of Germans who became POWs during that operation. Following their capture, he recalled, "a rumor circulated that Germans had killed some civilians, and this American officer came up and picked out ten of us to be shot for revenge. I was one of the ten. He lined us up and told us to face this stone wall. A command was given, and we heard the ammunition being loaded. We knew they were lining up their machine guns. . . . To this day I don't know whether they were just trying to scare us or whether some higher-ranking officer ordered them not to kill us."[75] Ernst W. Floeter, also captured in France, had a far different feeling after being captured: "When the first American came up with his machine gun, I threw my rifle on the ground and thought, 'Thank God, no more rifle drills.'"[76] These men entered the well-established Nazi-dominated POW camps in the United States.

Welcome to America

Some American communities desired the construction of prisoner of war camps to boost the local economy through POW labor, government funding, civilian jobs, and the influx of soldiers' money. As a result of existing military policy, citizens of the community remained abreast of the planning stages for the POW camps. The military chose an "advance man," who went to the area and conferred with local officials, government agencies, reporters, and citizen groups.[77] During these conferences, the military representative stressed that "prisoners of war are coming to this community at the request of local citizens."[78] He explained the treatment of prisoners of war, showed how private citizens could employ them, and described how the Geneva Convention bound the United States and how it applied to the POW program.

The curiosity of American citizens and interests of local employers and businesses peaked in anticipation of the POWs' arrival. Many Americans hoped to catch a first glimpse of the captive enemy. At Concordia, Kansas, dozens of spectators watched the first large trains of POW unload and their transfer to the Concordia POW camp. On August 7, 1943, the third train of POWs disembarked at Concordia. One reporter described the event as a "circus day," since it was after dark, and the town lit up under army lights as throngs of curious townsfolk watched the POWs being unloaded.[79] The local newspaper carried reports of all the arrivals of POWs and events taking place at the POW camp, from the first arrival of POWs who required hospitalization to the final groups arriving by train, who brought the camp to its 4,000-man capacity.[80] Reporters discovered that some of the POWs were officers who had commanded "various units of the Nazi army in action against Allied troops." The press speculated that "today they are being introduced to the routine of life at the prisoner of war camp north of town and possibly comparing the scenery of Sibley township, Cloud County, Kansas, with that of the country where they donned the knee length shorts many of them still were wearing."[81] One of the final trainloads of POWs arrived at Concordia on August 26, 1943. By this time, American guards had became accustomed to the unloading and transfer of the POWs, but even the "spectators who have become veteran 'assistants' at the unloading thought they noted an improved technique in the detraining procedure because of the speed with which it was accomplished."[82]

Many of the reports told of a defeated and demoralized enemy. *Time* described the POWs at Fort McClellan, Alabama, as "troops of the once great *Afrika Korps*. . . . Most . . . are Bavarians, blond, stocky and young. Except for four doctors, a dentist, and a tall, hatchet-faced pharmacist, there are no officers among them. Dressed in faded blue denim P.W. uniforms or, occasionally, the patched-up uniforms which they had on when they were captured, they looked arrogant, meaty, well-fed."[83]

Beverly Smith, writing for *American Magazine*, was among the first to witness the POWs entering the Crossville, Tennessee, camp:

> These are the warriors of Hitler and Mussolini, captured on distant seas and battlefields. They glance about with a puzzled expression. For them, the Axis glory trail has led to Main Street, U.S.A., opposite the "Last Chance Café," the filling station, Cole's Cash Store, and "New and Used Shoes Repairs while U Wait." Some of them wear the gaudy uniforms, faded and rumpled now, of high ranking officers. Many have the iron cross and other decorations for bravery in action. The majority of the Germans are from Rommel's once dreaded Afrika Korps. Among the Italians I see the insignia of the Bersaglieri and the Centauri. There are fliers, parachute men, artillerymen, panzer men from the German tank divisions. Now they blink briefly in the waning Tennessee sunlight before climbing into the waiting trucks and buses to be whisked off to the near-by-camp which will be their home until the war ends.[84]

Some accounts underestimated the POWs. John A. Moroso III reported that the POWs were "dudes, plunderers, and crybabies." He continued: "They were part of the once proud Afrika corps and many of their monocled officers still were proud and disdainful and dudish despite the thin layer of African dust that coated their bemedaled uniforms." He also stated that the "enlisted men... all were tanned and well fed—contradicting reports that they had been poorly supplied in Tunisia." Moroso stated that when guards threw the mixed German and Italian POWs cigarettes, they "fought and shoved like savages to get them." Others held "plunder" from all over Europe, including "French perfumes, such things as tinned Norwegian sardines and other fish, chocolate from Czechoslovakia, tobacco from London, cigarettes from Cairo."[85] One colonel alone had "17 bottles of stuff designed to keep one beautiful" and others "howled" upon discovering that two of the enlisted men that searched them were Jewish.[86] Another article claimed that "iron crosses and other decorative hardware doled out by the Nazi overlords are a dime a dozen among the group." This report also stated that the POWs preferred to sing while being transferred from trains to prisoner camps, but "they weren't singing 'We're Marching on England' nor the 'Horst Wessel' song... both... these selections are understood to be losing their popularity to some extent, especially among the Germans in Allied prison camps."[87]

Not everyone underestimated the POWs. One POW at Camp AuTrain in Michigan's Upper Peninsula recalled that sometimes the prisoners on work detail threw candy to local children, but once "some kids were chased away from a lumber job after they taunted and infuriated the SS soldiers, telling them Germany was losing the war."[88] The lack of restraint on the part of the civilian population forced the army to issue a warning to civilians against wearing clothes with *PW* painted on them. The military reported that "numerous incidents had been reported in which high school students and other civilians had painted prisoner-of-war inscriptions on their clothing as a joke." The army warned, however, that those wearing *PW*-marked clothes could be mistaken and shot by accident. The article concluded by stating that "many prisoners work from time to time on farms and are transported over public highways" and "the presence of pranksters in or near such areas would be extremely dangerous."[89]

The POWs should not have been underestimated by anyone. Another war would soon be fought once they were behind barbed wire. This explosive and volatile mix of nationalities, ethnicities, languages, religions, and ideologies entered U.S.-operated prisoner of war camps, as well as those of other Allied nations. POWs captured after the North African campaign contended with an existing Nazi regime in American-operated POW camps. Opponents of Nazi ideology soon learned that the consequences within American POW camps could be as swift and severe as in the Third Reich. Language problems plagued U.S. efforts to communicate. Few U.S. personnel spoke German, so many POWs served as translators at every stage in the POW process. Once behind the wire, some POWs disobeyed American authority and others attempted to escape. The mistake of not segregating the POWs based on nationality and ideology only came to light after rumors of threats and signs of violence and murder appeared within the camps, and many prisoners pleaded with American personnel for safety. Eventually the United States established separate camps for the various ideological groups represented by the prisoners. For many, this was too little, too late.

Chapter 3

Igniting the Powder Keg: Nazi Influence within the Camps and the Last Acts of Defiance among POWs

The prisoner of war "congregation" gathered on the night of November 4, 1943, at Camp Gruber, Oklahoma, to listen to *Hauptfeldwebel* Walter Beyer's "midnight sermon." All understood that the late-night meetings passed for courts-martial within the camps. After accusing *Gefreiter* Johannes Kunze of treason, the "pastor" and the faithful grew quiet. A sweating and nervous Kunze contemplated the impending visit of the "Holy Ghost" moments before members of the group ritualistically attacked him in an orgy of violence.[1] Shortly after, silence again dominated the mess hall. The POWs returned to bed, but broken dishes and spattered blood remained to mark the killing of Corporal Kunze. The powder keg within the POW camps ignited and burned with explosive effects for a long time before being extinguished.

Germans and non-Germans, hastily thrown together by overwhelmed American officials, filled prisoner of war camps in the United States. Members of the elite Afrika Korps, Kriegsmarine, and Luftwaffe, some hard-core Nazis, nearly all veterans of the blitzkrieg years, mixed with less desirable Wehrmacht recruits captured later in the war, non-Germans, communists, socialists, and convicts, all threatening, beating up, and murdering each other in American camps. In the eyes of most Americans, all Germans were Nazis.

Guards and officials eventually learned that not all Germans were Nazis and not all German soldiers were even German. Conflicts between Nazi and anti-Nazi POWs proved the most dangerous. The Afrika Korps, by virtue of being the first captured, established an administrative system within the camps that closely resembled that of the Third Reich. These hard-line patriots demanded discipline, and anyone suspected of defeatism, lack of support for the regime, or being overly cooperative with U.S. personnel was classified as anti-Nazi. These men, once labeled by the Nazis, became grouped with the decidedly anti-Nazis, including socialists, communists, criminals, and foreigners who served with the Wehrmacht. A simple slip of the tongue landed many otherwise loyal soldiers in this group.

As long as they abided by the rules set forth by the United States, POWs governed themselves. This meant that the United States recognized the Nazi position as the legitimate authority within the camps. The Nazis established a regime that terrorized and brutalized noncompliant elements, policing the camps imposing discipline and order. They censored POW mail, newspapers, magazines, and anything that interfered with their manipulation of the facts. Nazi control ensured that the camps operated smoothly. At first this created a seemingly satisfactory relationship between the POWs and U.S. officials, but the limits of this arrangement would soon be revealed.

In most cases the Nazis ensured this domination with threats. Nazis at Camp Crossville, Tennessee, reminded their fellow POWs to "remember that you are still members of the German Army, whose duty it is to work for Germany."[2] One Nazi explained to U.S. officials that Germany intended to repay them for the good treatment its POWs received. "When Germany wins the war," he stated, "that will be at least one good mark on your record."[3] Herston Cooper, the U.S. commander at Crossville, complained that the Nazis created "a little Germany, where persecution of anti-Nazis was thorough and violent."[4] The Nazis made good on these threats when they deemed it necessary. Franz Josef Veltin, a POW in Oklahoma's Camp McAlester, tried to be "especially careful when reading an American newspaper or talking with any Americans."[5] Werner Baecher, after translating the news for his fellow POWs, was branded a traitor for "repeating enemy propaganda."[6]

The Nazis scrutinized every aspect of POW life, including religion. Radbert Kohlhaas, a former POW at Camp Gordon, aspired to become a Benedictine monk and received threats from his fellow POWs. The Nazis in the camp disliked his cooperation with the American chaplain. They considered Kohlhaas a defeatist and a traitor and threatened retaliation against his family in Germany unless he straightened up. The Nazis would find a "soldier who was going to be repatriated" and "give him the documents necessary for the police to interfere in Germany."[7] In another instance, a POW at Fort DuPont, Delaware, stood outside church and "warned would-be churchgoers that if they entered he'd note their names and they would discover the consequences when they got back to Germany."[8]

Helmut Hörner, captured in France in late 1944, kept a journal of his captivity. He described a conversation with several of his comrades concerning the Nazi activity. He commented that "part of them have been prisoners since 1942 and don't know about the situation in Russia or France. But they have newspapers here, for Hell's sake. They must know what is going on." His friend Siegfried added that "the best thing for us to do is keep our mouths shut. Otherwise there will only be trouble and that doesn't help anyone."[9]

The category of anti-Nazi included anyone not ardently in support of Nazi policies within the camps. The anti-Nazis feared the consequences if they voiced their real feelings, even after officials ultimately segregated them based on ideology and nationality. Sometimes camps became unofficially segregated, as occurred at Camp Stark, New Hampshire, which by coincidence housed more anti-Nazis than Nazis. Despite this, "there were always some ardent Nazis among them and the anti-Nazis had trouble maintaining a solid front against the Nazis." The Stark anti-Nazi group worried about "the triumph of fascism in America." They found "the American guards' preference for dealing with 'obedient' Nazi prisoners of war rather than democratically inclined anti-fascists who discussed and questioned everything" disturbing.[10]

In other situations where anti-Nazis outnumbered Nazis, such as at Camp Blanding, Florida, which housed naval POWs, the results proved different. Twenty-four ardent Nazis, including Lieutenant Berndt von Walther, segregated themselves from the 216 strident anti-Nazis. Walther claimed that "the camp was full of Reds, criminals, and traitors. I slept each night with a large stick by my bed, fearing for my life. We adamantly refused to go into the main compound and eventually persuaded the commanding officer to erect a 'dead line' separating us from the 'anti-Nazis.'"[11] These men pleaded with Major W. H. Lowman, the U.S. officer in charge of the camp; the PMGO; and the Swiss legation for a transfer to Camp McCain, Mississippi.

Still, Nazis dominated most camps. Continued Nazi threats, attacks on fellow POWs and occasionally guards, and forced suicides and murders caused officials to separate the POWs. The best-documented example of violence between Nazis and suspected anti-Nazis occurred at Camp Gruber, Tonkawa, Oklahoma, on November 4, 1943.[12] Corporal Kunze, a member of the Afrika Korps, gained the distrust of his fellows during the transfer from the battlefield to the POW camp with his defeatist comments and disinterest in the course of the war. His choice of authors, Immanuel Kant and Karl Jaspers, not to mention his use of the phrase *insa'Allah* (May Allah grant it) on his enclosure to a letter to his wife, drew more suspicion.[13] The Nazis monitored Kunze, using an intercepted letter to his wife and a note he wrote about Hamburg, Germany. These items, coupled with his being questioned by American intelligence officers, prompted the aforementioned "trial."[14]

An investigation of his murder revealed that nearly all the POWs believed Kunze had committed treason. His demeanor during the trial became a damning point even before Beyer ascribed the letters to Kunze. The announcement of Kunze being a traitor sent the crowd into a frenzy. Some attacked Kunze, others threw plates and items in the mess hall, most watched attentively, and few left. No one attempted to stop the attack. By the next morning, guards had found Kunze's body outside the mess hall. Stonewalling and fear among the POWs undermined initial attempts at investigating the murder. The Nazis declared Kunze a traitor and the other POWs knew that cooperation with the investigation may result in a midnight visit by the "good" Germans.[15]

Eventually, investigators offered to protect and transfer cooperative POWs, and many came forward. Their testimony resulted in the trial and conviction of five POWs.[16] Walter Beyer, the commanding officer and organizer of the meeting, protested that he neither struck Kunze nor ordered the beating. He claimed that he lost control of his men, but that as a traitor, Kunze deserved his fate. U.S. officials informed Beyer that Kunze had only shared useless common knowledge and old information. Beyer still called Kunze's act treason and responded that "when a man as foul as Kunze, with a wife and children in Germany, behaves this way, I don't wish to protect him. He committed a dirty crime." "I am only sorry that Kunze met his death here instead of Germany," he added. "I have no guilt in this matter."[17]

The United States tried the five men in a secret court-martial, the first trial of German POWs in an American court. The case proved problematic for the prosecution, who had to prove premeditated intent to kill rather than assault. Nearly all the witnesses said that the POWs only beat Kunze and that the wild melee made it impossible to identify anyone involved. Difficulties in translation arose, the Germans had trouble understanding the questions, and the translators seemingly took liberties with their responses.

During the trial, defense attorney Lieutenant Colonel Alfred C. Petsch and his colleague Major Murray B. Jones received assistance from Frederick Opp, a German POW and former lawyer in Germany. They argued that the POWs possessed the right to try and punish treason just as in the German army, and that American POWs under similar circumstances would act the same. They described the murder as not premeditated or intentional but a result of the administration of punishment. The defendants, therefore, should be charged with manslaughter, not murder. They denounced the legality of the POWs' earlier admissions of guilt or complicity in the crime, arguing that since this evidence had been recorded before the trial and was not based on purely voluntary statements, but given under duress and without aid of legal counsel, it should be inadmissible. The prosecution, led by Leon Jaworski, the trial judge advocate, refused to reduce the charges and destroyed the defense's case.[18]

Wilma Parnell, author of *The Killing of Corporal Kunze* and stenographer during the trial, questioned the proceedings. She felt that the defendants did not receive fair treatment during the trial. *Time* magazine, however, claimed that "the trial had leaned over backward to be fair" by permitting the defendants "a German lawyer, selected from among their fellow prisoners," and allowing them to "refuse to testify against themselves. They waived this privilege, insisted that their sworn testimony be heard, and proudly admitted their part in Kunze's liquidation."[19]

The court found the POWs guilty of "riot" and "murder"; sentenced them to death on January 25, 1944; and transferred them to Fort Leavenworth, Kansas, to await execution.[20] Some of the men hoped to be exchanged for American POWs awaiting the death penalty in Germany. Two of the former Afrika Korps men considered appealing, but their leader, Sergeant Walter Beyer, reminded them that "you are German soldiers.... I will not allow you to crawl before the enemy." They sat on death row until hanged in July 1945, becoming the first German POWs executed in the United States.[21]

U.S. officials and some historians have viewed the Kunze killing as a simple case of Nazi versus anti-Nazi, but in reality, it went much deeper. Four of the five men accused of the killing were members of the Nazi Party, but one held membership in the German Social Democratic Party, which opposed the Nazis on most issues.[22] Perhaps the inmates knew more of Kunze and his alleged treason than they admitted and felt betrayed by one of their own. Witnesses for the prosecution included non-Germans and members of the 999th Penal Brigade. Also, three of the damning testimonies against the perpetrators came from non-German nationals, two Poles and one Czech, men who had personal conflicts with the Nazi element.[23]

There were numerous other cases of murder and forced suicides. Captain Felix Tropschuh, held at Camp Concordia, Kansas, a "defeatist" condemned by his diary entries, received a choice from other POWs of suicide or allowing his entire family to face repercussions in postwar Germany. Tropschuh chose the former and on October 19, 1943, after slightly more than three months in captivity, hanged himself. At the request of the POWs, he was buried away from the POW graveyard, and none of the POWs attended the services.[24] Two POWs hanged Horst Günther, a POW at Aiken, South Carolina, on April 5, 1944. Sergeant Erich Gauss and Private Rudolf Straub, convicted of killing Günther, explained that he had favored the American guards over the German POWs when distributing food. President Franklin D. Roosevelt denied an appeal to commute their death sentence and they were hanged in July 1945.[25]

Hugo Krauss, captured in North Africa, gained the suspicion of his fellow POWs and suffered a visit from the "Holy Ghost" on December 17, 1943. Naturalized in the United States, Krauss sympathized with the Nazi Party and, after returning to Germany, joined the Wehrmacht. Although he joined the army, expressed pro-Nazi sentiments, and served in the Soviet Union and North Africa, he quickly changed his views once behind barbed wire at Camp Hearne, Texas. He claimed defeat loomed for Germany, criticized its government and military, and told other POWs that he was both "a German and an American."[26] Segregating himself from many of the activities practiced by his fellow POWs only deepened the suspicions against him. The Nazis in the camp alleged that Krauss had not only exhibited defeatism but, more seriously, also delivered information to the Americans.

The Nazis' case against Krauss seemed to convince even the less ardent POWs. They called him a traitor and a spy. They beat him in his barracks under the cover of lights out, giving him skull fractures and broken arms. He died six days later.[27] The United States questioned many POWs in the Krauss case; some admitted that they may have heard the commotion, but no one "officially" saw anything. Despite "exhaustive investigation" by the PMGO, including interviews of "forty-nine witnesses ... five being American personnel," the guilty parties remained unidentified until two years later, when a guilt-ridden Guenther Meisel admitted he was one of eight men who had participated in the attack. Nearly everyone in the camp hated Krauss, he affirmed, and "not one person in the entire company [of all the POWs, not just the eight assailants] said one word against the action. Everybody approved of the beating, but many of them were too clever to join in. They encouraged us by talking for it."[28] To avert suspicion, the attackers had come from a different barracks and struck at night. The POWs in Barracks 1, where Krauss slept, knew of the impending assault and had orders to "stay in bed and be quiet."[29] They used sticks and pipes, and Meisel admitted that he hit Krauss with enough force to break his stick. As he returned to his own barracks, he recalled the men of Barracks 2 watching him pass by. "I shall never forget those faces. Someone asked if Krauss was dead. I knew then the affair was serious. I had not intended to kill Krauss or to help others kill him. I just wanted to beat him. I had tried not to hit him on the head because I did not want him to die."[30] Meisel based his decision to come forward on the advice of his girlfriend, a devout Christian and an American, whom he met while on work detail. Meisel received life in prison, later reduced to fifteen years, while the four other men also received prison terms but were all paroled "after only three years in prison" and returned to Germany in 1949.[31]

These cases exemplify the many instances of murder and forced suicide within the camps. According to one estimate, Nazis put to death as many as three hundred men.[32] Investigators faced similar difficulties in each case, and although they made arrests, violence continued. Officials prosecuted the accused using the "Disciplinary and Control Measures Applicable to Prisoners of War," which complied with the Geneva Convention and scaled punishments to the offense.[33] Murder earned a court-martial followed by a prison sentence or the death penalty. More paperwork accompanied a court-martial, including the WD-AGO Form and the "Check List for Records of Trial of Prisoners of War by General Court-Martial, as to Compliance with the Geneva Convention."[34] Fort Leavenworth usually housed the accused. Many of those found guilty of murder received the death penalty, but the sentence was not given out until after V-E Day to avoid retaliation against German-held American POWs. The PMGO and the judge advocate general kept records of all the cases and listed those accused or found guilty of murder in the "General Courts-Martial of Prisoners of War" summary.[35]

German and Non-German

Obviously not all acts of violence or disruption in the camps centered exclusively on Nazi POWs, since, contrary to the prevailing belief, not all Germans were Nazis. In the same vein, not all anti-Nazis were political outcasts, criminals, or non-Germans. Often mischief, theft, and violence among POWs originated from nationalism, ethnicity, or just plain greed rather than Nazism. These early assumptions and mistakes in observation, however, make it difficult to ascertain what political or national group deserved responsibility for the myriad of obstructive and murderous activities within POW camps.

The greatest degree of separation of nationalities within the camps occurred between Germans and Austrians, despite many cultural similarities. Austria was a Catholic nation and Germany largely a Protestant one, although large segments of the southern population were also Catholic. While the voting procedures proved questionable, the Austrians voted for the Anschluss, which had annexed their country to the Greater German Reich. Once in American custody, many Austrians sought complete and total separation from the Germans, in essence ending the "Greater German" unity within some POW camps. Some feared that the American guards or government would repay the Germans for atrocities committed during the war and did not want to get lumped in with them. Many Nazis suspected their Austrian allies of defeatism and disloyalty, and this caused many Austrians to close ranks.

The Free Austria Movement, an organization devoted to establishing an independent Austria, reinforced this separation by giving and receiving support to and from Austrian POWs. It claimed that "Austria has been overrun and brutally oppressed by Hitler and the Nazi bandits, and that the Austrians serve in the despised German army only because they were forced to do so." The Free Austria Movement struggled to "show the world . . . that Austria was the first victim of the Nazi barbarism and that she has the undeniable right of her reestablished independence."[36] According to the historian Allan Kent Powell, the Austrians held "the Germans responsible for the war and considered themselves the victims of German militarism."[37] At times, these national divisions also took an elitist turn. In the Logan, Utah, POW camp, the Vienna "elite" segregated themselves from their Austrian cohorts and dominated the POW end of the camp's operations.[38]

This rivalry became apparent on the playing fields as well as in more dangerous ways. Former POWs Georg Hirschmann and Eric Kososik remembered how Austrian-versus-German soccer games that started in rough play often ended in fighting. Hirschmann, a German, also recalled being placed in an Austrian compound. His experience lasted only one night and the Austrians were happy to be rid of him. As he put it, "although I was no Nazi, for the Austrians if you were a German you were a Nazi."[39]

There was also rivalry between the Italians and Germans, who sometimes shared POW camps. According to the camp guards, the Italians posed less danger and were less fascist than the Germans, often getting them better treatment. Once the Italian government actually changed sides and joined the Allies, the Italian POWs received many privileges as they awaited repatriation to join Italian field units.

The Germans looked with contempt upon the treatment and behavior of their one-time Allies. At Crossville, German POWs commented on the frivolous requests and questionable sexual nature of their Italian counterparts. The Italian officers insisted that they be able to take baths, a privilege enjoyed in the Italian military, instead of the showers provided in the POW camps. They also demanded partitions with working doors between the commodes. These men threatened to contact the Swiss representatives to ensure that their demands were met, and the United States quickly complied. Elated at the victory, "even the taunts and insults hurled at them from the German compounds failed to disturb their joyful concentration on the anticipation of the satisfaction of their simple want."⁴⁰ Education among the groups became another method of segregation. German POWs completed correspondence credit for college and high school classes, while the Italians, among whom "there was a high illiteracy rate," learned "the three R's."⁴¹

Italian Service Units (ISU) caused jealousy among and bad publicity for the Germans. The U.S. government created the ISU from among the former Italian POWs. These men cooperated with their former captors, worked for the military, and received benefits such as weekend passes. A lot of ISU men used their new privileges to date American women, and some of these women became pregnant, angering their families and the public. While the ISU men "lived it up," the Germans remained behind barbed wire, but most Americans did not distinguish between them. Americans generally thought that "prisoners were prisoners, enemy was enemy, and many knew that their sons were dying in Italy. If these ISU men were helping us, if they really were our allies, why didn't they go home and fight? If they were prisoners why didn't they stay behind barbed wire where they belonged?"⁴² Many Germans considered the ISU men traitors to the Axis cause.

Captured Soviet nationals serving the Wehrmacht caused consternation for all involved. Once in POW camps, many of these men claimed that they had been forced into service and wanted nothing more to do with the Nazis or the Germans. Many Soviet conscripts and volunteers in the German service jumped ship to gain favor with the United States. This stance did not endear them to the Nazis. The United States, in accord with an agreement with the USSR, exchanged these men for American soldiers liberated by the Red Army. These men were doubly damned. By alienating the Germans, they tempted the "Holy Ghost"; by returning home, they faced a court-martial for treason, probably accompanied by a summary execution. When they learned of their eventual exchange, many Soviet POWs reacted suddenly and violently with eruptions in camps across the United States. They officially protested, claimed citizenship from other nations, rioted, and sometimes committed suicide. The United States had to subdue them before they could be exchanged.⁴³

The Three "Worst" Camps in the United States: Concordia, Kansas; Clewiston, Florida; and Crossville, Tennessee

Most of the powder keg's explosions were loud and violent. Fortunately, it seemed that as suddenly as it erupted in one camp, it subsided again, but nothing prepared the United States for the intensity and volume of the problems in the three worst camps.

The Concordia, Kansas, camp had six murder-suicides by POWs, a POW shot and killed by a guard, a riot, and the shooting of the camp commander's wife by a guard. Many of the problems at Concordia seemed traceable to its commander, Lieutenant Colonel John A. Sterling, recalled from retirement to run the camp. Under his administration, supervision of guards was lax and the facilities had many deficiencies. The POWs lacked a recreation area and had poorly planned heating and latrine systems. Nazi control of the interior, however, maintained complete order.

The POWs maintained order and efficiency, even dotting their barracks with pictures of pinup girls and cooperating with U.S. officials, but behind this innocent-looking facade, the Nazis dominated.[44] The Nazis oversaw several court-martials leading to forced suicides, including those of a German captain who hanged himself "with a bath cord" after one week in camp and an Austrian anti-Nazi private who slashed his wrists.[45] Concordia is also where Captain Felix Tropschuh's forced suicide occurred on October 19, 1943. During the winter of 1944, Concordia authorities realized that Tropschuh's death and other murders and suicides had been politically motivated and acted to move four politically "at-risk" POWs to other camps.

Other instances of Nazi bullying and threatening abounded, but at Concordia POWs also feared the guards. They had gunned down one man, a POW named Huebner, as he crossed the deadline to retrieve a soccer ball.[46] A POW witness, Gerhard Gruenzig, stated, "Several times the ball went into the security zone, and the guards permitted us to get the ball. Then they would not permit it anymore and the guard shot our comrade through the head as he stood."[47] Another account, however, stated that Huebner disregarded a warning, intentionally kicked the ball into the dead zone, and then followed after it while "looking back over his shoulder and laughing at the guard in the nearest sentry tower."[48] The POWs reacted to the shooting, according to Gruenzig, "with stone-throwing and a two-hour demonstration."[49] All the camp guards on leave were recalled and civilians evacuated the camp in reaction to the POW protest. One of the guards recalled that "the prisoners got in their formations and started marching up and down the road in the compound singing German songs. They kept it up for 48 hours or longer. We were kind of outnumbered, four to one, and didn't know what was going to happen."[50] Eventually, the POWs returned to the barracks and the riot ended.

The night of October 23, 1943, made the situation even tenser for the guards and camp officials. The incident centered on Lieutenant David Roberts, the commander of the 456th Guard Company, based at Camp Concordia. On the night in question, despite being the officer on duty, he had a few drinks in the officers' club. He later claimed that he did not become inebriated.[51] During the evening, a heated argument began between Roberts and the wife and daughter of Captain King, the transportation officer and president of the officers' mess. Roberts admitted that he became enraged, pulled his pistol, and fired at least three shots at Captain King's wife. Mrs. Sterling, wife of the post commander, stepped between Mrs. King and Captain Roberts and received a bullet through the abdomen. Mrs. King and her daughter attempted to subdue Roberts and held him until the male officers of the club arrested him.[52] Authorities feared that Roberts's mental state might trace back to his four years of service in World War II with the British.[53] This incident marked the low point of the troubles within the camp, and a new commander with stricter discipline prevented further problems.[54] The historian Lowell A. May stated that "by this time, Camp Concordia was getting a bad reputation in the local press and throughout the Army as the worst POW camp in the country."[55] May and citizens near the camp were not the only ones who noticed the problems. Reports filled papers in the United States and even appeared in the *London Daily Mail*.[56] Headlines included "Berserk Captain Shoots Wife of Col. Sterling," "German Prisoners End Lives after Camp 'Court-Martials,'" and "Nazi Terrorism Specter behind Prison Camp Deaths."[57]

The POW camp at Clewiston, Florida, established in February 1944 as a branch camp of the Aliceville, Alabama, camp, was identified as the "worst in all America" by Guy Métraux, the IRC investigator.[58] The location of the camp, in a sugar-cane field devoid of shade and pounded by the Florida sun, created terrible living conditions for the POWs and the guards. The Florida *Palm Beach Post* stated: "If there were a perfect hell for German prisoners, this was it: Temperatures as searing as 103 degrees in summer, dust even thicker than the mosquitoes, back-breaking work in the cane fields. And if you tried to escape, there was no way out—if the swamps didn't get you, the snakes might."[59]

Among the problems that the Red Cross found were the presence of "only 12 latrines for 293 prisoners; only two had seats. It had three showers, one of which sometimes had hot water." There was evidence that "prisoners were deliberately injuring themselves in hopes they would be transferred to northern camps with more hospitable facilities."[60]

The prisoners at Clewiston were as tough as the conditions. Within the camp lurked 310 hard-core nationalists, according to the local paper, "arrogant Nazis," and most from the Afrika Korps.[61] A continual assault upon the POWs by Florida snakes broke up the monotony of the hard work and dreary living conditions. Catching and skinning these snakes became a sport and pastime. Clewiston also shared the political and ideological problems faced by other POW camps.

There was the mysterious "suicide" of Karl Behrens, who escaped but was later found dead, hanging from a tree just two miles from the camp.[62] Authorities and prisoners alike questioned why Behrens would wait until after he escaped to hang himself with his own duffel bag. Rumors that other POWs or angry guards had caught him and killed him abounded. Behrens's brother, Bernhard, believed it to be a suicide. He said that his brother had "difficulty dealing with the hard labor, the homesickness and depression, and the intolerable heat" and that "his father had tried to kill himself several times.... Karl never got over the shock."[63] Behrens was one of just four POWs who escaped from the camp. The camp also suffered from poor administration. For long periods, the POWs lacked hot water, cigarettes and beer, and adequate recreation areas—in other words, things that they were entitled to by the Geneva Convention.[64]

The prisoner of war camp at Crossville, Tennessee, had its own problems. Much of the trouble stemmed from a handful of individuals, mostly officers within the camp.[65] Escapes became commonplace. Captain Wolfgang Hermann Hellfritsch, who fled on October 23, 1943, had the honor of being first to break free. He remained at large for a year before being apprehended while working on a farm outside Lexington, Kentucky.[66] Officials at Crossville faced other problems. Former POW Emmerich von Mirbach recalled that to pass the time at Crossville, "a group of officers, by design, shipped off conflicting complaints to the Swiss. Some said their quarters were too hot, others found them much too cold. Food was highly seasoned, too bland, contained too much starch, too little starch, was monotonous, skimpy, and so on."[67] The POWs also "refused to write home" for such a prolonged period of time that the Swiss, as the protecting power, began to question how the camp was operated. Eventually, the "Americans were asking the Germans to *please* write to their families."[68]

The POWs continued their nuisance attacks. When forced to attend the lowering of the U.S. flag, they saluted with three *Sieg heils*. A U.S. officer claimed that the POWs were "like boys in prep school, always experimenting to see what they might be able to get away with."[69] *Fregattenkapitän* Jürgen Wattenberg, although not the highest-ranking officer in the camp, became leader and one of the chief agitators. The camp was divided between enlisted men and officers, with a public road running between the two sections. Wattenberg wanted all the men to stand near the fence by the roadside with signs pleading for the American people to come to their aid. Although never put into action, the plan demonstrated the mischievous thinking of the POWs. The final act of nuisance involved POWs August Maus and Fritz Guggenberger attempting to spend their canteen credits. These men, without permission, ordered from the Sears catalog "a smoked turkey, rings, watches, a set of dishes, and several items perhaps of use to a potential escape." They only received the dishes, which they kept and divided after repatriation.[70]

The Nazis worked within Crossville as well. Many became agitated when a U.S. officer of Jewish descent was put in charge of one of the compounds. They responded by committing arson and other acts of defiance. Eventually, a German officer spoke to Herston Cooper, the commanding officer of the camp, and explained that he pitied him for failing "to deal sternly with your prisoners [and for] actually be[ing] kind to them. You, therefore, do not possess the qualities of a good soldier and are considered by us to be easy prey." He ended the conversation with the threat: "You will be killed."[71] Cooper urged that since they were alone, he do it now, but the POW officer walked away.[72]

The threat of that conversation did not bear fruit until February 1943. On this day, the German POW officers refused to vacate their barracks for inspection.[73] Cooper recalled asking one of the influential German officers apparently not directly involved in the incident to assist in making his comrades get out. The German replied that there was nothing he could do to stop "the battle of Crossville," and the officers refused to leave until forced by an armed guard.[74] About an hour after the barracks check was complete, the POWs were escorted back to their compound. At this point, a signal was given by the same POW officer who had commented about the battle of Crossville, and a group of POWs rushed the stockade commanding officer.[75] The guards reacted quickly enough to stop most of the group, but one man grabbed the stockade commanding officer and applied a "hammer lock" on his arm. This man was pried loose only after being kicked by the stockade commanding officer's steel boots and prodded by the guards' bayonets. According to Cooper, he even "grabbed the gleaming bayonets with his hands."[76] Once in the hospital, this man "continued to scream that he wanted to die for his Fuehrer in the battle of Crossville. He wanted to be left alone to die for Germany."[77] The next morning, he died. He was buried with military honors in a nearby cemetery. Later, almost as a last act of defiance, the POWs requested that he be exhumed and buried in a new cemetery nearer the camp.[78]

Historian John Hammond Moore's account differs slightly from Cooper's. Moore stated that after the guards appeared in riot gear, an agreement was reached whereby two to four of the German officers would accompany the guards on the search of the compound while the other POWs waited in another compound. After the search ended, "a guard, overzealous and irritated, hit an officer named Graf in the stomach as he was leaving—why is not entirely clear. Graf died of internal injuries a few days later."[79] The differences in Moore's brief account, which favored the POWs, might be attributed to the fact that interviews with the POWs housed at Crossville and involved in this incident constituted his major sources.

American Guards, German Prisoners of War

Wide differences in background and experience among American camp guards affected the treatment of POWs. Initially, security concerns led to a ratio of one guard to every three POWs, placing immense manpower strains on the use of POW labor outside camps.[80] Recruiting camp guards ranked low on the scale in manpower competition within the military. Many guards had been unfit for regular military duty because of age, infirmity, or other reasons. Some of them had been sent home from the battle fronts for various reasons.[81] Major Maxwell McKnight, chief of the Administrative Section of POW Camp Operations, explained that in assigning guards, "we were pretty much dredging the bottom of the barrel. We had all kinds of kooks and wacky people. Men were selected in haphazard fashion, often merely because they knew a few words of German."[82]

The use of more experienced soldiers sent home from the battle fronts because of injury, transfer, or rest and refit did not necessarily mean better adherence to the Geneva provisions. They brought preconceived notions of the enemy developed in Europe or the Pacific. Even guards who did not serve in combat overseas knew that the POWs attempted to kill American soldiers. These notions led to mixed results as the guards carried out their duties. Most guards did their job well, but these accounts pale in comparison to the number of violent reactions to the POWs and the even larger number of fraternization cases.

The Germans at Camp Leonard Wood, Missouri, remembered the hostile attitude of the guards: "There was one guard to every ten prisoners during work. They tried to make themselves look important in the eyes of the girls. To show off, the guards would sometimes use the stocks of their weapons on us. It was also a laughing matter to us that the guards habitually had their fingers on the triggers of their weapons, ready for use on us if needed. . . . [They] were always looking for trouble. They were ridiculed even by their fellow Americans on occasion when they used their power to subdue a helpless POW."[83]

A POW at Camp Bliss, Texas, complained that "American guards 'speak very freely of shooting whenever an infraction of the regulations had been committed, just as if we are criminals.'"[84] At Camp Clark, Missouri, POWs accused the guards of insulting and mistreating them. These claims were of dubious reliability, as Camp Clark personnel established a reputation for cooperation and friendship with the camp's Italian POWs, and the accusers had been transferred to Clark from other camps largely based on their poor behavior.[85] False claims like these caused problems between guards and POWs across the nation. When coupled with instances of POWs insulting the guards, according to the historian Allan Kent Powell, it became "easy to understand why a guard might 'bust them in the nose or shoot in the air' if pushed too far. On one occasion at a Missouri camp the guard fired his rifle at the prisoners because they defied his orders against smoking. Luckily he did not hit any of them."[86] In another instance, a guard pointed his pistol at the German spokesman in order to get the prisoners to follow orders to work.[87]

At times the guards acted with excessive force. At Camp Carson, Colorado, the POWs claimed that the guards attacked them with tear gas without provocation or warning while they were en route to their labor assignment. Camp officials responded that "the captives were not guinea pigs for army maneuvers but were inadvertently driven through a tear gas demonstration on the main post."[88] At Camp Barkeley, Texas, two escaped POWs complained that when they were apprehended, the guards "beat them unnecessarily with blackjacks, otherwise brutalized them, and subjected them to public ridicule by parading the POWs in front of civilians while handcuffed."[89] An investigation validated these charges. In a separate instance another POW recalled that "blue, yellow, and green marks could be seen on our comrades after they had concluded their time in the stockade."[90]

The POWs feared that their complaints would fall on deaf ears or exacerbate the situation. American officials sometimes made communication difficult, as was the case at Camp Patrick Henry, Virginia. Lieutenant Kugel, the assistant executive officer of the Intellectual Diversion program, created to administer the reeducation program, earned the dubious title of "Der Propaganda Minister" among the German POWs. According to Captain Herman W. Graupner of the Special Projects Division, Kugel's activities caused a "considerable set back at this camp" and he "attracted attention to himself by his super secretive mannerisms, by constantly carrying a brief case and by many ill advised remarks made to the prisoners of war."[91] Failure to create an understanding among the guards, officials, and POWs occasionally led to tragic results.

At Salina, Utah, on July 8, 1945, Private Clarence V. Bertucci, considered mentally unstable and already with two courts-martial, received guard duty after returning from non-combat service in England. During the night he turned the guard tower's .30-caliber machine gun onto the tents of the sleeping POWs, killing eight and wounding twenty. He later explained that "he had hated Germans, so he had killed Germans."[92]

Major Paul Neuland, chief of the Field Service Branch, interviewed Colonel Leonard Smith, commander of Camp Atlanta, Nebraska, during a field service visit and reported that he found "the appearance, attitude, and morale of the guards unsatisfactory. The transfer of one-third overseas soldiers into his guard personnel has been detrimental. These men for the most part are mentally unstable and what he terms *trigger happy*. They are sullen and make the worst possible impressions on the German prisoners of war. A good number of them have had to be discharged." He "recommended that greater attention be given to the type of American personnel assigned to prisoner of war camps." The program would "fall short of its goals if the worst type of American personnel were used in the camps."[93] Neuland added that "this has been a general complaint on the part of every commanding officer interviewed thus far."[94]

The varying numbers of guards at the prisoner of war camps also compounded the problems. Some camps had too many guards, others too few. James M. Alexander, inspecting the POW camp at Indiantown Gap Military Reservation, Pennsylvania, noted that only ninety men provided the entire administrative and guard detail for the POW installation and none of the American personnel could speak German, although "several of them are very much interested in studying German."[95]

Black GIs, German POWs

The color line provided another source of tension between guards and POWs. Black soldiers faced discrimination within and outside the camps. They suffered "gratuitous humiliations [such] as the segregation of black plasma and even the refusal of service in restaurants where German prisoners of war dined."[96] Segregation on base often prepared African American soldiers for what to expect in town. They protested that POWs received better treatment than they did. A wounded African American soldier complained that "the sick and disabled [black] soldier is treated worst than a Jap, or German Prisoner ever dreamed of."[97] Another soldier at Camp Livingston, Louisiana, lamented that "German P.W.'s here have more rights and freedom" than black soldiers.[98]

Another African American soldier, Eugene Gaillard, contrasted the racism blacks faced from southerners at Camp Robinson, Arkansas, to the relationship at Fort Dix, New Jersey, between black guards and German POWs, who "were very courteous, very nice."⁹⁹ Eddie Donald, a GI at Camp Claiborne, Louisiana, commented that black soldiers faced a great deal of racism from their white counterparts, but even northern whites suffered catcalls of "'Yankee' and adjectives of the uncomplimentary kind were generally attached." He recalled that the German POWs had better quarters and more freedom than black soldiers: "They were given passes to town when black soldiers were confined to the area and did not have their privileges." In this instance he may have been confusing the ISU men with Germans, although the essential point remains the same. Donald added, "This was one of the most repugnant things I can recall of the many things that happened to Negro servicemen."¹⁰⁰

David Carson Jr., a black soldier from Michigan serving at Camp Gordon, Georgia, received the same treatment "as the Negro civilian population living in the area" despite his soldier status.¹⁰¹ He witnessed firsthand exactly what that meant during a layover in Texas. While searching for a restaurant that served blacks, he observed that at the train station restaurant, whites and German POWs were "comfortably seated, laughing, talking, making friends, with the waitresses at their beck and call. If I had tried to enter that dining room the ever-present MPs would have busted my skull, a citizen-soldier of the United States."¹⁰² Richard Carter had a similar experience while crossing through Texas. When he searched for "colored" facilities, he spotted "American MPs and some of Hitler's bully boys, now prisoners of war, . . . having a ball together, wining and dining! It was sickening."¹⁰³

According to the *Atlanta Daily World,* "German prisoners of war have started here a system of working hat in hand with the Bourbon South in the matter of giving the Negro soldiers another slap in the face."¹⁰⁴ Black soldiers, frustrated with discrimination and witnessing preferential treatment being given to prisoners of war over African American soldiers, had little recourse. Protest or violence in this situation typically resulted in the black soldiers being on the losing side of a physical and legal confrontation.

Housing prisoners of war in the United States obviously led to many problems and many concerns. Some of the American guards and civilians resented the Germans for what they had done in Europe, for the Nazi regime, and for the treatment they received. Good treatment of POWs also brought to the fore the poor treatment of African Americans, specifically those in uniform. The events within the POW camps reached a boiling point. POWs threatened, attacked, and murdered each other and defied orders from the guards and camp commanders. In at least one instance, they attacked the camp commander. U.S. authorities, the American public, and many of the POWs had had enough. To make matters worse, each time an incident of violence or escape occurred, the public became informed through a chain of communication from the military to the local police to the local news agencies. Some of the manhunts required the FBI and the media to be involved. Any attempts to enforce a media blackout failed; too many civilians worked on base and POWs in the community, not to mention the occurrences of guards telling family and friends. Through these same channels the public knew of the murder and mischief within the camps and Americans reacted vocally and harshly to these Nazi attempts to control the United States from the inside. The POWs also earned the enmity of many guards and civilians, and it was time for the "coddling" of these individuals by the U.S. military to end and for greater restrictions to be in place. It appeared that by early 1944 the Nazis and other troublemakers within the camps had soured the United States on housing German prisoners and threatened the success of the entire POW program.

Chapter 4

Love Thy Enemy: Coddling, Segregating, and Fraternizing with German POWs

> *I've got no love for these blankety-blanks. When I first came here, it made me sore to see how well we treat them. But my father got word last month that my brother Phil is a prisoner of the Germans. If we treat these fellows here bad, Phil will take the rap for it. So now, whenever I do something for these blankety-blanks, I just figure I am doing it for Phil.*
> —Anonymous American solider

Americans reacted to the housing of the German POWs with mixed emotions.[1] The number of injuries and deaths of American boys overseas continued to rise and the army discovered evidence of German military atrocities. GIs taken captive by the enemy suffered torture and deprivation while POWs held by the United States enjoyed dry clothes and warm food. News of POW escapes, violence, and mischief reached the public through the press, police dispatches, military releases, and the rumor mill. Confidential information sometimes leaked out of the camps; often it poured out. The local prisoner of war camps usually created the biggest news for the area communities and proved irksome for citizens whose family members were away at war. An American public that already hated the German enemy and especially the Nazi scourge became incensed at the activities of the Nazis "next door." The actions of a few prisoners brought much negative attention to all German POWs.

Citizens charged the military with coddling the enemy and complained bitterly about this treatment in newspapers and to politicians. Camp guards often expressed their anger toward the POWs more directly and violently. In the midst of this distrust, misunderstanding, and violence, the reactions also ran to the other end of the spectrum. Guards allegedly escorted POWs out on the town and engaged in drinking parties. Employers allowed prisoners to roam freely and invited them to dine at their houses. POWs engaged in sexual activities with their female co-workers. These charges of fraternization fed directly into the accusations of coddling. Military officials used the Geneva Convention as a defense of humane treatment but at the same time investigated and took measures to end the problems in the camps.

POWs' fraternization with civilians and guards presented a problem, and army regulations forbade it. The cooperative attitude of many war prisoners, their hard-working nature, and the fact that some of the Americans either felt sorry for them or themselves were of German ancestry made preventing these relationships difficult.[2] In many cases, guards and camp officials fostered friendships to prevent problems within the camps. These attitudes made POWs more cooperative in camp life, labor, and providing information to the U.S. officials.

The actions of the guards colored the reactions of the POWs. Leonhard Reul, a former German POW, recalled that "we always got along well with our American guards." He remembered one guard who "was a colorful character who used to say 'Fuck the army' or 'You damn Germans make me sick. Instead of watching you sons of bitches, I could be at home making a lot of money.' I used to cool him down by telling him at least he didn't have to go to the front line." Reul added that "we Germans were never offended by his crude remarks because we too were familiar with a trooper's tongue."[3]

Former POW Alfred Schmucker, who spent time in Arizona and California camps, commented on the lack of respect GIs gave American officers: "Many times we noticed that a GI did not take his hands out of his pockets while talking to an officer. We are all human beings; there are good ones and bad ones, there are intelligent ones and there are dummies. That applied to the prisoners as well as to the guards."[4] Schmucker recalled the limited interaction with the guards on work details because of "the language barrier which prevented the exchange of a meaningful conversation." In addition, "during their 8-hour shift, there was nothing for them to do but to stand around, sometimes in other people's way."[5]

At other times mutual respect and friendship formed the basis of the relationships between guards and POWs. Former POW Heinrich Kersting remembered playing ping-pong with the guards and the friendly competition the guards arranged between POWs. He became friends with his civilian employer Elmar Ruehling. Kersting told Ruehling that he met his "future wife when we were 11 years old and that we had planned to marry on her 21st birthday in 1944. For a carton of cigarettes, [Elmar] got me a 14-karat gold wedding ring. From that ring we made two rings. Later, my fiancée and I put these rings on our fingers when we married. We wore them until her death in February 1986. Today the rings are worn by my daughter and the wife of my eldest son."[6]

Former POW Rudolf Hinkelmann recalled that "when the guard who was watching us had to let down his pants behind a nearby bush, he gave me his loaded rifle and told me to watch it. He could have given it to any other prisoner because nobody would have threatened or harmed anyone with it. Why should we have? Secretly we were glad to be in captivity and in safe hands."[7]

Al Griego, a former guard at the Louisiana Camp, Missouri, remembered the trust that he placed in POWs on labor details: "I would set my gun down in the corner and just watch the Germans work." He added that "I could have gotten by without even taking my gun. A lot of people laugh about it and say 'Griego, damn it, the way you left your rifle lying around those Germans could have downed you right now.' But I wasn't scared."[8]

The relationships between guards and their POWs in Missouri camps became so amicable that some German POWs sold purses made of snakeskin and replicas of German medals made from toothpaste tubes to their guards.[9] At Weingarten, Missouri, "after a . . . guard accidentally shot himself while loading his gun, camp authorities refused to issue any more ammunition," apparently believing that the dangers some guards posed to themselves were greater than any they might face from the prisoners.[10] Teresa Drury, an area resident, witnessed a shocking incident when a POW work detail passed by. She saw the guard riding in front of a wagon with several POWs holding pitchforks riding behind him and "feared the prisoners might kill the guard; however, she soon realized that this was a common sight at Weingarten."[11] At one Missouri branch camp, guards even planned to take POWs to a football game until the War Department intervened.[12]

Extreme "trust" barely begins to describe the relationship between American guards and German POWs at the Lake Wabaunsee POW camp in Kansas. The local newspaper stated that "both the Army men and prisoners are delighted with the prospect of living at Lake Wabaunsee this summer."[13] POWs often worked "without any guards" and "considered the [barbed wire] fence to be only 'symbolic.'"[14] Roger Schwalm employed POWs on his farm, including Ernst Künzel, who once wandered through the pasture unattended with a loaded shotgun, looking for rabbits. He returned with ten rabbits.[15]

The POWs affected civilian co-workers differently, and these relationships had various results. Anti-fraternization regulations applied to civilians, and the military especially hoped to prevent POWs from forming sexual relationships with the women who lived nearby. Werner Gilbert, a former POW at Camp Cooke, California, recalled that we were forbidden by the American authorities to establish personal relationships that might lead to romance with American women who were working at Camp Cooke. Most POWs, myself included, abided by this restriction. Some of us established good friendships, however. One co-worker from the shoemaker's shop went a little further and was caught with a woman. Instead of reporting the POW, the GI simply borrowed the woman for three days. In another instance, one of the kitchen helpers had an affair with an American woman. The couple, who were in a car, were unexpectedly interrupted when a second love pair showed up wanting to get inside the car with the first couple. It turned out that the second girl was the daughter of the one already in the car.[16]

At least two POWs at Camp Cooke engaged in romantic relationships with civilian female employees, and these may be the same ones to whom Gilbert referred. In one instance a POW bus driver used his access to the bus for romantic interludes in more remote areas of the camp, and a different encounter concerned a mother of nine caught in the act with a German prisoner.[17] Major Cecil Parshall recalled that "those Germans out at Papago Park were a fine bunch of men—smart, good-looking, well-built. Hell, down at Florence we had to put machine guns on top of the trains to scare off the women when those Italians arrived. Says something about our patriotism, doesn't it?"[18]

Sexual misconduct among prisoners also posed a potential problem. At Crossville, Tennessee, the camp commander felt that the Italian POWs were "too contented" and "suspected a social regime of homosexuality."[19] The German POWs, by contrast, posted a sign that read: "Ein guter soldat muss verzichten Konnen (a good soldier must learn to do without)."[20]

Apprehension, Fear, and Coddling

Reports of escapes, murders, threats, and mischief within the prisoner of war camps worried the American public. Citizens also knew of the strained relationships between guards and POWs and recognized that, despite the problems caused by prisoners of war, they still received good treatment, warm clothes, shelter, and food in quality and quantity unavailable to the average citizen. They also understood that American boys were suffering in Europe and in the Pacific and facing death and hardship, while the enemy in custody lived easy behind barbed wire. The American people may not have appreciated the extent to which the Geneva Convention guaranteed that German prisoners had access to the same caloric content, clothing, and facilities as U.S. soldiers, which typically exceeded that given to civilians. For example, soldiers received more meat in their diet than the average citizen, and the German POWs became entitled to these same privileges and comforts. Many citizens feared and disliked the German POWs and claimed that the U.S. Army coddled the enemy.

The charge of coddling erupted suddenly and forcefully in late 1943 and gained strength over the next two years. Plenty of evidence seemed to validate this claim. The menu of prisoners of war provided damning evidence in the eyes of an angry population. F. G. Alletson Cook, writing for the *New York Times*, produced one of the first rallying cries on the topic and voiced the thoughts that occupied the minds of many Americans in his article "Nazi Prisoners Are Nazis Still."[21] Cook visited the POW camp near White Sulphur Springs, West Virginia. He never used the word "coddling" but instead discussed how POWs worked, respected the American officers, and never tried to escape. He also talked about the POW food allowance, stating that "in the matter of food they are certainly better off than the average citizen 'on the outside,' for they have no rationing troubles and no shortages of anything. In their modern kitchens I saw piles of juicy hams, plenty of butter, steaks and sausages."[22] The author continued, however, "They get exactly the same rations as the American soldier, but cook what they get in the German way."[23]

After Cook's article, the discussion of coddling became more frequent. A December 24, 1943, *New York Times* letter to the editor queried why POWs were well fed when many families had to forgo a turkey for Thanksgiving and Christmas. The writer stated that no one would object to the U.S. soldiers receiving the small quantities available but asked why part of this allotment went to POWs. He bluntly stated that "it is known that German, Japanese and Italian prisoners do not know that such a thing as food rationing exists ... that they suffered from no dearth of turkey on Thanksgiving [and] that large roasts are not unusual in prison camps.... [It] becomes time to overhaul conceptions as to the proper treatment of prisoners of war."[24]

The feeding of prisoners of war struck a negative chord with Americans not only because of their own hardships at home but also because of the treatment of U.S. soldiers being held captive by the enemy. Germany signed the Geneva Convention and generally operated under its provisions. A German soldier's diet, however, typically consisted of far fewer calories than that of his U.S. counterpart. This caloric content became more restricted as the war dragged on and Germany's food and supply lines reached a critically dangerous point. These facts provided cold comfort to American GIs being held in Germany and to their friends and relatives at home in the United States. Philip B. Miller, a B-24 crewman, became a POW after being shot down over Ludwigshafen, Germany, in April 1944. He recollected an erratic meal schedule, sometimes being fed only once a day, and variations in both food quality and quantity. Miller recalled eating barley that often had "grubs and insects boiled in" and bread "baked with sawdust as a partial filling and wood chips were sometimes in the loaves."[25] Animals slaughtered in the war often appeared in soup and stew served to the GIs. In one case the appearance of a horse's eye became an envied "prize" for a lucky POW.[26] American POWs supplemented this food with parcels received from the Red Cross. But the cans in these packages had often already been opened by the German guards.[27] American POWs described this as the "Hitler Diet."[28] POW camp life in Germany differed in other ways. Many of the GIs received little in the way of blankets and clothes and were often housed in poor facilities with inadequate heating, cover, and toilets. These conditions had noticeable effects. Many Americans in captivity experienced a marked loss of weight, while German POWs held in the United States frequently wrote home about their massive weight gain.

The Pandora's box concerning German POWs opened slowly at first but picked up speed over the next two years. The issue of food remained central. Citizens complained in editorials across the country. Reporters and politicians questioned the policy. This attention caused some immediate change in certain locations. POW workers in Illinois faced a food cutback in April 1944 after the AFL and CIO complained about the preferential treatment given POWs over civilian laborers.[29]

The coddling issue became an international concern. In May 1944, the Soviet paper *Izvestia* criticized the treatment of Axis POWs held in the United States. According to the report, U.S. officials "not only did not resist, but 'cultivated' an insolent attitude among the German prisoners of war." Further, it stated that "anti-fascist literature was not permitted among the prisoners but that they were allowed at Trinidad [Colorado] to publish their own newspaper, thus keeping up the 'National Socialist spirit.'"[30]

Robert Devore, writing for *Collier's,* discussed POW treatment in his article "Our Pampered War Prisoners." He used Camp Concordia, Kansas, as a focal point to demonstrate the potential problems in the camps. According to Devore, "American officers had a far greater interest in social gaieties than in prisoners. Every night used to be fun night at Concordia, and often the fun began at 11:30 in the morning at the bar in the officers' club. Saturday night, of course, was the big night. That's when the boys and girls whooped it up in true boom-town style until, one Saturday night, someone shot the colonel's wife.

With the camp administration thus preoccupied, the dominant Nazis could attend to dissenters in the better traditions of the Party."[31] Devore added that the situation at Concordia and other camps had since improved. He felt that Americans had a difficult time understanding the dual concepts of reciprocity and the Geneva Convention.[32] The importance of this article cannot be discounted. Despite frequent news leaks or official releases when POWs escaped, the camps were restricted areas, and such in-depth coverage of camp life was scarce. At a time of heightened emotions from the coddling charges and Nazi atrocities, articles like Devore's reached a large and receptive audience.

Through the winter of 1944 and 1945, politicians loudly questioned the treatment of U.S.-held POWs. In some cases, the threat of investigation provoked changes in camp policy. Officials quickly altered procedures at the POW camp in Clarinda, Iowa, to avoid even the perception of coddling after Iowa representative Charles B. Hoeven made a February 1945 speech to Congress. He charged that the military coddled POWs, and he complained that he knew "of a prison camp in the Midwest which is supplied with every luxury—innerspring beds, the newest type of Frigidaire, and the finest food. At the same time I know of a hospital which has been trying to get a priority on a new Frigidaire and has been unable to get it."[33]

The protests became more frequent, the words more harsh. The PMGO saved a sampling of letters to the editor and editorials from across the nation. Although individuals' names were not included, they provide a gauge of public sentiment. A February 19, 1945, letter in the *Huntington (W.V.) Herald-Dispatch*, queried, "If they could speak, we wonder what the two-score American soldiers who were lined up in that field near Malmedy and mowed down by the Germans would say about our policy of coddling Axis prisoners." The author continued:

> Despite the many documented accounts of German atrocities, despite every proof that American prisoners have been mistreated and practically starved in numerous instances, authorities of this government still prate about the Geneva Convention and permit Axis prisoners to parade their insolence and contempt for our softheadedness and softheartedness. The most recent instance of this disgusting policy is enough to make one vomit. American citizens in a railway diner were made to change tables and even wait while a group of German prisoners are seated comfortably together and fed—fed first and fed the finest food available.[34]

A letter to the *Wilmington (N.C.) Star* softened the blow by stating that "perhaps we have been following a kid glove policy in the treatment of prisoners but we have been rather helpless in the matter. We must follow the international rules in the hope that the enemy will adhere to some of them."[35] The *Star-Telegram* of Fort Worth, Texas, declared that "no objection is raised against humane treatment of German prisoners or observance of the Geneva Convention but merely against pampering." It postulated that "it is certain that if these camps were administered by former American prisoners in Germany, there would be no coddling of Nazis."[36]

The *Montana Standard,* however, made one of the most condemning arguments against coddling that occupied the PMGO's newspaper collection. It stated that "Americans in German prison camps are not pampered, nor are they permitted to scoff openly at their guard or establish 'dictatorships' under the noses of their keepers." It contended that GIs in Nazi Germany were fed little not only because "the Nazis themselves are desperately short of food" but also because "the aim of the Nazis is, of course, to break their prisoners' spirits." The *Standard* advocated that recently returned veterans be reassigned as camp guards since these men "would know more about the kind of treatment the Nazis deserve and they would be strong-hearted enough to see that they get it." The *Standard* asserted that American veterans "have seen the Nazis keep their machineguns going until the last moment, mowing down Americans by the score, and then shouting, 'Eamerad,' [sic] and thereby saving themselves for a 'pampered' existence in a prison camp in the United States."[37] More complaints and angry questions appeared in papers across the nation.

Regardless of the authenticity of these accounts, many of which were based on rumor or overstated, they provoked continued citizen protest and a government response. Richard F. Harless, an Arizona congressman, charged on April 22, 1945, that German prisoners continued to be coddled and that Nazis ruled the camps to the extent that guards were "sometimes afraid of them."[38] Harless and his colleague Robert Sikes, a Florida congressman, urged an immediate and thorough investigation. Harless claimed to have "plenty of evidence" and to have received "fifteen to twenty letters a day reporting 'soft' treatment of German prisoners."[39] Sikes concluded that "German war prisoners should be thoroughly indoctrinated into the workings of democracy. . . . although . . . forcible indoctrination is prohibited by the Geneva Convention, force should be used, if necessary, because the United States is the only country to observe the convention."[40] Following the complaints of the congressmen, the rations of German POWs were cut and types of food substituted. Major General Thomas A. Terry, the commander of the Second Service Command, claimed that the reduction resulted from difficulty obtaining food in his area. This also affected civilians in the region, and even the soldiers in his command had their meat quantities reduced. This decreased POW daily caloric intake to 3,560 calories. Terry added that the claim of coddling by Harless and others had nothing to do with the decision and that "no complaints of 'coddling'" had been received in his command area.[41]

In May 1945, Major General Archer L. Lerch, the new PMG, responded to the mounting charges of coddling of German prisoners of war in the *American Mercury*. Lerch insisted that the intent was not to give special treatment to POWs but to give them fair treatment so that similar treatment would be given to Americans in enemy hands. The "Geneva Convention, I might emphasize, is *law*," he added, and any changing or disregarding of the responsibilities charged to the United States was tantamount to sacrificing "the place of honor and moral leadership that it has earned in the eyes of the world" and would sink it "to the level of Japan, whose emissaries talked peace while its army went to war."[42] The American Red Cross backed army policy by praising the "scrupulous attitude of the American Army in fulfilling the Treaty of Geneva toward enemy prisoners." They added that this strict adherence was anything but "mollycoddling." In fact, its policy of treating the men "strictly but fairly" allowed "regular communication" with American POWs in Germany and "obtained from [German POWs] millions of valuable man-work hours." Lerch concluded that any retaliation against the German POWs for acts committed by the German military or government during the war would simply result in a "contest of cold blooded murder. There is no end once retaliation has begun."[43]

The provost marshal's statement preceded a shift in the tone of press reports. The *Lima (OH) News,* stated on April 29, 1945, that "we could have been more strict with our prisoners of war without offending the Geneva Convention and still have made captivity more attractive than belligerency to any German but a rabid party-man. But while American prisoners in Germany did not get full benefit of Geneva Convention rights, it seems that they really were fed better, treated better, in general, than any prisoners except perhaps Britons."[44] The *Grand Rapids (MI) Press,* in an April 30, 1945, article, endorsed Lerch by explaining "that word of the contented lot of German prisoners in the United States, reaching Nazi troops, has caused them to give up in droves." The article supported Lerch's "evidence that our surrender propaganda, dropped from the skies, has fallen on more willing ears because of our liberal interpretation of the terms of the Geneva Convention. Perhaps we have erred on the side of kindness, but thereby we may have helped to shorten the war and bring more American sons, husbands, and fathers home safely."[45] The *Bayonne (NJ) Times* and the *Springfield (IL) Register* both reported in June that the "coddling" of German POWs saved the lives of Allied airmen held in Germany when German officers refused Hitler's orders to execute them as a reprisal for the Dresden bombing.[46] The *Reno (NV) Gazette* declared on June 26, 1945, that with the reduction in POW menus and caloric intake, the last remnants of coddling had finally disappeared from POW camps.[47]

As Americans read Lerch's words in the *American Mercury*, they were unaware that changes had been made as early as March 1944 to make the military's operations beyond reproach. The two biggest problems at this time involved prisoner-on-prisoner violence and murder and fraternization and "coddling" of the prisoners by the guards and civilians. While regulations that forbade fraternization existed, and new ones could be created, they proved difficult to enforce. POW problems within the camps seemed the more pressing issue and ideally easier to solve. The military began a detailed screening program identifying the nationalities and political leanings of POWs. Once the military completed this process, it segregated these POWs by designating separate camps for the different groups.

Ideological Segregation

Initially, only hard-core troublemakers, those guilty of crimes, and prisoners of war who asked for protection from their fellows received transfers. Those charged with or convicted of crimes often awaited trial or served sentences in Fort Leavenworth, Kansas, or another suitable location. The troublemakers and protected individuals, early on, might only be sent to another camp, secure only by their anonymity at the second location.

Military inspections and investigations of POW camps produced results that shocked some authorities but had been facts of life to the POWs. Detailed investigation allowed the United States to categorize the Germans in several ideological groups: "the super-Nazis, who constituted approximately 15%; the Nazi followers, who believed in the doctrine of National Socialism, if criticizing certain parts of it, about 50% (this includes the opportunists); the politically neutral, of whom the majority have no political opinions, due to ignorance and/or rural backwardness, and of whom small groups are neutral for religious reasons, about 30%; and the anti-Nazis, who made up about 5%."[48] On the basis of these categories, the military directed on March 23, 1944, that the anti-Nazis and "rabid" Nazis be transferred to separate camps, or separate compounds within camps, to prevent contact between them and the other prisoners. This request created difficulties. Camp officials now had to screen the POWs in their charge and army officials had to locate housing for them. Personnel records and reports of POW activities from within camps provided some help. Brigadier General Edward F. Witsell, acting adjutant general, told U.S. personnel in November 1944 that many members of the SS "are tattooed under the left arm about one inch below the arm pit. It is believed that this tattoo is the badge of membership in the above organizations [and] many prisoners of war bearing this mark have attempted to obliterate it, either by having a new design retattooed over the old, or by using some caustic or acid to burn it out."[49] Administrators examined POWs during routine physicals or as part of the screening process. In the midst of the ideological screening, officials received an order to identify all non-German citizens, which caused even greater confusion.

Camp Campbell, Kentucky: Anti-Nazi Haven?

The military initially designated three camps to house anti-Nazis: Fort Devens, Massachusetts; Camp McCain, Mississippi; and Camp Campbell, Kentucky. Each camp shuffled men or created new barracks to provide space. The unique process of screening, segregation, and transfer led to new problems. As one of the first and largest of the anti-Nazi camps, organized after much trial and error, Camp Campbell became a model for other segregated camps.

Initially, Campbell housed all 1,000 anti-Nazi POWs located west of the Fifth Service Command Area within one compound. Two other compounds, located across the base, housed Nazi POWs. According to authorities, this allowed "complete segregation" and masked the "identity of the camp" because distinguishing Campbell as a "Nazi or Anti-Nazi [camp] is impossible. The War Department thereby hopes to avoid retaliation against the families of Anti-Nazi prisoners by removing any clue on their political beliefs that might be obtained if only Anti-Nazi prisoners were known to be interned at certain camps."[50]

In March 1944, construction of a second compound, DD, provided space for 1,000 anti-Nazi prisoners. Lieutenant Colonel Carl Byrd, commander of the POW camp, requested space for seventy-five more anti-Nazis, including "Austrians, Poles, [and] Czechs" who gave "valuable intelligence information and would be more willing to divulge further intelligence if they were assured of being transferred to a camp where they would not fear molestation."[51] The declaration that the two compounds provided a haven for anti-Nazis who now cooperated with officials so that they would not have to fear repercussions, while the other two compounds, located at some distance, housed ardent

Nazis blissfully unaware of their former comrades on the same base, was not accurate.

The anti-Nazis from Compound DD reported in September 1944 that they volunteered for transfer to escape the Nazi terror and that "we don't know how many Anti-Nazis become a sacrifice of Nazi-atrocities. We know we lost the strength and power of the best sons of [the] Anti-Nazi movement by the[ir] murder in American P.W. Camps."[52] These men provided labor prohibited by the Geneva Convention such as "repairs of military vessels" and "the loading of guns, military equipments and weapons."[53] They claimed that they never complained or asked for favors but, on the contrary, objected that "the social conditions in our camps are far under the standard of the fascistic camps. In a much higher degree we are urged by the guards to work more, our payments are not so punctual as in Nazi-Camps."[54] They also protested that "many newspapers, magazines, and books [are] prevented ... material ... necessary ... to eliminate the poison of nazistic infection of the German soul. It is forbidden for us to comment on radio and news-paper announcements, forbidden for us to announce to the American camp-leadership well-known Nazis which were sent to this camp to spy, to work as agents, men who recently persecuted Anti-Nazis. These agents have in short time confidential post inside the camp."[55] These anti-Nazi men claimed that "when they bring forward their wishes or propositions, being declared as troublemakers and elements who endanger the peace of the camp," their concerns typically fell on deaf ears.

First Lieutenant Walter Schoenstedt of the Special Program Section reported in November 1944 that at Campbell "the smooth functioning of this camp is constantly being handicapped through the unpleasant mixture of several different types of Anti-Nazis, Nazis, non-Germans, run of the mill, and criminals. Although the great majority of the prisoners consider themselves Anti-Nazis, the camp, or even single compounds, cannot be described as such."

According to Schoenstedt, the spokesman for the two anti-Nazi compounds (DD and VW), Catholic priest Sergeant George Rupprecht, managed both compounds despite the five-mile distance between them but was "not strong enough, in a military sense, to run the Nazi compound."[56]

The anti-Nazis also took exception to the mixing of criminals in their compounds as a "discrimination against the majority whose reputation is being kept at a low artificially." Schoenstedt found that "strife and disunity between groups, awkward military attitude, weak leadership and the civilian background of the prisoners (artists, doctors, writers, professors, actors, etc.) do much to prevent an understanding of the problems of those prisoners on the part of the American officers and the camp commander." Yet the Nazis in compound XO, under the leadership of Staff Sergeant Otto Guenther, gave "the appearance of a 'smoothly' run compound, very much to the satisfaction of the American personnel." This led to the Nazis receiving a greater deal of respect than the so-labeled "nuisance" and "trouble maker" anti-Nazis, "who write petitions and forget to act like soldiers."[57]

Other anti-Nazi camps faced similar problems. Brigadier General Blackshear M. Bryan, assistant PMG, discovered that at Fort Devens, Massachusetts, four men reported to the camp officials that they "were Gestapo agents" and that having "secured all the information they desired about the anti-Nazis in that compound . . . they now wished to be transferred to a Nazi prisoner-of-war camp." Bryan added that "these four men are still at Fort Devens and are well-subdued by the anti-Nazis."[58]

The Nazi Camp: Alva, Oklahoma

Camp Alva, Oklahoma, gained distinction for housing rabid Nazis. Yet, just as at Camp Campbell, the screening and transfer process left much to be desired and created problems for which officials at Alva received blame. The most startling revelation concerned the definition of an "ardent" or "rabid" Nazi. Seemingly, no two people defined these terms similarly. The Alva camp, intended to house only Nazis, became a catchall camp. Camp commanders shipped as many as possible of their problem POWs to Alva. POWs who caused some minor problems, refused to work, or disobeyed an order and other borderline troublemakers, along with Nazis, rapidly filled the limited space available.

Captain Alexander Lakes, investigating Alva on April 25, 1945, discovered that "many of the prisoners of war at this camp cannot be considered subversive or rabid Nazis." According to Lake, haste and misunderstanding produced these errors. To improve the situation at Alva and elsewhere, Lakes recommended that "The [Eighth] service command should require camp commanders to provide corroborated evidence to substantiate the classification of a prisoner of war as an incorrigible before approval is granted to transfer such prisoner of war to this camp. The 201 file of each prisoner transferred should contain complete information about that prisoner," and he should again be screened once at Alva so that "all prisoners incorrectly classified as subversive and incorrigible" could be returned.[59] These recommendations created delays in transferring POWs to Alva. In the interim, as earlier mistakes were corrected, the Nazis awaiting transfer roamed freely in other camps.[60]

The official ideological screening and segregation process initiated in 1944 allowed the Nazi POWs nearly two years of domination within the POW camps. Yet even once implemented in 1944, the process hit snags. Nazis still exerted influence at Campbell, and non-Nazis ended up at Alva simply because of inefficiency or convenience. A process that placed POWs into diametrically opposite ideological camps was bound to overlook members of both groups within the "ordinary" camps, as inspections in 1944 and 1945 revealed.

An investigation conducted by Captain William F. Raugust at Crossville, Tennessee, on January 31, 1945, with the help of anti-Nazi informants, uncovered "the existence of a well-organized Nazi underground" that operated in a "dictatorial manner" and used intimidation, misinformation, and court-martials to keep the other Germans in line. In this case, he recommended that the anti-Nazi "informants be given every protection and that complete files be built up on the ringleaders of the subversive activities."[61]

The ideological segregation program became more sophisticated and more camps were designated for Nazis and anti-Nazis. Camp Blanding, Florida, housed anti-Nazi German navy personnel, and Camp McCain, Mississippi, became designated for all non-navy anti-Nazi officers. Papago Park housed navy personnel not "classified as anti-Nazi" but apparently not specifically Nazi either. Enlisted anti-Nazis went to Fort Devens, Massachusetts, while anti-Nazis who "might suffer punishment, beatings and other untoward incidents at the hands of other German prisoners of war" went to Camp Campbell, Kentucky.[62]

The next stage of screening and segregation consisted of identifying non-German nationals. It began in 1944 but gained the most momentum in 1945 as POWs holding nationality to Allied nations received repatriation. In November 28, 1944, the War Department issued orders that POWs holding citizenship from Poland, France, Luxembourg, Belgium, or Czechoslovakia be segregated from the German POWs and transferred to Camp Butner, North Carolina. Men sent to North Carolina had "to have been impressed into the German Army," "be physically qualified for service in the Armed Forces," and "hold political beliefs in accord with the tenets of the United Nations."[63] The men received an initial screening at the camp of origin and a second screening at Butner before being repatriated to the armed forces of the nation to which they belonged.

Locating and segregating German prisoners of war of Soviet origin proved more troublesome. As late as July 1944, no official provisions for Soviet nationals existed.[64] Camp commanders had orders to identify all German POWs holding or claiming Soviet nationality; explain that they would be repatriated; and ask them individually, "Do you claim Soviet citizenship?" If so, they were "considered a Soviet citizen and reported as such by name, rank and serial number. However, if the individual reveals by words, acts or deeds that he does not desire to be returned to Russia, and claims protection under the Geneva Convention, he will be reported by name, rank and serial number as a Soviet citizen not desiring to return to Russia."[65]

By February of 1945, the United States was in direct negotiations with the Soviet Union concerning prisoner exchanges and the Halle Agreement was signed on May 22, 1945. This agreement with the Soviet Union was made largely because the Soviets had occupied or would soon be advancing upon parts of Germany or German-held territory where American POWs were being held, and ultimately liberating Japanese-operated camps in Manchuria that also held American personnel. In order to ensure the speedy and full recovery of these men, the United States had to agree to repatriate all Soviet nationals, those liberated by U.S. forces and those captured by U.S. forces while wearing German uniform.[66] As the historian Arieh J. Kochavi noted, "Given the Kremlin's indifferent attitude to its citizens, not least its own POWs, the [U.S.] administration had reason to be apprehensive and in any case refused to take any chances, especially as it had no interest in keeping Soviet citizens."[67]

Many Soviet nationals feared repatriation, some lied about their nationality, and others violently resisted returning home. Even Secretary of War Henry L. Stimson noted the potential problems with this agreement. "The Russians . . . wish to have turned over to them German prisoners that we have taken who are of Russian citizenship, and the State Department has consented to this in spite of the fact that it seems very likely the Russians will execute them when they get them home."[68] Yet we still sent them home.[69]

Between the Angels and Devils: Ending Fraternization and Violence between the Guards and POWs

The final step toward ending the problems within the camps concerned putting a stop to fraternization. Beginning in 1944, the War Department investigated claims, issued directives, and implemented disciplinary measures to educate camp personnel. In January 1945, Captain William F. Raugust found at the Crossville POW camp that "the general appearance, attitude, and morale of the guard personnel is good. Their recreational facilities are adequate." He "recommended that regular orientation lectures based on the Geneva Convention and War Department Circulars be prepared for them."[70]

At Camp Peary, Virginia, USN, an agent of the Special Projects Division discovered that the "installation commander, on two or three occasions took some Naval personnel to a variety show presented by prisoners of war," but they were "completely segregated from prisoner personnel." Further investigation revealed that "three naval chaplains taught prisoners to play softball, but in no instance did American personnel participate in sports events with prisoners of war." The Special Projects Division recommended that camp officials "stop the practice of Americans attending variety shows." It was indicated that the commander had been notified of "our displeasure and embarrassment."[71]

Enforcing newly enacted anti-fraternization regulations where none previously existed proved difficult. Major General J. A. Ulio, adjutant to General Somervell, found that "statements in the press and correspondence from public and private sources indicate that the fraternization between prisoners and American military and civilian personnel concerned with their treatment is increasing."[72] In some cases, there was a marked "laxity in the enforcement of prisoner of war directives relative to the maintenance of order and discipline in prisoner of war camps." Officials had to personally intervene to "insure a stricter compliance with all War Department circulars and directives relative to prisoners of war, and a tightening up of prisoner of war discipline."[73]

Ulio outlined the types of prohibited activity in ASF Circular No. 39, which listed "any activity or conduct not specifically required by the Geneva Convention" that would give "the general public the impression that prisoners of war are pampered." He added that "recalcitrant or contemptuous attitudes on the part of the prisoners resulting in their refusal to work will be answered promptly by the 'no work, no eat' policy."[74]

Ulio noted that fraternization between POWs and guards had not ended and that it threatened to unravel the POW program. He declared that "prisoners' letters indicate that guards have participated in drinking parties with prisoners, exchanged gifts with prisoners, delivered messages outside of camp at the request of prisoners, and permitted prisoners to accept the hospitality of civilians while on outside work details." He also discovered that "prisoner of war communications are carried to and from the camps by civilians or are mailed by civilians at the request of prisoners who are outside of the camp on work details.[75] He also added that U.S. officials understood that sometimes the "statements written by prisoners of war are subject to a certain amount of distortion and exaggeration, but the fact that these statements are repetitious and have been written from widely scattered camps lends credence to them."[76] In short, the declaration by the War Department, underscored by Ulio, indicated to all U.S. officials that further fraternization or waning of discipline regarding POWs would not be tolerated.

Tomorrow Will Be Better...

The military announced most of the changes as they were implemented in 1944 and 1945. They prohibited the Nazi salute; reduced POW diets twice, once on July 1, 1944, and again on February 2, 1945; and determined that returning veterans would be utilized in POW camps. The military even invited a congressional committee to investigate the camps.[77] Although none of these measures provided perfect or immediate solutions, combined, they helped the United States recover from the most serious political problems facing the POW program, specifically the problems generated by POWs of various ideologies and nationalities. The abuse by and fraternization with American personnel would no longer be tolerated. With the lives of American POWs at stake, the POW program in jeopardy, and the U.S. reputation of adherence to its international obligations and treatment of POWs endangered, military authorities acted. Tomorrow would be better. The "cleaning up" of the program ensured that even though problems still existed, measures were being taken to reduce and eliminate them. The prisoner of war labor and the quality of camp life benefited from these changes. Segregation of the worst elements meant that those POWs who could be "reasoned" with might still be saved by American democracy.

Colonel George Chescheir (center), U.S. commander at Fort Benning, Georgia. Courtesy of the Kentucky Historical Society.

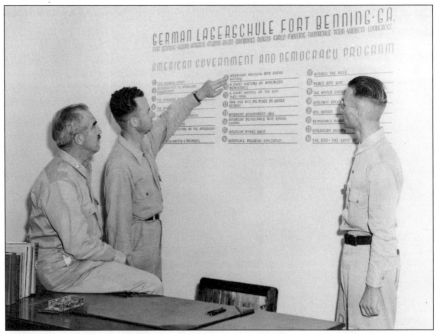
Colonel George Chescheir (seated) and the POW school at Fort Benning, Georgia. Courtesy of the Kentucky Historical Society.

POWs boarding the train at Fort Knox, Kentucky. Courtesy of the Historical Preservation Office, Fort Knox.

POW-constructed model castle at Camp Ruston, Louisiana. Courtesy of the American Foreign Policy Center at Louisiana Technical University, Ruston.

Examples of barbed wire surrounding camp. Note that the cleared areas provide good visibility and fields of fire for the guards. Courtesy of the Kentucky Historical Society.

POWs shopping at the canteen at Fort Knox, Kentucky. Courtesy of the Historical Preservation Office, Fort Knox.

POW-constructed stadium model, Camp Ruston, Louisiana. Courtesy of the American Foreign Policy Center at Louisiana Technical University, Ruston.

Yugoslavian POWs housed at Camp Ruston, Louisiana. Courtesy of the American Foreign Policy Center at Louisiana Technical University, Ruston.

POWs working in the kitchen at Fort Knox, Kentucky. The POW reaching toward the oven is Heino R. Erichsen. Courtesy of the Kentucky Historical Society.

POWs carving turkey at Fort Benning, Georgia. Courtesy of the Kentucky Historical Society.

POW buying cigarettes at the canteen at Fort Benning, Georgia. Courtesy of the Kentucky Historical Society.

Chapter 5

The Devil Is in the Details: German POW Labor and the American Home Front

> *Of all the horrible conditions left by the war, none can surpass in infamy the conduct of the nations which claimed to be fighting for freedom and have followed their victory by making slaves of their prisoners.... If Britain and France—not to mention Russia—are slave drivers, what are we but slave traders?*
> —"Uncle Sam in the Slave Trade"

Prisoner labor became one of the most beneficial and controversial aspects of the World War II POW program in the United States. The Geneva Convention permitted forced labor for enlisted prisoners and allowed officers to volunteer to work. Regulations, while vague, required that POWs be afforded the same benefits and treatment as civilian employees and prohibited their assignment to jobs directly related to the war effort.

The American home front desperately needed POW manpower, but figuring out the details of the plan became daunting. Military and civilian officials could not agree on what constituted a "non-military task," the amount that POWs should get paid, the amount employers should be charged, and how the contracts should be negotiated. Myriad other issues plagued the program as well. Many base camps were located too far from where POW labor was needed, leading to the development of the temporary and mobile branch camp system. Initially security concerns required nearly as many guards as POWs on work details, thereby restricting the amount of work done outside camp. The War Department looked to other government agencies to help overcome these problems. The War Manpower Commission (WMC), the War Food Administration, and the Industrial Personnel Division (IPD) cooperated with the PMGO, the ASF, and service commands in selecting appropriate tasks, determining pay, and establishing the number of POWs available to work. The extra bureaucracy helped set policy for the program but also sparked more trouble. Even when these agencies approved prisoner work, they had to contend with civilian labor unions, which often protested that POW employment stifled civilian opportunities and complained about the fickle nature of POWs, who tended to strike with little notice.

Although prior to the war, more agricultural workers were available than jobs, and farm labor constituted "16 percent of the national labor force," by 1942 demand in the military and war production industries drained so much manpower that many farmers doubted their ability to raise crops.[1] Emergency government action and nearly two million military deferments for agricultural workers proved to be too little too late. Debates on how best to help farmers continued throughout the war.[2] Government attempts to retain farm labor and ensure fair wages, coupled with the infusion of foreign labor, especially from Mexico, angered farmers, some politicians, and farm unions.

In the midst of these manpower demands, the War Department and the cooperating agencies formulated labor policy, which changed as the war progressed. Ultimately POWs worked for the military and civilians both on and off base.

Early Labor Interpretations, 1941–1942

Although the Geneva Convention allowed the utilization of POW labor, it provided only general regulations.[3] The United States typically treated POWs the same as civilian labor, with comparable hours, working conditions, and injury benefits. POW officers choosing to work held supervisory roles "unless they expressly request a remunerative occupation."[4] Other articles stipulated that POW labor "shall have no direct relation with war operations" and prohibited "unhealthful or dangerous work."[5] The Convention required that the German prisoners be paid the equivalent to American GIs of the same rank and that this pay, as well as any money "taken or withheld" upon capture, be placed into an account for that individual.[6]

Using these Geneva provisions, U.S. planners published the April 22, 1942, manual *Civilian Enemy Aliens and Prisoners of War,* which contained in sixty-three pages the first U.S. interpretations of the Geneva Convention regarding POW labor.[7] The War Department, ASF, PMGO, Joint Chiefs of Staff, and Joint Staff Planners worked together on the initial drafts and relied partly on World War I experience.[8] Although it mostly dealt with civilian internees, it had some basic provisions anticipating POW labor. The 1942 plan envisioned employment of all enlisted POWs and determination of their job classification in three broad categories based on their health: heavy work, light work, and sick (no work). Additionally, POW labor was divided into Class I and Class II categories. Class I labor provided for POW and camp upkeep with no pay. Class II included all other work, including contract work in the private sector, and while employers could negotiate the amount paid to the War Department for POW labor, it could not be less than eighty cents per day per prisoner. This pay rate was established at the insistence of Allen W. Guillion, the PMG, as it was roughly equivalent to what U.S. privates made.

One statement contained in the manual under "Labor Limitations," however, created controversy before the final draft could be approved: "Internees may not be employed in any work which is directly connected with military operations. Neither will they be assigned to inherently unhealthful or dangerous work."[9] Some officials questioned whether any POW labor was not truly related to the war effort and clarification was needed to close potential loopholes.[10]

Upon agreeing to accept an emergency transfer of 175,000 British-held Axis POWs, officials reexamined the 1942 manual. On September 7, 1942, the Joint Staff Planners recommended that the POWs, most of whom were unskilled, be employed en masse on conservation projects, in agricultural work, or in manual construction. Officials also anticipated utilizing POWs to construct roads and buildings on or near POW camps and in work related to their own upkeep, including constructing barracks, latrines, and fences. The Joint Staff Planners held that this employment, even under the most conservative interpretations, constituted work not directly involved with the war effort. With this in mind, Guillion issued a new draft in September 1942 stating that POWs "may be used at posts, camps, and stations for maintenance and repairs of roads and utilities, in handling Quartermaster supplies and in the maintenance of station facilities," and generally where "prisoner labor detachments may be used to relieve Service Troops."[11] Major General George Gruner, the chief of administrative services, amended the draft before sending it to Somervell for approval by adding that "the plan also envisages the utilization of large numbers of these prisoners on agricultural and other projects not under War Department supervision where there is a recognized shortage in unskilled labor."[12]

A controversy erupted before approval of the 1942 draft plan. Colonel Archibald King, chief of the War Plans Division, Office of the Judge Advocate General, upon reading the proposal on September 25, refused approval. He insisted that plans for POW labor on the Alaskan Highway, a thoroughfare designed for military purposes, violated Article 31. He added that POW labor used on the construction of any road might constitute a violation of the Geneva Convention, as such employment was "within the spirit and purpose, if not the letter of the forgoing prohibition; and is equally objectionable," and that "the adoption of such a plan might cause the Axis powers to take retaliatory measures against American prisoners."[13]

Fearing limits on much needed POW labor, Guillion protested that King's interpretation was far too restrictive. He "admitted that interpretations of the labor provisions of the 1929 Convention were meager and scattered" but argued that American plans were in line with interpretations and uses of POW labor by other belligerent nations. He recommended that the POWs be allowed to work on all tasks "not in a theater of operations and not concerned with the manufacture or transportation of arms and munitions or the transportation of any material intended for combatant units and not unhealthful, dangerous, degrading, menial or beyond the particular prisoner's capacity."[14]

This definition was objectionable to Lieutenant General Dwight D. Eisenhower and Cordell Hull, the secretary of state, both of whom recommended changes in December 1942. Eisenhower, supreme Allied commander of the European Theater, desired that the phrase "any work not in a theater of operations" be changed to "any work not under fire in a combat zone."[15] Otherwise, POW labor in the European Theater would operate under the more limited provisions suggested by King. Hull's proposed changes prohibited POWs from working with any materials directly destined for combat troops. He also requested that the semantics of some work details be changed to clearly delineate them from tasks related to the war effort. These changes permitted the Department of State to be "in a strong position to protest the nature of work given Americans who were in enemy custody should it become necessary."[16]

While the provisions of the labor program were debated and revised through December 1942, Chief of Staff George Catlett Marshall concerned himself with the possible places of employment for POWs. Marshall toured Walter Reed Army Medical Center on Christmas Day 1942 and asked Brigadier General Shelly U. Marietta, commander of the hospital, about the feasibility of POW employment there and at similar facilities for a "great deal of dirty work." Marietta told Marshall that the "difficulties of housing, security, and mess facilities—plus the unknown reaction of local civilians—probably made the use of prisoners of war impractable." Undaunted, Marshall posed a similar query to Somervell, stating that POWs could be placed "within cantonments" and "the business of guarding could be carried out on a limited basis and the escape of a few prisoners would not be too bad in its effect." Marshall recalled "seeing German prisoners working on farms [in France during World War I]. I don't recall the arrangements for guarding them but I think there were almost none with a certain class of these prisoners."[17] He further added: "I understood that probably there would be a fine basis of employing these men perhaps in mines, on the beet fields and in similar work, possibly moving them by companies from crop to crop. However, to whatever extent it is possible for you to cut down on the Army's direct demands on the civil population, it will be very helpful in our battle on the subject of manpower."[18] Somervell informed Marshall that a plan for utilizing POW labor within the United States was already near completion.

The December changes to the 1942 draft plan led to the publication of the *War Department Policy with Respect to Labor of Prisoners of War* on January 10, 1943. The new War Department policy now affirmed that "any work outside the combat zones not having a direct relation with war operations and not involving the manufacture or transportation of arms or munitions or the transportation of any material clearly intended for combat units, and not unhealthful, dangerous, degrading, or beyond the particular prisoner's physical capacity, is allowable and desirable."[19] This ended the debate.

The January 1943 plan also advocated POW employment in "War Department owned and operated laundries; brush clearance and construction of fire breaks; mosquito control, soil conservation and agricultural projects, construction and repair of highways and drainage ditches; strip mining and quarrying; and other work of a character similar to the foregoing."[20]

1943: Critical Manpower Shortages, Contract Labor, and POW Pay

During 1943, U.S. forces captured small numbers of prisoners and enemy civilians on the high seas and added these men to the numbers of the British transfer. With plans for its first major offensive aimed at the Axis forces in North Africa, the United States anticipated larger numbers of POWs and saw a need to expand the labor program. No major objections had been raised to the January 10, 1943, policy, and the War Department moved toward developing a contract labor program. Considerations for employing POWs in civilian markets focused not only on the security of citizens but also on providing labor to the sectors that most needed the help and on not offsetting available civilian labor. The War Department required the assistance of the IPD, the WMC, and the Department of Agriculture in making these assessments, preparing contracts, and allocating POW labor.[21]

The critical shortages facing agricultural labor in 1943 forced the War Department to rush implementation of the contract labor program. In the midst of the labor shortage, farmers learned that they could soon hire German workers from the local POW camp. The contract program hit a few snags concerning POW pay and job sites. The first draft of the agreements drawn up by the PMGO and the judge advocate general contained the provision agreed upon from the April 1942 manual that POW labor could not be hired for less than eighty cents per day and employers would provide transportation and food. National and local labor unions protested that this low wage would displace civilian labor. James P. Mitchell, director of the IPD, urged that the employer pay the same wage that civilian labor received for the same task.[22] Guillion felt that local farmers and employers would not pay the prevailing rate since there were too many hidden costs, including language difficulties, potential for escape, damage from recapture attempts, and potential for unreliable work. General Bryan, assistant PMG, reiterated the concerns of the PMGO in a March 1943 meeting with the IPD. The IPD listed numerous advantages of employing prisoner labor, including immediate access to the exact number of workers needed, for the time needed, without fear of turnover. They argued that this balanced out any problems and therefore required that the POWs be paid the prevailing wage. Despite the March conference, revised contracts issued by Guillion in April 1943 stated that "the cost of prisoner labor should be estimated at 50 to 75 percent of the normal costs of free labor."[23]

After April, service commanders and individual camp commanders signed contracts at amounts in line with the PMGO, not the IPD. The camp commanders typically negotiated contracts directly with employers, and the price established for hiring the prisoners varied from one camp to the next based on local factors and the type of employment. Throughout the spring, the WMC and Department of Agriculture evaluated local labor needs and potential sites for new POW camps near high demands.[24] In March, because of the severe agricultural labor shortage, camp commanders received orders to transfer all workers from non-essential tasks to farm labor. This helped alleviate the agricultural labor problem by May, but at that time other areas suffered from lack of employment.[25]

While POW workers flip-flopped from job to job, the argument between the PMGO and the IPD continued. In early summer 1943, the IPD produced evidence that nearly all approved contracts provided POWs to employers at far less cost than available civilian workers. At this point Paul V. McNutt, chairman of the WMC, as well as some War Department officials who feared trouble with American labor unions, supported the IPD's position. Under this assault, the PMGO relented and retracted the April provision on POW pay.

Negotiations among the secretary of state, the War Department, and the chief of the WMC throughout the summer of 1943 resulted in an August 14 agreement. This resolved the compensation issue by requiring that employers pay the local wage earned by civilians doing similar tasks. POWs would receive eighty cents per day and the overage would help pay the cost of the POW program. Employers provided transportation to and from the POW camp and food for each prisoner and estimated the cost for the entire job, rather than simply per day. For instance, an area farmer with ten acres of tobacco to harvest figured out in advance how many POWs he wanted and for how long and estimated the cost of the entire project rather than paying farm labor daily or weekly, as was the normal practice. The prevailing wage was no longer an unknown, estimated, or negotiable amount. The WMC and the Department of Agriculture determined areas most in need of POW labor and set the wages. Camp commanders still negotiated the contract with local employers within these guidelines but also assisted by providing employers deductions based on the cost of transportation at the rate of twenty-five cents per prisoner per day, and lunch at twenty-one cents per prisoner per day, and further reduced the price if the POWs proved troublesome through escape attempts, refusal to work, or inefficiency.[26]

The August 24, 1943, "Employment of Prisoners of War off Reservations" came ten days after the War Department–WMC policies further clarified the process of hiring POW labor.[27] Requests from employers no longer went directly to the POW camp commander but were sent to the WMC, which approved or declined the request. Approved requests went to the service commanders, who forwarded them to the local camp commanders. Individual commanders then carried out the contract. The new forms continued the agreed-upon method of paying the prevailing wage for each POW but now specified that employers providing transportation received a deduction. This changed from requiring the employer to provide transportation. In the interest of security and performance, POW work details might be accompanied by POW noncommissioned officers, who performed only supervisory tasks and were paid by the War Department, not the contractor.[28] These new policies became effective September 17, 1943, and did not interfere with current contracts or the full employment of POWs.[29]

The WMC, concerned with the needs of civilian workers and labor unions, ensured that POWs not only received the prevailing wage but also had the same working conditions as civilian labor, and that employers sought labor from unemployment agencies before agreeing to any POW contracts. The resulting labor program provided a readily available source at reasonable cost without displacing civilian workers or angering labor unions. On September 24, 1943, the War Department published Prisoner of War Circular No. 1, the first of a series of fifty-four circulars distributed to all the agencies involved in the POW program.³⁰ The circular contained all the provisions regarding POW handling, care, and upkeep, including the labor provisions. It contained the agreed-upon labor regulations and cleared up some confusion regarding POW pay.

These policies, debated and agreed upon during 1943, were timely, since in March there were already 2,755 POWs: 1,334 Germans, 1,359 Italians, and 62 Japanese. By December the number had jumped to 123,440 Germans, 49,323 Italians, and 116 Japanese, a total of 172,879.³¹ The provisions of the labor program had been established. The determination of pay and labor and the balancing of security with full employment, however, continued to be debated.

Officials became concerned over the quality and quantity of work performed by POWs and devised ways to increase productivity. Numerous complaints from contractors, coupled with proof that many POWs performed inconsistently, working well some days and slacking off on others, led to the creation in 1944 of incentive pay and task systems. These systems were implemented by the employers, not the prisoners. Under the incentive system, POWs worked on a piecework basis. If a POW produced the allotted amount of work, he received a full eighty cents per day. Less work resulted in less pay, but industrious POWs who exceeded the daily production rate could earn up to $1.20 per day. Under the task system, POW workers had a set task to perform each day. If the POWs worked diligently, they could return to camp early but still receive the full day's pay.³²

In addition to wages earned through work, the United States provided an allowance to all enlisted POWs of $3.00 per month. This pay allowed all prisoners to purchase items as wanted or needed from the camp store and was provided in addition to any normal wages earned. Officers received pay based on rank, ranging from $20 to $40 per month.³³ All money earned by POWs was placed in an account, from which canteen coupons could be issued. Prisoners redeemed these coupons at the camp canteen or store for toiletries, snacks, sodas, and beer. Any remainder was reimbursed upon repatriation. The United States compensated sick and injured workers as well.³⁴

One of the problems with the employment system concerned officers and noncommissioned officers. These POWs could not be forced to work, and when they worked, it had to be in a supervisory role at the higher rate of pay. Many of the prisoners, however, had their *Soldbücher*, the basic personnel records that accompanied all German soldiers, confiscated prior to arriving in camp and thus had no proof of rank. Helmut Hörner, in a group of noncommissioned officers whose records had been confiscated, many when they first arrived in New York for screening, recalled that he and others without documents worked as enlisted men. A noncommissioned officer spokesman told his fellows that "there is no other possibility but to compile a list and request verification of your rank from the International Red Cross in Geneva. But that takes weeks. In the meantime the Americans will require you to work and assign you to work groups. The trick in New York was successful."[35]

Problem of Full Employment versus Security

The War Department's effort to ensure full employment of POWs was limited by its concern for maintaining security. The August 14, 1943, directive stated that the service commanders must ensure that "prisoners of war will be employed to the fullest possible extent, and in this connection, when no work of higher priority is available, prisoners will be used in doing the most useful available work on or in connection with military reservations."[36] It also stated that if the camp commander had to decide between security and full employment, then "the safeguarding of prisoners conformably to the requirements of internal security is considered paramount."[37] POW camp commanders, in the interest of following this order and maintaining security, ordered POW work details to be heavily guarded. Since the manpower shortage also affected the number of men available as guards at POW camps, however, this severely curtailed the number of prisoners employed. The subsequent policy of individual camp commanders and officers "overguarding" POW work details with nearly as many guards as POWs reduced POW employment off base to roughly half the number of men actually available to work.[38]

In February 1944, the heads of the service commands met with other executive officers of the prisoner of war program to discuss how to secure full employment of POWs under the current security restraints. Unemployment not only damaged the ultimate goal of utilizing the POWs to benefit home front labor and offset the cost of their housing but also proved detrimental to home front morale. The military feared reactions of overworked Americans whose family members were fighting overseas when they discovered that not only was the captured enemy living well, but their lack of employment was actually providing an additional drain on the already taxed economy. Despite these concerns, most of the service commanders preferred the added security. General Somervell and Carl L. Restine, the acting inspector general, disagreed. They argued that not only were the POWs not contributing to their upkeep or home front labor, but their idleness within the camps allowed them too much free time, which was "loaded with dynamite." Somervell explained that it was time to take a "calculated risk" and "balance the risk of prisoner escape against the value of the work to be done."³⁹ Guard details were subsequently reduced to one guard for every eight to fifteen POWs, depending on the POWs' characters, attitudes, and work performed.

Full employment also carried over to handicapped and crippled POWs. At Camp Sidnaw in Michigan, POWs worked primarily in logging. Several disabled POWs arrived from Camp Grant, Illinois, in March 1944. Captain William D. Home, commander of the POW installation, requested their transfer. He stated that "these men would be better off in a camp, where other type of work is done or a camp more suitable to their physical condition." He added that it would benefit "the morale at this camp, if all men were able to work at the logging operation."⁴⁰ Colonel A. M. Tollefson, assistant director of the Prisoner of War Division, in an April 10, 1944, letter, urged the personnel at Camp Grant to familiarize themselves with the basic labor provisions to ensure that in the future "only prisoners who are physically fit" and "qualified by civilian occupation or by training" would be selected for such arduous work.⁴¹ He requested that the men in question be returned to Grant to be given a thorough medical exam while fit replacements were sent from Grant to Sidnaw.⁴²

POWs Working in America

Prisoners of war began working as soon as they arrived in the United States. They engaged in a variety of tasks ranging from beautifying the camp, planting gardens, and constructing necessary buildings for their own upkeep (Class I) to working in agriculture, factories, construction, and timber by contract with civilian employers (Class II) and, finally, useful but not necessarily important tasks in and around the camp and on the military installations, which might include picking up trash (Class III). Most POWs welcomed the opportunity to leave their camps and earn money for needed items or beer. Employers cited the effectiveness of POW labor as positive and sometimes developed lasting relationships with their POW workers. Colonel George H. Lobdell, commander of the Algona, Iowa, POW camp, recalled that at his camp, "Most of the Germans preferred hard routine manual labor, 10 to 12 hours a day. We had one camp in Clinton, Iowa, that worked around the clock . . . with two shifts, each 12 hours, handling 11 different kinds of products each in 100 lb. sacks." Under his command, "every P.W. was to work every working day and have every hour of his day filled in either with work, studies or recreation and religious services on Sunday."⁴³

Preparing Employers, Guards, Civilians, and POWs

To ensure the most efficient use of POW labor, the military instituted a basic screening process to determine skills and suitability for tasks. Skilled laborers often worked on the military base, relieving soldiers for military tasks, while unskilled workers worked in agriculture, logging, and other industries. Prisoners of war often received training on the job, but sometimes brochures, pamphlets, videos, and lectures prepared them for the tasks.[44]

The War Department ensured that military supervisors had adequate training in handling their charges. Supervisors and guards received some instruction on the base or on the job, but the ASF and the War Department supplemented this with a series of manuals. The 1944 manual *Safe Work Practices for Prisoners of War (German)* included a supplement in both English and German that clearly outlined safety measures to be used on all tasks. It defined precautions for nearly every occupation that the POWs might be engaged in on or off base.[45]

The 1945 *Handbook for Work Supervisors of Prisoner of War Labor* adopted many of the policies laid out in the 1943 War Department *Handbook for the Director of Civilian Training*.[46] This new manual warned military supervisors and employers to continually use caution around the POWs, since "the Nazi system teaches its adherents to be constantly on the alert for weak points in the thoughts and behavior of the people of other nations, and to take advantage of those presented."[47] Employers were urged to "be impersonal, firm, and fair. Do not fraternize," and were instructed that "on every job possible the prisoner of war should be told how much work he must complete in a day."[48] It urged that meticulous production records be kept to prove the quantity and quality of work performed by the POWs and to keep track of damages and man-hours that contractors owed the War Department. Finally, the manual suggested that instructions be given in both languages. It warned those not fluent in German not to do this, since the POW "ridicules the use of poor German as we are inclined to laugh at broken English."[49] This proved difficult, however, as many employers and guards could not speak German. Many times a POW spoke both languages and interpreted the directions. This caused problems, since the POW translator, unskilled in a particular occupation, might not know what the directions actually meant. In other cases, POW translators purposely misinterpreted orders or POW laborers pretended not to understand. Finally, the manual informed employers and military supervisors that POWs could refuse to do certain tasks that proved unhealthy or dangerous.[50]

Contractors stayed abreast of War Department and WMC policies regarding prisoners through press and newspaper releases. More detailed policies covering the employment of POWs and the benefits of their labor appeared in national periodicals. Many contractors desired to hire POWs only to be told that none were available. To help employers understand that there were job priorities in the WMC's consideration for hiring out POWs, they published two brief articles in the *Monthly Labor Review* to clarify this system. The first, "Priorities in Allocation of Services of Prisoners of War," appeared in June 1944, and the second, "Policies for Employment of Prisoners of War," in July.[51] These articles helped, since the wide use of the military publications made it difficult to keep them in stock. Even as late as July 21, 1945, the WMC had difficulty keeping up with the demand for the War Department's technical manual on *Enemy Prisoners of War*.[52]

Work on Military Bases

Prisoners of war first worked on military bases, performing skilled and unskilled labor that fell into any of the three classes of work. Prisoner screening upon entrance into the United States determined if the men had any special skills. Skilled labor on military bases received pay, whereas some unskilled labor relating to the general camp upkeep did not. In other cases, the military contracted the POWs for construction or large projects that did not relate to the POW upkeep and therefore the men received pay. Since these men were available to a wide variety of contractors, including the army, air force, and navy, some confusion existed as to what jobs actually paid POWs. In 1944 the War Department created a rule-of-thumb policy that POWs would be paid if the task "required special training and qualifications" or was considered full time.[53]

Prisoners of war worked in agriculture, construction and repairs, dry cleaning, plumbing, and quarrying. The War Department ensured that all POWs employed on military bases worked daily. If any jobs had down days, the prisoners worked on agricultural contracts, which took precedence over most work on bases. To ensure that military supervisors used them efficiently, the POW camp commander often only hired them on a daily contract and appointed a Prisoner of War Action Committee to monitor contracts and check on POW labor on base.[54]

Some work relating to the war effort violated the Geneva Conventions regulations. It came to the attention of Brigadier General Blackshear M. Bryan, the assistant PMG, that POWs at Atterbury, Indiana, "were repairing jeeps. The military authorities stated that the jeeps were not going overseas. However, the papers on the inside of the pockets of the jeep showed that they were destined for overseas service."⁵⁵ The POWs learned of this direct violation of the Geneva Convention, which could have caused an international incident. Bryan ordered that in the future "no indication of overseas service should be left in a vehicle which is being prepared by a prisoner of war. In fact, prisoners should not be used to prepare vehicles designated for overseas service."⁵⁶

Initially, the army used German POWs on military installations and contracted Italians for civilian labor since the Germans posed a greater security risk. Obviously, however, due to the huge civilian demands for labor and the limited number of Italian POWs, this practice went by the wayside.⁵⁷ While the War Department and its branch agencies benefited from this labor, the POWs had mixed reactions to working so closely with the "enemy." The *Unteroffizier* from Camp Shelby, Mississippi, who waged an ongoing battle against efforts to force German POW labor, wrote in his diary on November 21, 1943, that "the next day all 20 men have fatigue duty and there you have to saw and chop wood for the kitchen, furthermore, we have to cleanse the lavatory. And new work crops up ever again so that I have in any case seldom leisure despite the nonwork."⁵⁸ Other POWs had fonder recollections of working on military bases. Paul Lohmann recalled that "sometimes we worked for very High Ranking Officers. Packing up their household goods for those coming in and shipping out. It was good work, sometimes they fed us and most times they gave small amounts of money."⁵⁹ Heinz Richter, held in Illinois, remembered that

> as November came, it got increasingly cooler. In a small hut close to where we were working there was a stove in which I had to keep a fire going. It was my job to keep all the tools clean in this hut. Our guard got cold too and rather than stay outside and guard where there wasn't anything to guard, he stayed inside with me the whole day. I seized the opportunity to speak with him, using the dictionary. He was very patient with me. Sometimes he fell asleep, but I wouldn't let him sleep too long because I wanted to learn English.⁶⁰

Agriculture

Agricultural areas suffered the most from the manpower shortage. From harvesting peas to picking cotton and peanuts and cutting tobacco, prisoners of war provided a needed boost. During the labor program, thousands of POWs worked on American farms more than in any other endeavor. POWs began working on area farms as soon as the first contracts were designed. The War Department and the WMC desired to keep POWs continually working to alleviate labor shortages and therefore carefully planned that the numerous changes in contracts would not negate earlier contracts. The military hoped that POWs could continue to be employed seamlessly between the expiration of old contracts and the signing of new ones. To ensure the hiring of POW labor in local communities, the War Department, the WMC, and representatives from the service commands and individual camps advertised in local news papers and magazines, with employment agencies, and through speaking engagements throughout the community. These efforts for employment were successful, as over 100,000 POWs of the 141,000 held by September 1943 were being employed.[61]

Most POWs worked on farms, alleviating, if not remedying, the manpower shortage. The tasks of these men ranged from working the cane crop with civilians and workers imported from Jamaica at Florida's Camp Clewiston to harvesting peas at Wisconsin's Camp Lodi.[62] These men provided relief for farmers, but it took time for employers and civilian co-workers to warm up to them. Complaints about POWs ranged from fraternization to poor performance. Most employers, however, appreciated the help. In some instances, POWs remained in contact with guards, employers, and co-workers long after the war ended.

For the POWs, working in the community held obvious advantages. Former POW Reinhold Pabel argued that "there was at least the illusion of freedom in the wide-open spaces; and . . . the trip to and from work gave plenty of opportunity to see things (including skirts), a temporary relief from the drabness and dullness of the prisoner compound. Besides, there was always an excellent chance to meet people for informal conversations, especially farmers who had not been trained previously to consider every German soldier as a potential troublemaker and bad boy in general."[63]

J. O. Warren, a farmer who hired POWs from the Lake Wabaunsee POW camp in Kansas, felt that "the POWs were nicer men than the CCC boys." He went on to say, however, that "the CCC boys were the scum of the earth."[64] Others who hired POWs from the camp did not add such qualifiers concerning their trust of the POWs. Some let the POWs play with their children, and one couple, the McKnights, not only "trusted their children with several POWs" but "sent Helmut Grahl on a pony to pick up their first-grade daughter at a rural school."[65] Roland McKnight had been unable to work for three months because of an injury, during which time the POW labor greatly helped his family. The McKnights "felt that the POWs were 'just like Kansas farm boys.'"[66]

The views expressed in Kansas echoed through most of the nation. Rudolf Ritschel, a former POW at the Scottsbluff, Wyoming, camp, remembered working on farms and then often being "a guest for dinner in the homes of farmers of German origin. Each of them was interested in talking with the German boys some time."[67] Paul Lohmann recalled that at Fort Dix, New Jersey, "our relationship with the American workers there was also very good. Several older women (in their 50's and 60's) had sons serving over-seas. They were very motherly towards us and would like to hear about our families."[68] *Feldwebel* Rudolf Hinkelmann recalled supervising labor details in California's peach orchards. He said that the "guarding by the Americans became very superficial." He also recalled that if the POWs finished their allotted work early, they "played cards in a tree house that we built for this purpose." Other POWs, however, "walked across the asphalt road to the various plantations staffed by Mexican field workers. They used to help the Mexicans increase their pickings and by doing so became friends with them."[69]

Lohmann remembered the way the guards treated them. He said that they

> thought it foolish to follow us around with their guns. They were tired of the War and the Army and wanted to go home. Since many of the GIs enjoyed an active night life, they were always tired during the day. We were all very young then and we talked mostly about girls, with our Guards. We fully understood their tired conditions and we hid them, so that they could sleep during the day. We warned them when the Sergeant of the Guard was approaching, to check on them. We always made sure that our "SLEEPERS" were up in time. We were very well organized.[70]

Hinkelmann added that at the "end of the work day, the order was given for all prisoners to gather at a single point even if they had been distributed during the day over a wide area. Occasionally, one of the men would get lost or arrive late. There was an unwritten law among us prisoners; fool around as much as you wish but don't make difficulties for the guards."[71]

In the Deep South, POWs worked the cotton crop. Former POW Hans Goebeler, held at Camp Ruston, Louisiana, recalled that "the backbreaking labor cured me of all my Jack London–inspired fantasies about the life of lumbermen. Picking cotton was even more odious. The cotton flowers tore at one's fingers, and the constant stooping and bending was agonizing."[72] Farmers complained that POWs working in cotton "simply could not catch on" and "where an experienced cotton picker would harvest 300 pounds a day, the prisoners frequently picked only thirty to forty pounds."[73]

By August 1943, there were already 160 contracts to employ POWs on farms in the Southwest. Local employers appreciated this manpower boost, although they complained that they "do not compare with free labor."[74] The POWs worked slowly and often failed to meet their daily quotas. On occasion, farmers discovered that POWs added rocks to their bags of cotton to make the weight. Investigations made near Camp Hearne, Texas, by Jim Potts, head of the Agricultural Extension Emergency War Service, found that in nearly all areas of employment, POWs worked more slowly than civilian workers, but also more meticulously. Their quality of work, whether harvesting cotton or engaging in other labor, seemed always high.[75] Reports from the Texas Extension Service, and similar reports nationwide, conflicted with some of the claims put forth by farmers. One report regarding POWs from Camp Maxey, Texas, stated that "German prisoners picked an average of about eighty bales of cotton per day."[76]

Hans Goebeler, a former POW working in Texas cotton, discovered a way to end preferential treatment by farmers as a way to increase production. The farmer he worked for rewarded cigarettes to the fastest cotton pickers in the group, angering the other POWs. Goebeler recalled one of the men exclaiming, "'Tell that asshole that he should give a cigarette to each of us or none of us or he can keep them.' So I had to tell him. He said, 'Listen, I give cigarettes to whom I want.'" Unable to sway the farmer, the POWs turned on the more productive workers. "As soon as we were getting close to the end, we watched those fellows who were trying to race ... and when they got close to the end we threw stones at them and they stopped."[77]

Lumber Industry

Manpower was desperately needed for harvesting lumber for pulpwood production. In the summer of 1943, pulpwood producers and the International Allied Printing Trades Association appealed to President Franklin D. Roosevelt, the War Department, and the War Production Board that without an increase in labor, many paper products would cease to be printed because of a lack of pulpwood.[78] On August 13, 1943, the House Subcommittee on Brand Names and Newsprint requested that industries associated with paper processing and manufacturing "be classified as essential in order to relieve newsprint shortages." It determined that the United States must have 20,000 more workers cutting timber. Even at this rate, however, the subcommittee stated that

Canada, which met 75 percent of U.S. demands for pulpwood, needed to institute a similar program, even though as of August 1943 they had "not designated pulpwood cutting as an essential industry." Representative Lyle II. Boren stated that POW labor should be employed, but "experience has shown that Italian prisoners could be used more easily than German because the latter had attempted sabotage and tried to escape on some occasions."[79]

Despite these demands, the dangerous nature of this occupation violated the Geneva stipulations, preventing POWs from working in the lumber industry. Yet these restrictions were lifted on September 1, 1943, once it was ensured that POWs would be used only to harvest small trees and would be under constant supervision by skilled supervisors.[80]

A civilian supervisor and guard detachment always accompanied the timbering detail. The POWs received training both on and off the job, which varied widely from place to place and supervisor to supervisor. Most of the POWs had no experience harvesting wood. Sometimes the guards had some experience from civilian life, but most of the time it was new to them as well. Historian Allen V. Koop described lumber details at Camp Stark, New Hampshire: "The foremen knew how the work was to be done, the soldiers held the authority, the prisoners of war did the work."[81] After they had shared the difficulties of summers and winters spent in the woods, these "distinctions blurred" and although "initially divisive, work became a unifying activity" for the men. Rudolf Ritschel, former POW at the Scottsbluff, Wyoming, camp recalled that "up in the mountains we lived in log cabins, as we knew them from wild west films." For Ritschel "it was the most beautiful time of my internment, and I will never forget it. Far away from human settlements in this mountain wilderness, the living together of prisoners with their guards developed into a most friendly fashion. Christmas Eve was celebrated together quite according to German custom. The men on both sides were deeply impressed with the entertainment presentations."[82] According to Colonel Lobdell, commander of Camp Algona, Iowa, POWs worked in harvesting trees through the "winter and summer and only stopped when it got below 45 degrees below zero; when the axes got too brittle to use."[83]

Utilizing POWs in American forests helped alleviate the labor shortage and increase pulpwood production. By 1945, about 22,000 POWs worked in the logging industry and accounted for as much as one-fifth to one-third of total production.[84] Despite the reservations of the War Department, the liberal interpretations of the Geneva Convention by local commanders, and assurances by local employers, the logging industry proved no safer for inexperienced POW laborers than for civilian labor. Numerous deaths and accidents resulted from the normal danger of the work involved but may have increased due to the POWs' inexperience and ignorance of proper safety conditions, despite both groups having copies of the Geneva Convention and the safety guidelines published by the War Department and ASF.[85]

There were other dangers in the forests not directly related to felling trees. Gilbert Hart guarded POW work details at Camp AuTrain in Michigan's Upper Peninsula and recalled the danger from deer hunters. He remembered that the guards "pulled strips of torn red cloth tight around the arms of the Germans" and that "we'd tell them to sing in German or make a lot of noise or something out there because we didn't want any hunters bearing down on those guys."[86] Hart blamed the conditions of employment for most of the accidents: "We were in swamps . . . the worst darn place to cut pulpwood. . . . It was cold and sometimes we'd have two, three foot of snow out there and those guys are out there trying (to) cut these trees down. They had a lot of accidents, a lot of injuries out there."[87] With the number of accidents, the POWs' inexperience, the Geneva restrictions, and eight-hour workdays, it was not surprising that POW production was reported to be less than that of civilian labor. The Southern Pine War Committee in 1945 found that the POWs produced less than civilian labor available before the war.[88] In some cases, such as at Camp Robinson and Camp Dermott, the daily quota for POWs was "considerably less than an experienced civilian worker could produce in the same time."[89]

Canning and Meatpacking

Prisoner of war work in canning factories and in the meatpacking industry created some difficulties due to fears that the Germans might poison the food or sabotage production. The need was as pressing in this industry as elsewhere. The governor of New York stated in September 1943 that without extra manpower, "the harvesting and processing of 2,000,000 tons of fruits and vegetables" would be lost in that state.[90] The Italians first entered this work in 1943.[91] German POW employment in canning and meatpacking began in 1944 and increased in 1945, although in areas such as Wisconsin, Germans worked making grape jam as early as October 1943.[92] Brigadier General Robert H. Dunlop, acting adjutant general, instructed that all "reasonable precautions will be taken to guard against opportunities for rendering food products unfit or dangerous for human consumption through sabotage procedures." This included alerting the Army Veterinary Corps inspectors to scrutinize POW activities and warning employers that POWs should not have access to "meat or other food products which will not be cooked or sterilized after such contact."[93] The shorter working hours of POWs caused employers to realize "the importance of fully utilizing them a full day."[94]

One of the problems that plagued workers in industry also affected POWs in other endeavors: fraternization with women. Special precautions were made to keep them away from American women in the community and female coworkers. Donald E. Bonk worked alongside POWs at the Chilton Canning Company, near the Chilton POW camp, and recalled "local gals flirting with the guards and the prisoners."[95] Richard Hipke owned a cannery in Wisconsin and "believed a couple of American girls working in the plant fell in love with German prisoners and continued correspondence with them after repatriation."[96] At Austin, Indiana, as at other canneries, the guards attempted "a physical separation, if possible, when PWs worked next to women."[97]

In canning, as in other industries, employers complained that the prisoners worked inefficiently. These claims were made even when agricultural agencies determined that both county- and statewide, the POWs produced amounts nearly equivalent to those produced by prewar civilian labor. As in other cases, investigations often found the reports baseless.[98] Cost and security considerations severely curtailed the employment of POWs in meatpacking industries.[99]

Refusal to Work

POW labor, by definition, is forced labor. Even though POWs were fed, paid, and given the opportunity to work outside the base camp, that did not change this basic fact. POW workers proved temperamental and attempted work slowdowns, produced shoddy work, and sometimes went on strike. The reasons that POWs did these things varied widely. They tried to use the Geneva Convention to protest work that they "considered . . . to be a part of the American war effort."[100]

One historian felt that "shared attitudes toward work do not follow lines of nationality. Some people are workers. If they see work to be done, they do it. They will not sit idle. They must always be making, producing, carrying, rearranging. Others seem to live to avoid work. If there is a way out of doing something, they will find it. Most people fall somewhere in the middle, sometimes working enthusiastically, sometimes reluctantly."[101]

One POW officer housed at Camp Shelby, Mississippi, used the opportunity to work as a supervisor to cement solidarity with the enlisted men and passively attack the American labor effort. He stated that many of the German enlisted men did not like the fact that their officers supervised them without helping them work. He reported that the enlisted men "were unable to comprehend that our intention was solely to again deprive the American … of a laboring hand. (That every single man is of importance to him, his paper reports are proving)." When a "group of 10 men went out, one *Unteroffizier* was always with them"; he "stood there without doing a thing." He admitted that this boosted the morale of the Germans, but soon the Americans discovered the plot and not only kept these POWs officers away from the men during work details but, according the German officers, made threats to completely "segregate us from the men." He added, however, that even attempts to fence out the men from each other failed since they were still able to "wander" between compounds.[102]

Helmut Hörner and his co-workers caused problems when a farmer tried to teach them to hoe beets. The farmer asked which of the POWs had farming experience, but the men replied that "we are all students or shopkeepers." Upset, the farmer approached an officer in the group but received the reply "I am a pastor from Bavaria." Finally the frustrated farmer exclaimed, "Well, I can't do anything more. Please begin."[103]

Instances like this were repeated throughout the nation. Methods of dealing with POW work slowdowns and strikes varied as much as the reasons for them. Some farmers felt that proper treatment, friendliness, and good food promoted a strong work ethic. In most cases this tactic worked. Former POW Fritz Ott claimed that when not fed or treated well, POWs would often "piddle along."[104] Colonel Lobdell felt that at his camp in Algona, Iowa, "most of the Americans treated their job with dignity, neither fraternizing with the Germans nor maintaining a cocked gun attitude. They simply did a good job treating their prisoners as soldiers and maintaining to the letter those international laws which govern our activities."[105] Lieutenant Colonel Lester Vocke, a cavalry officer at Concordia, stated that with POWs, "You don't barter with them. You tell them. And they respect you for it. I am not a missionary. I am a soldier."[106]

Methods of punishing recalcitrant prisoners for not working were few and mostly involved reducing or taking away privileges. The army discovered that these troublemakers, "normally confined within a restricted area, had only a few privileges and did not regard admonitions and restrictions in the same light as did American soldiers."[107] The *Unteroffizier* from Camp Shelby wrote that

> ever again the Americans touch upon the problem of work and now even coupled with threats. Something else could happen in case we do not go to work voluntarily, they are telling our company leader. Pressure always produces counter-pressure and this

is in our case too; now we wouldn't do it for spite. As usual nothing turns out of our complaint to the Colonel, a complaint which naturally has to follow such a threat. On the other hand the Americans do nothing to confirm that threat. The business is being carried on as (usual).[108]

Former POW Rudolf Ritschel felt that "They (the Nazis) thought they were doing their country a service, when they did damage to the farmers in the fields or refused to work."[109] The struggle between POWs and the War Department concerning labor was one that the military was determined to win.

The Geneva Convention vaguely described ways of dealing with noncompliant POWs. Article 32 stated that "any aggravation of the conditions of labor by disciplinary measures is forbidden."[110] The War Department published its interpretations of the acceptable forms of punishment on October 27, 1943, in the manual *Administrative and Disciplinary Measures*.[111] Permissible forms of compulsion included verbally reprimanding POWs; restricting privileges; withholding pay; and, in accordance with Article 55 of the Geneva Convention, placing POWs on a bread-and-water diet. Military regulations stipulated that diet restrictions could not last more than fourteen days, that POWs must be given at least eighteen ounces of bread and unlimited water, and that the restrictions could be repeated after an interval of fourteen days, during which the POWs' diet returned to normal quantity and quality of food given the general POW population.[112]

The "no work, no eat" policy proved effective at stopping strikes, but not preventing them. POW pea pickers at Utica, New York, went on strike in July 1943 because they were not permitted to remain outside until ten PM.[113] At Stockton, California, five hundred POWs protested against a newly announced nine-hour workday.[114] Strikes occurred at Camp Rupert, Idaho, because the privates "refused to work in Southern Idaho pea fields alongside non-commissioned officers"; at Camp Perry, Ohio, where POWs working at Crile General Hospital protested "harsh camp rules"; and elsewhere.[115] In each case, restricted diets helped end the strike, but other administrative pressure typically accompanied this punishment. At Stockton, in addition to the restricted diets, the strikers were denied "baseball equipment, music and canteen facilities." At Utica, they received solitary confinement, while those at Rupert "were required to sleep in an open field within the prison camp enclosure, without cots and with only one blanket apiece."[116] A potential strike in Buffalo, New York, was averted when Colonel M. McDowell ordered the guards to read and translate chapter 3, verse 19, of the Book of Genesis. POWs who complained bitterly of the working conditions at their food-processing plant listened to the words "In the sweat of thy face shalt thou eat bread till thou return unto the ground." It apparently worked, as "the 200 prisoners quickly got the idea and went back to work to eat."[117]

In another instance, a work stoppage resulted from interference by the employer. POWs from Camp Cambria, Wisconsin, worked at the nearby Columbia Canning Factory. Civilian co-workers became angry and jealous that the POWs "worked only eight hour shifts and got a ten minute break each hour." The employer attempted to "convince the PWs to work longer and forgo their breaks. After that 'discussion,' the PW's and their guards marched back to camp."[118] POWs farming beets in Wisconsin quit on the job because "the coffee was cold." The guard told the farmer's wife, "No hot coffee—no work!" Once fresh coffee was brought, the men returned to work.[119]

As demonstrated by some of the complaints and comments, many POW laborers worked more slowly and produced less than their civilian counterparts. Employers quickly pointed this out but overlooked the discovery by many military supervisors that POW labor was more reliable and performed at a higher quality. It was written into contracts that the military would provide compensation when POWs paid a regular wage rather than for piecework failed to perform to employers' expectations. While this clause was open to interpretation, invariably some employers hoped to use the loophole to their advantage. Given the large number of employers who expressed satisfaction and the relatively few documented cases of POWs purposely sabotaging their work, some of these claims were suspect.[120]

Union Troubles

The biggest opposition to the employment of POWs came from American labor unions. In nearly every state that POWs worked, local and national labor unions protested the German workforce. The WMC stated in its "regional operations bulletin" that "where union agreements are in effect, the represented union shall be consulted and given every opportunity to assist in recruiting free labor before certification is submitted for prisoner-of-war labor. When possible, the concurrence of the represented union in the utilization of prisoner-of-war labor shall be obtained."[121] Both the WMC and the War Department tried to work with labor unions, but their goal of alleviating the manpower shortage and seeking full POW employment often put them at odds with organized labor.

A major problem erupted between the WMC and labor unions in Michigan in 1944 concerning POW employment in lumbering. It started on January 5 when Alex Legault, president of the United Auto Workers, wrote to John B. Bennett, Michigan congressman, that the Ford Local 952 took issue with the employment of POWs in Michigan forests. Legault felt that "if the War Manpower Commission would make an effort to clean up conditions and wages it would be no effort to get men for the jobs."[122] Bennett, in turn, forwarded the complaint to F. W. Hunter of the WMC and requested more details on the POW program in the western portion of Michigan's Upper Peninsula.[123] The WMC forwarded a statement of its policies to Bennett and began an investigation.

Similar complaints resulted in a meeting between members of Timber & Sawmill Workers Union and the WMC in January. This meeting did nothing to clear up the union's confusion about how and why the POWs were to be used in Michigan. On January 7, 1944, Harold E. Arnold, acting president of the union, wrote to Robert Goodwin, WMC regional director (for the region including Kentucky, Ohio, and Michigan) and Paul V. McNutt, director of the WMC. Arnold queried why the union was not contacted by the WMC prior to the placement and employment of POWs in the timber industry. Arnold bluntly stated that "it certainly looks as though Labor will have no voice in the placement of these war prisoners in the lumber industry. The Union feels that if they are to get something crammed down their throats, the least the War Manpower Commission could do would be to check on conditions in the camps of the operators who have asked for war prisons. They would discover that, in most cases, camp conditions are such that they have been the reason for the insufficient amount of manpower or free labor necessary to carry on operations."[124]

Goodwin followed up by contacting Edward L. Cushman, the acting director for Michigan, on January 8 regarding specifics of the complaint and the employment of POWs in the region in question. John L. Craig, acting deputy director for Michigan, replied on January 11, 1944, that he and Cushman had "several discussions with CIO officials with respect to labor supply prior to the submittal of prisoner of war justifications."[125] He added that there had been no other complaints that concerned the WMC previous to the current issue. Therefore, according to the agreement reached between the WMC and the union on December 13, 1943, POW labor had been approved.

These meetings provided cold comfort to an already enraged Timber & Sawmill Workers Union, which issued an official protest in mid-January. It stated that the WMC awarded "anti-union employers, who have refused to maintain union wages and conditions," with POW work.[126] Undaunted, R. L.

Shaw, acting chief of the Division of Placement of the WMC, stood by the decisions of the Michigan WMC branch in his January 17, 1944, letter to the WMC headquarters. Shaw stated that prior agreements had been reached with the local lumber unions whereby the WMC would first attempt to locate available civilian labor and then use POW labor. He added that the only firms in Michigan's Upper Peninsula that agreed to the use of POW labor were those with no union ties and only two firms held union membership. Even then the International Workers Association representative protested that "as a National policy they were opposed to the use of prisoner-labor." Yet he also "admitted" that there was not enough available labor. "We gathered from this comment that opposition would be slight if prisoners-of-war were brought into the Upper Peninsula." Shaw concluded that "obviously, it is desirable in the interests of good public relations to avoid the antagonism of any labor organization regardless of its size or relative unimportance within an area. We do not feel, however, that we can permit an organization with such a limited membership to control the WMC labor supply policies over such a large area as the lumber industry touches its operations in the Upper Peninsula of Michigan. Nevertheless, we did not approve the contracts for the firms where the CIO held bargaining arrangements nor do we have any intention of doing so."[127]

In another case, the Snider Packing Company of Fulton, New York, complained that the cost of POW labor should be reduced because the "the Army allows two different classifications in factory work, what they call men's work and women's work."[128] The WMC forwarded this complaint to the Prisoner of War Division. Colonel Clifford S. Urwiller, the assistant director of the Prisoner of War Division, responded that the military had no such policy and adhered to the prices set by the WMC. He added that the WMC "makes no difference between male and female labor" and that "the wage rate is established for the type of work and that the Government is entitled to full payment at the rate so established."[129]

The War Department won another victory by refusing to allow labor dues to be deducted from POW checks. Labor unions watched the labor program carefully from its inception and secured agreements that the War Department and the WMC would work with them to keep from displacing civilian labor. No agreement had been reached concerning POWs working in certain industries paying labor dues. The unions took this to mean that they could deduct union dues for POW labor. At Seabrook Farms in Bridgeton, New Jersey, owner Jack Seabrook claimed to operate a closed shop, but because of the extreme manpower shortage, the Amalgamated Meat Cutters and Butcher Workmen "agreed to let the matter go until after we got the men."[130] Leon Schachter, the business manager of the local branch of the union, responded that even when American soldiers were hired temporarily "to save the 1943 tomato crop," union dues were deducted. He stated that the union did not wish to deduct the dues from the POW pay, but rather from the overage that went to the Treasury Department. He made clear that the union felt the "argument is not with the Government, it's with the company."[131] The War Department responded to the claim that organized labor had a right to deduct union dues from POW pay or from the government with a resounding no. They stated that "neither the prisoner nor the United States Government will pay the money" and added that "the only way for unions to collect check-offs for work done by war prisoners would be to get it directly from the employer."[132]

The War Department and the WMC attempted to work with the unions where possible but, as these three cases make clear, stood their ground on issues that proved unfair to their stated terms. As national and local newspapers covered the stories, disagreements between the two government agencies and the labor unions became common knowledge to American citizens and POWs. The *Unteroffizier* from Camp Shelby commented that "these papers bring in principal certain interesting things. So for instance it is evident from them that 150 to 200 thousand miners are on strike in the coal mines. The government seems unable to settle this strike with drastic means. No one resumes work until the demands are satisfied. A thing like that at home would be impossible. That these trade unions do not tolerate interference in their affairs by the State, we have noticed even here in the camp."[133]

Labor Returns

By 1945, the problems with the labor program's policies had nearly all been resolved and the contracting agencies more clearly understood what constituted permissible work and how to get the most out of POWs. The percentage of POWs being employed increased to nearly 96 percent. Germany's surrender allowed the United States to remove restrictions from employing POWs only on non-military tasks, but only if "it were a temporary expedient."[134] At about the same time, the United States began making plans for the future repatriation of the POWs. While the War Department slowly shifted prisoners to larger camps in preparation for return to Europe, smaller camps began to close. The cooperating government agencies ensured that each closing camp announced plans early enough to allow civilian workers and soldiers returning from the European front to replace POWs. Obviously, beginning in the summer of 1945, the overall production of POWs decreased. Even by the winter of 1945 and

1946, however, POWs continued to supply large amounts of labor. In December, 194,306 POWs worked, out of a total of 212,722 available to work (not including noncommissioned officers, officers, and sick and injured POWs).[135] By June 1946, all POWs, with the exception of those sick, injured, and incarcerated, had been repatriated.

The success of the labor program needs to be measured in terms greater than just as a method of keeping the POWs busy. The United States had never implemented a program on this scale and the Geneva Convention provided only vague guidelines. Despite continual difficulties, the War Department created a flexible set of guidelines to permit a new source of labor during the war years. The POWs saved hundreds of acres of crops and provided needed man-hours of production to save local farms and industries. Nationally, the infusion of nearly 200,000 workers who could be transported to branch camps across the country as needed allowed the government flexibility in providing relief and freed up thousands of U.S. citizens to serve in war industries and the military.

Chapter 6

Idle Hands: Recreation and Intellectual Diversion behind Barbed Wire

> *The point is not that these Germans, from a cattle-breeder's standpoint, are great, strapping huskies who can on occasion smile and murmur expressions of gratitude and touch our too-easily-touched hearts. It is not the bodies of these men, however formidable, which are our enemies. It is their minds. These have been corrupted by beliefs which, in Hitler's proud boast, have "brutalized" their holders. These beliefs are contrary to everything in which we ourselves believe and for which we hope. They not only contradict, they deny and imperil what are the foundations of our faith.*
>
> —John Brown Mason

By the end of World War II, nearly half a million Axis POWs resided in camps in the States, almost 400,000 of them Germans. The United States began holding prisoners as early as December 1941; the last left in 1947. Such a large number of men held for this long period of time caused trouble if left unoccupied.[1] The labor program proved helpful but only filled eight to ten hours a day. Many did not work and all were guaranteed one day off per week. This meant that prisoners spent most of their time in the camps. The Geneva Convention only vaguely mentioned recreation and intellectual diversion. Article 16 allowed freedom of religion within the camp, and Article 17 stated simply that "so far as possible, belligerents shall encourage intellectual diversions and sports organized by prisoners of war."[2] The War Department, the ASF, and the PMGO had to interpret these articles. They did so in a broad fashion while providing government support in ways that benefited the POWs' physical, spiritual, and intellectual well-being.

Religion

The U.S. government supported POWs' practice of religion. When there was no German priest or preacher in the camp, civilian clerics performed services. Nearly all the German POWs belonged to either the Lutheran or Catholic faith. The Wehrmacht, like the U.S. Armed Forces, had chaplains who accompanied soldiers at the front. These men, like medical personnel, represented a protected class of POWs but many performed as active soldiers rather than members of the clergy. John Brown Mason, a member of the Internees Section of the Special War Problems Division of the Department of State, noted the difficulty locating POW clergymen, since the "German Army provides only one chaplain for each division, as against between one and three for an American regiment."[3] The PMGO discovered that only nine POWs officially acted as chaplains and most of them were "members of the Gestapo or other police organizations and their assignment as chaplains constituted a secondary duty."[4] These men of the "cloth" were prohibited from preaching to the POWs.

This left the military to rely on POWs who had been preachers in civilian life but through draft or enlistment had become regular troops. These soldiers were treated unofficially as protected personnel. When they were in camps with the POWs, they performed the religious ceremony. Even then, some of the Nazis slipped through the cracks and used the platform to spread their own message. For example, Captain William F. Raugust recommended that Protestant POW preacher and officer Rudolf Sebold be stopped from conducting services at the Memphis ASF Depot because he was "noncooperative and troublesome."[5] Sebold's position of authority within the camp concerned the military to the extent that General Archer Lerch, the PMG, ordered that he be monitored or removed. By February 17, 1945, about a month after the visit, Sebold's true Nazi character had been revealed and Major Maxwell McKnight, acting director of the Prisoner of War Special Projects Division, transferred Sebold to the Nazi camp at Alva, Oklahoma.[6]

Individuals conducting religious services, whether POWs, army chaplains, or civilians, had a set of rules to which they adhered. They could only discuss religious matters, could not relay written messages, and had to be accompanied by U.S. military personnel.[7] The mission of the military, therefore, became one not only of adhering to the Geneva Convention but also of using religion to control and eventually reeducate POWs. American churches had a similarly sincere mission—to bring the POWs back into the Christian fold.

The division of POWs into separate camps and compounds and the separation of officers from enlisted men led to many groups not having access to religious personnel. When this happened, the military allowed the U.S. Army chaplain or a representative from local churches to perform services. The POWs were most happy when a German American conducted services in the absence of someone from their own group. The PMGO noted the army chaplain's difficulty "exercis[ing] a helpful influence over the prisoners because of their inherent distrust."[8] Among many Germans, "reading the Bible had gone out of favor along with churchgoing as Nazism became a religion as well as a political ideology."[9] Situations like that at Fort DuPont, Delaware, where a "Nazi posted himself, pencil and paper in hand, outside the compound church," taking names of those who entered, did not instill much trust in the POWs concerning religion.[10] Georg Kroemer, a former POW at Camp Cooke, California, probably echoed many of the POWs' thoughts when he said, "Religion was not much in demand at Camp Cooke. After all, the origins of Christianity are rooted in Judaism."[11] Some of the POWs were openly and deeply religious, however, and others kept their faith or desire to learn about religious matters a secret. The United States hoped to foster those feelings among the POWs and encouraged religious activities.

The Lutheran Church responded to the religious needs of German POWs by establishing a Lutheran Commission for prisoners of war under the leadership of the Reverend Dr. Paul E. Kretzmann, a professor at Concordia Lutheran Theological Seminary in Saint Louis, Missouri.[12] The Lutheran Commission held its first meeting on September 30, 1943.[13] Kretzmann felt that since nearly half of the POWs were Lutherans, there was "evidently a God-given opportunity before the Lutheran churches of America to promote [their] spiritual welfare."[14] He explained that through the commission, religious services had been conducted at POW camps; devotionals and hymnals distributed; and textbooks, classics, and records given out. He noted that books on "politics are excluded, as are all books making reference in any way to Fascism, Nazism, and the like."[15] Individual churches and other Lutheran organizations had been active on a smaller scale since the arrival of the first POWs, and many, including the National Lutheran Council, pooled their efforts with those of the Lutheran Commission for Prisoners of War.[16] These Lutheran organizations provided an important link in the POWs' religious planning and communication with the War Department agencies.

The Catholic Church also set up services for the POWs and local branches sent personnel to the camps. The National Catholic Welfare Conference organized a War Relief Services Branch in June 1943. This organization provided services to numerous groups in need of help during World War II, including POWs held in the United States.[17]

Initial planning for POW camps called for the construction of a chapel, but many camps had no designated building for religious services. In these situations, the camp commander worked with the POW clergy and spokesman to find a building suitable for holding services. The Indiantown Gap Military Reservation POW camp in Pennsylvania utilized an upper room above a barracks. This small space seemed suitable for the equally small average attendance of about sixty-five Catholics and twenty-eight Lutherans at two separate Sunday services.[18]

As time passed and especially after Nazi segregation, the POWs became actively involved in religious activities. Karl Gustaf Almquist reported that at the Memphis ASF Depot, both congregations planned a Saturday activity, Eine Kirchenmusikalische Feirstunde, which, he felt, "would mean quite a lot for the future."[19] Olle Axberg, inspecting the camps for the army, reported that during February and March 1946 there were three Protestant services each week at Camp Shelby, Mississippi. About 150 men attended the weekday services, and double that number on Sunday. He noted that Catholic interest dropped, with only about 200 attending Sunday mass. This might have been due to the shifting of many POWs from Shelby over the winter months.[20]

Whether Lutheran or Catholic, POWs had an opportunity to grow as a Christian community in the United States. Living behind barbed wire provided a more nurturing religious environment than Germany, where soldiers and civilians practiced their faith, but the Reich discouraged this activity and preferred that they place their faith in Nazi ideology and Hitler. In some ways, the Reich demonstrated its reliance on the "old faiths" by placing clergymen in combat roles and placing political officers in the positions of faith within the army. The U.S. government, although having ulterior motives, worked with established churches, which allowed religion to flourish within the camps.

Sports

In addition to religion, POWs had access to different types of sporting equipment and organized athletic teams. They played ping-pong and tennis and boxed, but soccer took precedence over all other games. POW Reinhold Pabel commented that "all Germans are soccer fiends. Matches for the camp championship were always gala affairs and the GI guards used to shake their heads sadly about our wild enthusiasm for the game."[21] The POW newspaper *Das Echo,* published at Camp Forrest, Tennessee, cleared up the uncertainty about American football. POWs read about football in American newspapers and were understandably confused. The staff at *Das Echo* explained how soccer had branched off in England and evolved into rugby, and how American football had derived from rugby. They informed their readers that *Fussball,* called soccer in the United States, although played, was far less popular among Americans than other sports.[22]

It did not take long for American observers to see just how devoted the Germans were to soccer. Olle Axberg, acting in his role as camp inspector, attended a soccer game during his visit to Camp Shelby, Mississippi, and found hundreds of spectators. On the other hand, he saw limited interest in other sports.[23] When he visited Camp Shanks, New York, however, he discovered ample sports equipment but little effort to organize games or create teams to utilize it.[24] B. Frank Stoltzfun discovered that crowding of the recreation area by new construction forced POWs "to a playground some distance from the camp for football games."[25]

Boxing proved another popular sport for POWs. At Camp Forrest, Tennessee, the POWs organized boxing tournaments approximately once a month that featured up to nine matches a night. Nearly 1,000 attended the second tournament. The sportswriter for *Das Echo* described how the boxers from one compound of manual laborers repeatedly defeated other POWs with less demanding work. He stated that "a person generally has the impression that wood cutting and other hard works are a more favorable influence on the body conditioning than applying plaster, taking temperatures and distributing pills!" In one fight, the boxing director, Guenther Pfeifer, lost his match in the second round. The writer claimed that Pfeifer had "too much book dust in his lungs, for he was very soon out of breath."[26] Over 2,000 attended the third tournament, held in January 1946. The night ended badly as a result of foul-ups by the POW referee, which led to the final heavyweight match getting called early.[27]

Some of the sports and recreation activities were very well organized. Camp Indiantown Gap had one of the most structured programs. Hans Bodenmiller, the spokesman for the camp and director of athletics, organized 125 POWs volunteering for athletics into a total of thirteen soccer teams, five handball teams, and eight volleyball teams, based on skill and age. Additionally, 40 men competed in boxing and 154 men entered ping-pong tournaments. An inspection report noted that nearly all the POWs used the recreation room and facilities and actively engaged in wood carving, metalwork, and painting.[28]

The United States went beyond the normal means of providing recreation areas for the POWs, allowing guards and POWs to organize teams, games, and competitions, and provided sporting and recreation equipment in the canteen for the prisoners to purchase. The United States took the extra step of allocating $1.00 per POW per year (based on the estimated number of POWs in June 1944) to a special fund under the "Supply and Transportation of the Army."[29] A standard package of indoor and outdoor equipment was gathered and placed into a kit. Every camp received one kit for each 250 POWs. Despite the attempts by officials to satisfy the recreation needs of the POWs, some still complained that the kits did not contain certain materials, like woodworking equipment.[30]

Lieutenant Colonel Earl L. Edwards, assistant director of the Prisoner of War Division, assumed responsibility for shipping the kits. This meant that he monitored the number of POWs entering the camps to ensure that they had the correct number of kits. This simple activity produced mounds of correspondence between Edwards and the Prisoner of War Division, the numerous camps, and the nine service commands. Edwards closed most of his correspondence by instructing camp commanders that it was solely their responsibility to distribute the kits and that they were only for POW use.[31]

Another problem, besides American soldiers procuring equipment for themselves, concerned contractors not meeting requirements on equipment. This caused obvious delays in the POWs receiving the goods.[32] Of course, some of this generosity may have been prompted by a May 1942 provost marshal report concerning the Fort Oglethorpe, Georgia, Enemy Civilian Internment Camp. Allen W. Guillion found no work or athletic equipment for the internees and observed that they entertained themselves "by playing volleyball with a paper-filled sock." He recommended that for $75, sufficient equipment could be purchased for them, but for other camps, seventy-five cents per prisoner should be used as a guideline for recreation funds.[33]

POWs came to expect the kits, and failure to deliver them led to complaints. One of the earliest came on October 12, 1943, from the German POW spokesman at Camp Trinidad, Colorado. On behalf of his colleagues, he wrote to the IRC Committee in Geneva, Switzerland. On his second contact with the organization he pleaded: "Is there a possibility that you will again contact the authorities concerning the supply of sports equipment? Our sport's [sic] field is now ready and the question of physical activity seems to us one of the most important factors. If it is not possible for the authorities to supply us with sport's equipment, we are ready to spend our savings on footballs and basketballs and medicine balls, etc."[34]

Alfred L. Cardinaux, assistant to the delegate from the IRC Committee, forwarded the request to Brigadier General Blackshear M. Bryan in the PMGO and also to the Catholic National Welfare Conference. Bryan ordered that Major Earl Edwards investigate the matter. Edwards discovered that four kits had been sent to Camp Trinidad on August 14 and six more on September 29. He sent this information back to Bryan, Cardinaux, and the chief of the Second Service Command, along with a statement that he would investigate and discover what happened to the kits.[35]

Music and Theater

The military encouraged POW involvement in music and theater. The only restrictive regulation was that "costumes which would aid in escapes were avoided."[36] Musically inclined and dramatically trained POWs resided in nearly all the POW camps. Some of these men had performed professionally in Germany before the war. The POWs acquired musical instruments, sheet music, scripts, and theater props through the YMCA, the Red Cross, church groups, and other aid associations. The YMCA alone shipped about 50,000 musical instruments, 3,780 gramophones, and 220,000 records to POWs held by the Allies and the Axis.[37] Prisoners also used their canteen money to buy musical instruments and theater props.

Once the materials became available, POWs organized orchestras and plays for the rest of the camps. While these events varied in size, often determined by the number of instruments available to the prisoners, they provided another distraction. Camp Aliceville, Alabama, had space for a forty-man orchestra, a six-man chorus, and a fifty-man theater troupe that performed various classical plays, including *Faust*.[38] The members of the eighteen-piece orchestra at the Memphis ASF Depot enjoyed being under the direction of a former conductor from Stuttgart.[39] The Sunday night concerts performed by the thirty-eight-piece orchestra at Indiantown Gap, Pennsylvania, drew audiences as large as 200 men. Thirty-two men performed plays, including *Stille Nacht, Heilige Nacht*, but the number and size of performances were curtailed for lack of sufficient space.[40] Camp Sharpe, near Gettysburg, Pennsylvania, operated as a branch camp of Indiantown Gap and housed about 277 POWs, a relatively small number. While the POWs at Sharpe did not have access to a record player, plans were made to organize their seven musical instruments into a POW orchestra. The theater troupe at Sharpe under the leadership of POW Uffz Buesch consisted of fifteen men, who performed the German folk-style plays that Buesch himself created.[41]

Obviously, the band music and plays performed at most camps were limited only by availability of materials, funds, and space, not lack of talent. Many of the industrious theater groups enjoyed a luxury that orchestra members did not, namely, being able to build the materials that they needed (props and scenery) from scrap wood and other commonly available items. The number of POWs engaged in these activities and the scores who attended the performances prove that both music and theatrical endeavors provided a needed intellectual diversion among the POWs and that the United States went to great lengths to ensure that they were well supplied.

Movies

Many POWs also enjoyed the luxury of attending movies shown in the camps. The availability of movies, like musical instruments and theater necessities, was limited by the ability of the military and civilian groups to procure them. In addition to the space and the movie itself, the camps had to acquire projectors. When these items could not be procured because of the cost, the POWs often pooled their money and purchased a projector from the canteen. Initially, the only restrictions on movies concerned current political topics, and all movies had to be approved by the PMG and the camp commander prior to screening.[42] One index of approved American films included titles from Columbia Pictures, Metro-Goldwyn Mayer, Paramount, and ten other production companies. The titles on this list ranged from such American classics as *The Westerner, The Adventures of Mark Twain,* and *Abe Lincoln of Illinois* to World War II titles, mostly dealing with the Pacific War, like *Back to Bataan, Guadalcanal Diary,* and *Thirty Seconds over Tokyo.*[43] The War Department issued new restrictions in its Prisoner of War Circular No. 4, published on January 23, 1945. This included a list of German titles that the War Department received on a reciprocal basis from the German government through the YMCA. The War Department approved most of the available films. The excluded pictures were *Die Drei von der Kavallerie, Die Reiter von Deutsch-Ostafrika, Drei Kaiserjäger,* and seven others.[44] In most camps where movies were available, nearly 100 percent of the POWs turned out to see them. Movies were typically shown once or twice a week, but sometimes more often. In instances where the facility used to screen the movie was too small, a second screening would be conducted to allow all the POWs who desired to attend to do so. Certain movies cost the U.S. government to screen them, so POWs often paid a small admission fee that varied, depending on the camp and on the movie.

Camp Newspapers

Prisoners of war received permission early during their imprisonment to produce their own newspapers. The military reserved the right to censor the newspapers prior to circulation and limited distribution to POWs in the camps where they were published.⁴⁵ The first camp newspapers appeared during 1944, and by 1945, over 137 had been created.⁴⁶ The POWs supplied the creativity and the physical materials for their newspapers. In spite of these limitations, nearly every camp that desired a paper created one and some had two or three in circulation.⁴⁷ Camp Butner, North Carolina, actually had four papers: *Lagerfackel, Mitteilungsblatt für die Österreichischen, Kriegsgefangenen,* and the *European*.⁴⁸ Since the desired audience of the newspapers was POWs, nearly all were published in German. The writers and editors must have understood the censorship guidelines, since most of the newspapers did not appear to be censored after publication.

Much like civilian newspapers, the POWs discussed any newsworthy or interesting topics and covered a broad range of issues. At Camp Butner, an issue of the *European* typically consisted of about twenty pages and included editorials and sections on history and current events at the camp. Many of the camp newspapers used the front cover to reprint a quote from a famous person. The Camp Breckinridge, Kentucky, paper *Die Brücke* often cited noteworthy Americans such as Abraham Lincoln and George Washington. A quote from Voltaire graced the cover of the August 26, 1945, issue of the *European*. The pages of one of the POW newspapers at Camp Campbell, Kentucky, *Der Neue Weg,* were filled with numerous photographs, drawings, and puzzles. Many of the other papers were similar to *Der Neue Weg,* publishing puzzle and joke pages and answering letters from POWs. Sports, theater, and music reports commonly appeared in all the papers. After the POWs had been ideologically segregated, and even more after Germany surrendered, they discussed the prospects of life in postwar Germany.

Not all the publications accepted POW camp life or the idea that Germany would be defeated or that Nazism was dead. The newspaper *Die Bruecke,* produced at Crossville, Tennessee, contained overt pro-Nazi ideology. This indoctrination could be found in nearly all articles and even in the poetry and puzzles. *Der Zaungast,* published at the POW camp in Fort Francis E. Warren, Wyoming, had stories "whipped up in a way that every reader is induced to believe that New York will soon be destroyed by V-3 bombs and that Germany cannot fail to win the victory."⁴⁹

The newspapers provided the POWs with another activity and intellectual diversion. Military authorities quickly learned the value of supporting POW endeavors in producing newspapers, as it not only gave the men something to do but also gave officials a means to gauge the sentiments in the camps and among individual POWs. Major William B. Gemmill, from the Executive

Division of the PMGO, believed that the "German P/W newspapers give a clear picture, like a mirror, of the educational standard, political opinion and intelligence of the P/W's and the whole camp atmosphere in which they are living. Not all of them deserve that name because they are only pamphlets or wastepaper."[50]

Libraries and Reading Materials

The PMGO realized that providing German POWs with libraries and reading materials was more than a matter of politeness. By engaging the minds of the POWs, libraries and reading materials occupied them, hopefully preventing them from engaging in "mischief." The PMGO authorized numerous agencies to provide books. These ranged from organized religious groups, both on the national and local levels, to the YMCA and the IRC, as well as the German and American Red Cross. Packages containing reading materials also arrived from German government agencies, and from individuals in Germany and the United States.[51] Censorship controls prevented the POWs from accessing sensitive or dangerous information. The U.S. government realized late in the POW program the degree of influence they had over what POWs could read but eventually used this to provide certain titles to prepare the POWs for life in postwar Germany rather than simply limit the books to which POWs had access.

The War Department published the first guidelines for POW literature in September 1943 in Prisoner of War Circular No. 1. It prohibited any books that could aid the POW in escape or sabotage and defined these generally as technical manuals and literature on weapons, logistics, map reading, meteorology, sailing, explosives, and chemistry.[52] To ensure censorship of all reading material, only approved agencies could provide books or magazines. Materials had to be new and unmarked. Camp commanders distributed magazines on the basis of one for every ten prisoners each week, and newspapers on the basis of one for every twenty prisoners each day. The camp commander used his own discretion in allowing the POWs access to magazines or newspapers, and in every case they were censored before being delivered. Donations from U.S. citizens, while allowed, had to be ordered directly from the bookstore and delivered by the bookstore to the Office of Censorship.[53] Magazine and newspaper subscriptions had to be ordered in the name of the camp commander, who censored and then distributed them. Additionally, individuals could send only one five-pound book package per month.[54]

Relief organizations realized the difficulty of working under these restrictions. Many sent books to both Allied and Axis POWs and tried to set up cooperative guidelines concerning books allowed and books available. In addition to the restrictions placed on books entering U.S.-operated POW camps by the U.S. government, the German government outlawed any books written by Jews or German émigrés. While they could not directly enforce this upon German POWs in the Allied countries, they prohibited these from entering German-operated camps.[55] Mathilde Kelly and Ruth Utter, working for the Chicago Public Library, devised a list of books allowed to reach American servicemen held by the Axis powers. Kelly and Utter stated that "compiling the list was no easy task. Almost all the newer books had to be eliminated, collections of plays, short stories and poetry invariably included proscribed material, books of cartoons which might be so welcome on this type of list were out because of the war humor, and we thought it best to exclude, for the most part, American historical novels since they might be open to accusation of propaganda."[56]

Yet even with these restrictions, the POWs devoured the reading material that they received and wanted more. Andre Vulliet, a representative of War Prisoners Aid of the YMCA who toured many of the American-operated camps, discovered that the libraries "were the busiest center of any PW camp."[57] Lawrence B. Meyer, a civilian Lutheran preacher ministering to POWs, wrote to the Lutheran Commission asking for donations of religious material. He stated that "with little or nothing to do and less to read, these soldiers are hungry for something to read, and the Bible is the most available, if not the only book they have at present."[58]

Camps began organizing libraries to house the material they received and to regulate access. IRC delegate M. Schnyder reported on a visit to Camp Cooke, California, on June 9–10, 1945, that its library contained 2,500 books. This seemingly impressive number, however, was insufficient, as POWs at branch camps also borrowed books from the main library.[59] When hard pressed for reading material, POWs purchased their own. At Camp Shelby, Mississippi, the library only contained about 2,000 books, but the POWs purchased many for themselves.[60] Vulliet stated that despite the best efforts of the concerned agencies, "for the millions of men interned [not just German POWs in the United States], there were not enough millions of books. . . . The average for PW camps in the United States was 0.55 book per man."[61] As late as December 1945, Olle Axberg discovered that the library at Camp Shanks, New York, had been "poorly supplied with books."[62] The demand for books proved so great that the YMCA took to printing and reprinting thousands of copies for distribution to POW camps. The books were read so thoroughly and used so often that the YMCA also delivered bookbinding materials to camps, as the spines and bindings quickly fell apart.[63]

The PMGO reduced restrictions on reading material in 1945. A wider range of newspapers, both foreign and American, and magazines became available to the POWs. The military also gave POWs direct access to a wide range of these publications by making them available for purchase at the canteen, including the most recent issues of *Newsweek, Time,* and *Collier's,* among others.[64] The POWs soon realized, however, that news in the United States came from a variety of sources, some unreliable, and that some Germans never completely trusted American news sources.[65] One POW writing for *Das Echo* warned his fellows, "The American knows how to pick the 'Chaff from the Wheat.' Many of us who read English do not interpret the facts correctly. Remember that when you attempt to read and analyze newspapers and magazine articles."[66]

Education

Reading by the POWs led directly into development of the POW education program. War Prisoners Aid of the YMCA spearheaded the education efforts by offering textbooks and helping to establish courses and exams. American POWs took classes prepared by the U.S. Armed Forces Institute, with the Educational Administration Center in Geneva acting as the clearinghouse by keeping records of classes and exams.[67] A similar program became available to POWs in the United States. German POWs began taking courses leading to high school diplomas and college degrees and for general interest. Some classes were very informal once-a-week discussions held in the cafeteria and led by a member of the local community. Others were more rigorous classroom-type experiences conducted by qualified civilian or POW instructors. These classes had formal exams and led to credit through cooperating German schools or American universities.[68] Andre Vulliet praised a Kentucky POW camp that "offered almost as many trade and vocational evening courses as a regular trade school and, in addition, went in for experimental horticulture and American agriculture with a class of 180 and an American instructor."[69]

Many of the POWs realized the importance of furthering their education to prepare for return to civilian life. These men had the time and opportunity to work toward higher degrees and vocational training during their imprisonment. At Camp Gruber, Oklahoma, Walter Schmid worked diligently to learn English. He recalled that "there were supposed to be English language classes, but there weren't any books. I still had Beer's English dictionary, but it was incomprehensible to me. One of the teachers learned that I had it and asked whether I would lend it, to which I agreed, as long as I could take part in the class."[70] For Schmid, learning English proved fairly difficult. "Most of the men in the class could barely speak some English from school days," he recalled. "I didn't learn much. Then another class was held, and I stayed in that one, too. This went on until I was able to speak some English. Later, it helped me a lot. Most of the other POWs refused to learn English and felt that if the Americans wanted to speak to us, they should learn German."[71] Another POW, from Camp Forrest, encouraged his fellows by arguing that "we are realizing more and more that it is an advantage to be here in normal conditions of life, and by this we are able to prepare ourselves for the work of our future. The serious situation in our homeland should increase our sense of responsibility. In this connection it is very important to make full use of the precious time which is here at our disposal, especially in order to train our minds and increase our knowledge."[72]

While a large number of POWs actively participated in these education programs, others did not. Olle Axberg reported that at the Memphis ASF Depot, relatively few POWs took classes, despite a selection that included English, French, math, physics, and bookkeeping.[73] He later reported that the only class offered to POWs at Camp Shanks was English, and that "most prisoners after work do not feel like going to school."[74] On the other hand, some camps had well-organized education departments. At Camp Indiantown Gap in Pennsylvania, POWs chose from courses in English, bookkeeping, French, Spanish, Latin, fruit culture, agriculture, biology, chemistry, history, geography, shorthand, arts, and German. If the POWs did not find a course from the list offered at the POW camp, they could look through the correspondence catalogs from American universities. In March 1945, four men were taking classes through the University of Texas. Albert Rosebrock ordered three classes in pharmacy. Three other POWs took courses from the University of California, two worked on electrical studies, and one took calculus.[75] According to Vulliet, in three years the YMCA "reprinted 337,000 copies of 23 German textbooks . . . and 71,000 dictionaries, mostly German-English and vice-versa."[76]

In many ways, German prisoners held in the United States had more freedom than in Germany. The United States attempted to provide a safe environment conducive to practicing religion, discussing ideas, learning, and self-expression. The fact that just over 2,000 POWs tried to escape while thousands of others volunteered in some aspect for these programs could be taken as a sign of success. The fact that dozens, if not hundreds, of former POWs held in the United States either aided the American occupation government upon their repatriation to Germany or returned to the United States and became naturalized could also be attributed in small part to these recreation and intellectual diversion programs. It would be difficult, if not impossible, to measure the direct impact of the recreation and entertainment program offered to POWs in the United States on the overall contentment within the POW camp structure or upon the postwar relationship between Germany and the United States. It would certainly be naive, however, to assume that these efforts by the United States to go above and beyond what was required by the Geneva Convention were made in vain.

Chapter 7

Exorcising the Beast: The Reeducation of German POWs in the United States

> *He who makes a beast of himself gets rid of the pain of being a man.*
> —Samuel Johnson

The reeducation program, dubbed the intellectual diversion program, was a belated and poorly orchestrated attempt to teach German POWs the value of democracy. This project began secretly because the Geneva Convention outlawed attempts to denationalize POWs. Any reeducation efforts might be seen as brainwashing or denationalization. The program began very slowly in 1944 with additional restrictions and specific additions to the reading materials already available to the POWs. Emphasis on German history and culture and American democracy and history within the normal education programs also constituted a subtle way of reeducating POWs. These methods remained largely voluntary and mostly secret until after Germany surrendered.

Once the war in Europe ended, the United States no longer feared reciprocal action against American servicemen held as POWs by Germany. The program picked up some momentum with the creation of a Special Projects Division (SPD) charged specifically with reeducation. A national POW newspaper, *Der Ruf,* written by a specially selected cadre of anti-Nazi POWs assisted by members of the SPD, provided carefully measured literature by POWs to POWs. Officials also scoured the camps to find groups of reliable anti-Nazi POWs to volunteer for four training programs being set up across the country. Programs at Camp Kearney, Rhode Island, and Fort Getty, Rhode Island, introduced the men to postwar government administration and democratic traditions. The POW camp at Fort Wetherill, Rhode Island, allowed the men to train to be postwar police officers. Camp Eustis, Virginia, provided a six-day crash course in democracy for nearly 20,000 POWs. Unknown to the POWs, those who volunteered received early and direct repatriation to Germany, while the rest went from the United States to France, Great Britain, or other countries, where they provided compulsory labor until as late as 1949. The program had obvious limitations. One of the most glaring was the relatively small number of POWs who received direct training, about 30,000 out of a population of nearly 371,000. A second involved the selection process. The POWs were chosen from among the reliable and trustworthy and, specifically, anti-Nazis. In other words, the men being reeducated about the German government and history were the ones least in need of it. Other problems included the haste with which the program was put together and the lack of properly trained or skilled personnel to run it.[1]

Ultimately, the segregation of POWs within the camps on the basis of nationality and ideology, designed to limit violence, transformed into a plan to reeducate them. The United States hoped that these men would reshape postwar Germany, and others foresaw using them as leverage against the Soviet Union in the coming Cold War. Henry Cassidy, in a November 1944 article in the *Atlantic Monthly* titled "What to Do with German Prisoners: The Russian Solution," suggested that the United States reeducate German POWs in democracy. He argued that the Russians had no qualms about converting their German POWs to communism and feared the impact that such forced indoctrination on such a large number of Germans would have on the political orientation of postwar Germany.[2]

The Impact of Books, Movies, and *Der Ruf*

Among the first things that the United States modified in seeking to reeducate the POWs were the list of books that prisoners of war were permitted and publication of the POW paper *Der Ruf*. POWs were now allowed only certain titles of books, and the publication of *Der Ruf*, which began to be published nationally. In May 1945, officials distributed copies of twenty-four different books published in German by the *Infantry Journal* under the series title *Bücherreihe Neue Welt* (*New World Bookshelf*) to the POW canteens and libraries. The titles included *Amerika* by Stephen Vincent Benet, *Achtung Europa* and *Lotte in Weimar* by Thomas Mann, and *Wem die Stunde schlägt* by Ernest Hemingway.

The military surveyed several camps to gauge the extent to which the POWs accepted these books. A representative from Halloran General Hospital at Staten Island, New York, commented, "We received the initial shipment of 105 books, and these were in the prisoner of war canteen the first day after their arrival," adding, "Your last shipment of 105 books were sold about an hour after arrival."³ The representative from the Richmond ASF Depot in Virginia said that "the books to date have been very popular and have enjoyed a sell out in the canteen and therefore suggest that you send us an additional 50 copies of each."⁴ Dozens of similar comments and additional orders poured in from POW camps across the United States. The official comment from the SPD was that "there is no absolute measure of the influence upon the minds of the Prisoners of War of the good books made available to them. But surely these books have exerted some influence, and perhaps a great one."⁵

The SPD felt that the books would affect postwar Germany long term: "It is expected that Prisoners of War will take many of these books home with them when they return to Germany. The Nazis knew the power of books and therefore burned them. But these same books are returning home to take up the battle again."⁶ The production of the *Bücherreihe Neue Welt* series demonstrated how, with the end of the war removing restrictions on literature, the War Department and the PMGO used the POWs' desire to occupy their time, to read, and to pursue knowledge to the advantage of the reeducation program.

The newspaper *Der Ruf,* or the *Call,* published at Camp Kearney, Rhode Island, was circulated nationally to the POW camps. As with the other papers, the staff and editors who produced it were all POWs. Unlike other papers, *Der Ruf*—written by anti-Nazis at Kearney, under the guidance of the Special Projects Division of the PMGO and headed by two POWs: Dr. Gustav René Hocke, a successful writer, and Curt Vinz, formerly an established publisher—had a direct anti-Nazi leaning. The newspaper began circulation in March 1945 and enjoyed a fairly wide readership, despite some POWs hiding the issues from their colleagues because of their direct anti-Nazi bent and the fact that much of the discourse was difficult for the average POW to comprehend.⁷

Of the movies selected for POWs to view by the SPD, the most important to the reeducation program were the *Why We Fight* series by Frank Capra and atrocity films taken by the U.S. military that depicted the aftermath of the Holocaust.⁸ Capra's movies, often shown to U.S. servicemen to foster an understanding of the current conflict, allowed the POWs to view the war from the American perspective. The atrocity films produced mixed results among the POWs. Some were shocked and angry, but most could not or would not believe that their nation had committed these crimes. Some saw it as American propaganda. Many were moved by the scenes.⁹ Historian Arnold Krammer noted that after the compulsory viewing of atrocity films at Camp Butner, North Carolina, 1,000 POWs "dramatically burned their German uniforms, and at numerous camps across the country, groups of prisoners voluntarily took up collections for the survivors of the Nazi concentration camps."¹⁰

Fort Philip Kearney, Rhode Island

The first formal reeducation program for POWs began at Fort Philip Kearney, Rhode Island. The camp functioned as a deactivated coast guard station but could be utilized in an emergency and had a nominal four-man guard. The PMGO sought a location to begin its reorientation program, and in January 1945 Captain Walter H. Rapp found Kearney to be a suitable site.[11] The PMGO had the camp reclassified in February and began moving its reorientation program to that location.[12] The staff of *Der Ruf* moved to the camp and the PMGO established the "experimental school" under the leadership of Lieutenant Colonel Edward Davidson, from the office of the PMG.[13] Davidson received assistance from some of the best military men and civilians involved in the prisoner of war program: Dr. Howard Mumford Jones, Dr. Henry Ehrmann, Major Henry L. Smith Jr., Colonel T. V. Smith, and Captain Robert Kunzig.[14] Captain Walter Schoenstedt, one of the military personnel involved with the program at Kearney, reported that of the entire faculty, Dr. William G. Moulton was among those who proved invaluable. Schoenstedt stated that the PMGO needed to exert every effort to retain the services of such men in the reeducation program.[15]

The POW reeducation at Fort Kearney began with a series of exams to determine the extent of the POWs' knowledge about world affairs. Then the POWs entered into the three-phase curriculum, which focused on English, military government, and democracy. These classes were supplemented by informal discussion groups, visiting lecturers, quizzes, and exams. The final stage included an interview to determine how much the POWs learned and how useful they could be to postwar Germany and the American military government to be established there. Once the POWs successfully completed the program, they became eligible for early and direct repatriation to Germany.[16] The POWs also provided services for the PMGO by working within the six sections of the program designed to screen materials being sent out to the POW camps across the nation. The Film Section, for instance, viewed movies and broadcasts before the general population of POWs and made recommendations on their appropriateness. The Camp Newspaper Section monitored the numerous POW camp newspapers with an eye toward the political leanings of each paper and camp.[17]

The faculty at Fort Kearney learned important lessons regarding acceptable candidates and avoiding problems. Initially the program design was for one hundred students, divided into three groups, to go through one class at a time. In the very first class, only sixty men arrived at Fort Kearney on

April 28 and 29, 1945. The staff waited to start them in course work until May 7, anticipating the arrival of forty more POWs. The additional men did not arrive until May 23 and 24, far too late to catch up with the others. The delay caused the relatively small staff scheduling problems in preparing classes and other activities and it also meant that the first group graduated before the second group.[18] This problem was exacerbated by the fact that the American military government in Germany asked for ten of these men to be shipped immediately. They hurried through graduation ceremonies and went to Germany on June 29. This left the staff in confusion regarding the graduation and repatriation date for the remainder of the students. They ultimately graduated and many were repatriated on July 6, 1945.[19]

These problems led the staff to suggest that in the future only groups of one hundred men could be accepted to begin courses and that they would all graduate together. Because of the large number of undesirable candidates, administrators also decided that future selections would be broadly anti-Nazi. Officials in charge of the reeducation program requested that camp commanders, when screening candidates for the program, overlook the very young men, as they did not have the experience for administrative work, and those who lacked basic English skills, since they would be of little use to the American military government.[20]

Captain E. Targum outlined several other factors that caused disruption in the program. Some of the POWs at Kearney complained about the loss of privileges when they transferred from their base camps. He argued that "the prisoners will feel themselves exploited if, on the one hand, an attempt is made to gain their confidence, while on the other hand they are treated according to the book, in the same manner as the great majority of prisoners."[21] On the other hand, when Major Frank Brown visited the camp, he found that when he entered the guard compound accompanied by an officer from Kearney, only one of the twelve guards stood at attention; the remaining men were sitting or lying on their beds. When Brown passed some of the POWs, they did not stand at attention or salute as required. Brown found the decided lack of courtesy to be coupled with ignorance when he was directly asked by camp personnel "where they stood in relation to supervision and requiring the camp to observe War Dept directives and to what extent SC [Service Command] directives would apply."[22] Brown forwarded this report to his superiors with a recommendation that the camp commander be promoted officially to commanding officer so that he and his personnel had no confusion regarding his authority. Brown personally began the paperwork to transfer some of the American guards out of the post. The PMGO received the report and corrected the lack of discipline at Fort Kearney by providing training and firm guidelines and transferring of some of the guards, as suggested by Brown.[23]

The experience at the "Idea Factory," or "the Factory," as Kearney was dubbed, proved successful enough in the eyes of the PMGO that its operations continued and more groups of POWs entered the reeducation programs. The Factory provided the nexus for other efforts as well. Three other reeducation programs were designed: Fort Getty and Fort Wetherill, in Rhode Island, and Fort Eustis, Virginia. Eventually, a core group from Kearney transferred to Europe, beginning in August 1945, to provide training for "teen-age prisoners" held in Europe "who have received little or no education during the Hitler regime and who might become a dangerous element which could be easily used against the interests of the United States and all peace efforts."[24]

Fort Getty and Fort Wetherill, Rhode Island

Rhode Island housed the next phase of the SPD reeducation effort. Fort Getty housed the administration school, also referred to as Project II. Fort Wetherill became home to Project III, the police school. These two programs were launched in the summer of 1945. Like Kearney, both of these projects were hastily assembled and quite ambitious in their goals. POWs only received sixty days of training before graduating. Officials, however, applied the important lessons gained from Kearney to the new projects. These lessons most specifically related to choosing POWs for the program. Military officials requested that camp commanders submit lists of "qualified" candidates for review. The military, the staff at Kearney, and the POWs at Kearney selected students from the lists. These selections, however, were made in conjunction with new regulations set by the PMGO.

Major Maxwell McKnight, acting director of the Prisoner of War Special Projects Division, used the suggestions from the Kearney project in preparing guidelines for Fort Getty and Fort Wetherill. Desirable candidates, according to McKnight, "must be anti-Nazi in the broad interpretation of the word, which is taken to include not only those who are actively opposed to Nazism, but also those who are merely non-Nazi." McKnight added that more importantly, these men must be "trustworthy, loyal, cooperative, industrious, sincere, in good health, and mentally stable." In selecting men for these projects, McKnight restricted anyone over the rank of captain, anyone under the age of twenty-five, and anyone who displayed militaristic characteristics. Final restrictions limited the program to candidates from Bavaria, Hessen, Hessen-Nassau, Württemberg, Thüringen, Bremen, and Bremerhaven. This last restriction, although McKnight did not fully clarify his reasoning, was probably to limit the candidates to the areas of Germany that would remain within the American zone of "Germany proper" after the war.[25]

The selective nature of the project excluded thousands of the POW candidates suggested by POW camp commanders. The SPD whittled down a list of 18,000 men suggested for the Fort Getty project to a scant 2,750 suitable candidates.[26] Much of the course work used at Kearney translated over into the classroom teachings at both Projects II and III. Obviously, those in Project III received specialized vocational training in police duties that differed from the administrative skills taught at Kearney and Getty. Dr. Henry Ehrmann, who taught at all three schools, stated that the three institutions resulted in a total graduation from Kearney of 73; from Getty, 455; and from Wetherill, 488. These relatively small groups formed a cadre of cooperative and reeducated POWs who, it was hoped, would play a direct role in the shaping of postwar Germany. These programs also provided the impetus for the most ambitious undertaking, the school at Fort Eustis, Virginia.[27]

Fort Eustis, Virginia

The reeducation program at Fort Eustis was easily the most ambitious and rushed of all the programs. The PMGO desired to reeducate as many as 25,000 POWs at Eustis. The biggest obstacle to this lofty goal was that the War Department planned to have all German POWs repatriated by March 31, 1946. That most of the personnel needed for this program were engaged in the other SPD projects and would not be available until December 15, 1945, only exacerbated the problem. Despite these constraints, planning moved forward and each service command had instructions to forward names of eligible POWs. On December 18, 1945, enough personnel were in place at Eustis to begin screening and other preliminary planning.[28]

The project at Fort Eustis originated from two factors. The first stemmed from what the SPD considered the natural expansion upon success of the Factory and Projects II and III into a larger reeducation effort. The second came from a summer 1945 announcement that the United States had agreed to repatriate German POWs to France, where they would continue to work as POWs, rather than directly to Germany. The members of the SPD felt that this transfer of "the more cooperative and anti-Nazi prisoners to France would negate whatever good results had been obtained by the re-education program."[29]

Screening of eligible candidates similar to that of earlier projects was conducted. POWs filled out questionnaires and the POW staff at Kearney assisted

PMG and SPD officials in culling the undesirables. The SPD anticipated, in accordance with the precedent of the earlier programs, that about 20 percent of those being screened would be rejected. In actuality, less than 10 percent were rejected. This caused a unique situation, since the program anticipated that only 2,000 men could enter at a time, but "the number of prisoners waiting to enter a cycle increased with alarming rapidity."[30] The SPD created space that allowed a larger number of classes to be conducted at one time in order to take care of the number of POWs available.

The POWs at Eustis went through a six-day program. Each day there were approximately two lectures, which resulted in the program goal of twelve, all of which had large democracy components. Following each lecture, the POWs had a discussion hour, which they ideally used to gain a better understanding of the material. Carefully selected movies and film shorts that augmented the lectures were shown to the POWs. The program outline for the six-day program was:

Day 1: Lecture 1—The Democratic Way of Life
Lecture 2—The American Constitution
Movie 1— *Abe Lincoln in Illinois*

Day 2: Lecture 3— Political Parties, Elections, and Parliamentary Procedures
Lecture 4—The American Educational System
Movie 2—*A Tuesday in November*
Movie 3—*The River*

Day 3: Lecture 5—Democracy and the American Economic Scene 1
Lecture 6—Democracy and the American Economic Scene 2
Movie 4—*An American Romance*

Day 4: Lecture 7—American Military Government
Lecture 8—Democratic Traditions in Germany
Movie 5— Power and the Land
Movie 6—*Displaced Persons in Europe* (later replaced by *American Military Government in Cologne*)

Day 5: Lecture 9—Why the Weimar Republic Failed? 1
Lecture 10—Why the Weimar Republic Failed? 2
Movie 7—*The Seventh Cross*

Day 6: Lecture 11—The World of Today and Germany
Lecture 12—New Democratic Trends in the World

Movie 8—*TVA*
Movie 9—*Toscanini*
Movie 10—*Hymn of the Nations*[31]

The POWs in the program at Eustis attended classes and watched compulsory movies for about eight hours each day. The staff arranged other films, discussions, recorded performances, physical activities, and talks at night. There were similar daytime diversions for the POWs who were waiting for their group to begin the six-day program and for those who had finished the program and were waiting to be repatriated to Europe.[32] Eventually 23,142 men graduated from the program and repatriated directly to Germany.[33]

Results of Intellectual Diversions and Reeducation

The military encouraged intellectual diversions as part of the required and necessary provisions within the camps as outlined by the Geneva Convention. The provisions of the Convention, however, were extremely vague and, like nearly all other aspects of the POW program, open to broad interpretation. That the ASF and the PMGO favored a version that allowed numerous diversions within the camps was a boon to the POWs held in the United States. The military not only allowed but encouraged these activities by providing equipment for the POWs to use. These actions on the part of the U.S. military, however generous, served a greater purpose. POWs occupied in programs that they helped create and the success of which they had a vested interest in kept these men from plotting escape, sabotage, or murder behind barbed wire. In the most basic sense, the military felt that a content prisoner would also be compliant. This treatment of POWs also paid propaganda dividends. In the first sense, POW-operated newspapers provided a gauge of sentiment within the camps. Officials stayed abreast of the developments with these publications and then took the necessary measures or precautions based on the political leanings of the POWs. Also, the POWs wrote of their treatment in letters home. This provided the United States with a source of propaganda when the families and friends of the POWs read these letters. While it would be difficult to measure the impact of this upon the German people, it undoubtedly had some effect on a war-torn German home front.

Critics of these efforts point to three limiting factors. First, these crash courses in democracy had little impact on postwar Germany or on the reeducation of those involved. Second, the small numbers represented from the total POW population immediately limited any potential success or gain.

For instance, what was the real benefit of 20,000 POWs out of approximately 371,000 receiving a six-day course on democracy? Third, the POWs selected were all considered anti-Nazi, and therefore the most compliant and least in need of reeducation. For instance, no reeducation candidates came from the ardent Nazi camp at Alva, Oklahoma.

The reeducation plans, however, had limited objectives. They desired to find the most compliant individuals to aid the American military government. Henry Ehrmann was the first to admit that the program "did not attempt to tackle the problem of reorienting the minds of convinced Nazis or active followers of the defunct regime. Neither available time nor the teaching staff was sufficient to undertake such a task."[34] As far as the Eustis project was concerned, the staff felt that the goal of the six-day program "was to send some 20,000 cooperative German prisoners of war directly back to Germany, via a six-day orientation cycle; this mission was accomplished."[35]

Historian Ron Robin pointed out several flaws in the reeducation program. One of the reasons that he gave for lack of success, if not outright failure, is that "With the exception of Harvard Professor Howard Mumford Jones, the members of the reeducation staff were not on the cutting edge of their respective fields. . . . [They] traded in ideas, but they produced few intellectual innovations. They showed a marked tendency to follow well-worn paths rather than break new ground."[36]

Robin also felt that a reeducation plan was doomed because

> The irreconcilable differences between National Socialism and democracy were perhaps, reason enough to expect limited success. But beyond this ideological obstacle lay a more mundane reason for the faulty dialogue between German soldiers and American educators. Once settled in the camps, these captive soldiers behaved much in accordance with the standard conduct of the prison inmate. The teacher was the warden, and, by implication, he was the enemy. At times the inmate would demonstrate varying degrees of acquiescence; but accepting the worldview of the warden was out of the question."[37]

Add to this the fact, according to Robin, that "a deliberate exclusion of behaviorists and other social scientists from the SPD staff further shielded reeducation officials from an understanding of the tensions affecting the lives of their wards."[38]

Critics must weigh the fact that planning for the first program at Kearney began in late 1944, at which time planners had to operate secretly because of restrictions of the Geneva Convention. Once the war ended, the programs could function openly but only until March 31, 1946, the date by which all POWs had to be repatriated. In reality these programs functioned for less than a year. Critics must consider that constraint along with the limited program goals. The result was limited means yielding limited ends, but this is exactly what the reeducation programs hoped to achieve. Therefore, one must conclude that the programs were somewhat successful.

Chapter 8

Leaving a Place Called Amerika

> *At one time, Camp Shanks and this lonely beach served the American invasion troops, which used this location as their springboard for their victorious push into Europe. Now we stand here, German prisoners of war with the same goal in our hearts, but instead intended on a peaceful return home. After they have pushed us around for years into all corners of the world, young Americans, our guards, stand with us also on the beach and shall return to the land of their fathers to keep the peace there. But the same joy is not to be seen in their faces as in ours.*
> —Former POW Helmut Hörner

With the surrender of Germany and the end of World War II, the United States began the repatriation process for the approximately 372,000 German POWs housed within its borders. The United States encountered and overcame a number of problems while housing these prisoners. Ultimately, it exceeded the guidelines set forth in the Geneva Convention. Although the Geneva Convention set some guidelines for establishing and operating the POW program, its vague articles left much room for interpretation. This required quite a bit of ingenuity, farsightedness, and compromise among the numerous agencies involved with the program. Government departments, civilian agencies, and labor unions all had a voice in the establishment of various aspects of the program, often causing much debate and delay in implementation of policy and procedure.

The POW program ended almost as quickly as it began. Branch camps closed and base camps consolidated beginning in 1945, often leaving no trace of their former inhabitants. The POWs realized that when the war ended they would go home and again they found themselves at their points of embarkation at Norfolk, Virginia; Camp Shanks, New York; and New Orleans, Louisiana. There they anxiously anticipated the arrival of U.S. transport ships, this time to return to Europe. While many may have respected the United States and others hated it, most desired to go home. Only the most intuitive among them and those privy to confidential information knew that they would be sent to France, Great Britain, Greece, Czechoslovakia, the Netherlands, and Norway, where they would remain POWs for up to three more years. The decision to transfer U.S.-held POWs to allied nations followed an agreement reached in November 1945 between the War Department and America's European allies to allow the POWs to aid in rebuilding these war-torn nations. Those POWs who participated in the reeducation program, however, returned directly to Germany in the hope that they would assume political offices and law enforcement positions.

The process of sending the POWs back to Europe took time. Practicality and a degree of stalling enabled American farmers to keep their workers for several months after Germany's surrender. The United States argued that with the war in Europe over, fewer transports existed for the Atlantic run. In fact, nearly all shipping now supported the war in the Pacific, which lasted until August 1945. Even with available shipping, the United States insisted that the administrative and security situation in Europe could not handle a large influx of POWs. One report from the *Washington Post* stated that "returning prisoners might soon band themselves into Freikorps, which could subsequently be united into a private army."[1]

By the end of 1946, however, nearly all the POWs had left the United States, and the last men shipped out on June 30, 1947. The War Department issued an official statement in August 1947 that all 435,788 POWs held in the United States, with the exception of the seriously sick or injured and twenty-four escapees, had returned to Europe. This included not only the official number of 378,898 Germans but also 51,455 Italians and 5,435 Japanese. A spokesman for the War Department added that "considering the numbers we feel we got them out in a hurry."[2] Nearly five hundred POWs died behind barbed wire in the United States, and they received burials in or near their camps.[3] The Western allies could weigh this against the situation in the Soviet Union, which released its last Axis POWs in 1956.[4]

In some ways the extended stay in the United States was a benefit for the Germans, but they did not understand that until it was too late. They were held under the liberal U.S. interpretations of the Geneva Convention, but after returning to Europe, many went to France and other Allied countries, where they worked to rebuild these nations. Anger overcame many of the POWs as they learned that their next destination was not Germany but work in the ruins of one of its former enemies. Helmut Hörner, boarding the *Empress of*

York on June 14, 1946, for what he thought would be the trip home, discovered the truth by accident. Above his bunk, someone had scrawled on the canvas: "10 March boarded in Camp Shanks. Goal Bremen—Hunger—Disembarked 22 March in Liverpool, England. Everything is only lies!"[5] After a bout of anger and depression, Hörner accepted his fate. England was still closer to Germany. In January 1948, he returned to Germany, finally able to see his wife. Walter Schmid was transported aboard the *Aiken* to Belgium. The POWs found it confusing that they received new serial numbers. Schmid called it "silly for the few days we'd be here, since we were about to be released. We were allowed to write a postcard home, to let them know we were on our way."[6] Schmid and his colleagues were again transferred, but this time to England, where they worked until sent back to Germany in May 1947.

Most of the POWs who have been interviewed or written memoirs have lauded their good treatment at the hands of the Americans. Many returned to the land of their former imprisonment. Heino Erichsen, a former POW in Texas and then at Fort Knox, Kentucky, returned in 1953. He moved to Minnesota and then back to Texas.[7] Reinhold Pabel, a Camp Grant, Illinois, escapee who was deported in the early 1950s after finally being recaptured, also returned to the state of his incarceration and the site of his arrest. In 1954 he came back to Chicago and to the American woman he had married and the bookstore he had established prior to his recapture.[8] Many of those who did not come back permanently came back to visit. They toured the camps, or the site where a camp once stood, accompanied by their families. Some of these visits passed in relative obscurity. For others, the local media and scholars accompanied the POWs, and the communities embraced their former residents. Some camps continue to host POW reunion gatherings. As time passes, however, these reunions become less frequent and, sadly, to many observers, as World War II becomes an even more distant memory, less important. Even the youngest of the former POWs are in their early eighties. Most of the surviving American personnel are even older.

In this study I have attempted to present a balanced and comprehensive analysis of the U.S. experience handling German prisoners. I have used untapped resources at the National Archives II in College Park, Maryland, and the Military History Institute at Carlisle, Pennsylvania; documents from the Special Collections at the Historical Center in Frankfort, Kentucky, and the Kentucky Building at Western Kentucky University; and other primary and secondary sources to support my conclusions.

While this study successfully gathers together most of the material available on the subject of German prisoners of war in the United States to provide an up-to-date overview, its major contribution is actually greater than that. Each chapter supports the thesis that the United States overcame major problems to maintain and even go beyond its legacy of humane treatment of prisoners of war, established as early as the American Revolution, and the requirements of the Geneva Convention. The chapters also examine aspects of the POW program that have previously received little attention.

The POW program began with some difficulty, since the United States had little experience housing such a large number of POWs and was relatively unprepared for such a task. Throughout this process, however, the United States maintained its reputation, which began with its experience in the American Revolution, as a world leader in providing humanitarian treatment to prisoners of war and adhering to international law.

Many historians writing about the subject make only passing reference to the troubles within the POW camps. They conclude that these problems were due to ideological differences between Nazis and non-Nazis and quickly demonstrate how the United States overcame these difficulties to support their thesis that the program operated smoothly. In this work, I have looked at the recruitment policies of the Third Reich and discovered that the differences among Wehrmacht troops were greater than Nazi and anti-Nazi views, and included religion, nationality, ethnicity, and ideology. While these differences created only minor problems in the military, behind barbed wire, they finally exploded.

Much of the literature suggests that the severity and longevity of these problems resulted either from ignorance on the part of U.S. soldiers or laxity on the part of the government. Both of these conclusions are rather shallow and erroneously place the blame for some of Germany's preexisting problems on the shoulders of Americans. Given that most American soldiers, youths themselves, had no idea that these potentially dangerous differences existed, that most GIs could not speak German, and that there were no orders to screen beyond separating Italians and Germans, American personnel could not have foreseen the conflicts that would occur among these men. Once alerted to the problems in the camps, officials acted quickly to segregate POWs and even created special camps for the most ardent Nazis and devout anti-Nazis. Once this separation took place, many of the problems within the camps either disappeared or could be controlled. In talking to several German POWs, I discovered that one of their greatest fears in being interviewed was that they would be viewed as Nazis. In the minds of many Americans then and now, those serving under Hitler were Nazis. However, this work shows that German soldiers could cause as much trouble behind barbed wire as their American counterparts and often had no affiliation with the Nazi Party. In fact, once the hard-core Nazis were separated, it was discovered that a relative minority controlled many camps through fear. At the same time, not all the problems that occurred between POWs stemmed from ideological causes.

The need to occupy the POWs' time posed another problem for the United States. This study takes an in-depth look at the utilization of POW labor, which has received little attention in the literature concerning U.S.-held Axis POWs. The labor program proved to be the most successful part of the POW program and provided the most benefit to the home front. The United States had little previous experience employing massive numbers of prisoners as workers, but necessity proved to be the mother of invention. Given the dire need for manpower on the home front, various government agencies were able to create the largest prisoner employment program in U.S. history. By constructing base and branch camps near places where labor was needed and allowing civilian and government contracts for POW labor, the United States eventually had a 90 percent employment rate for POWs. The POWs provided a needed boost to the economy. In many cases, they saved local crops from rotting. The importance of the POW contribution to home front labor is little analyzed in secondary literature. The focus instead is on how well the POWs and guards got along, and sometimes on how the POWs managed to get out of work or caused trouble. This work not only focuses upon how the United States utilized POW labor to complete necessary tasks and benefit the home front economy but also addresses the issue of what to do with the prisoners' idle time. The United States filled that time by providing various recreational outlets. Collectively, this work demonstrates how swiftly the government constructed the labor and recreation programs and dealt with problems that arose surrounding these programs.

Never before or since has the U.S. government attempted to handle prisoners of war in the numbers it received during World War II. It could not truly rely on the experience of the Civil War or the First World War, the most recent conflicts that required significant POW care. The United States held fewer than 2,000 POWs during the First World War, and while the number housed in the Civil War reached closer to 100,000, the inadequate housing and sanitary conditions of this conflict provided, if anything, only precautions for the Second World War. At the same time, the United States had a duty during the Second World War because of its own obligations under the Geneva Convention of 1929. With this in mind, it agreed to the transfer of 175,000 German and Italian POWs from Great Britain when that country claimed it could no longer house them according to the standards required by the Geneva Convention.

Housing facilities met the Geneva Convention requirements for size and sanitary conditions, and when the prisoners went without, so too did the guards. That the United States was able to construct camps, when none existed prior to 1942, to house all of the approximately 425,000 Axis POWs and provide conditions that met and even exceeded the Geneva requirements afforded the nation both national and international respect and set an example for future generations of Americans to follow.

The U.S. effort in housing its prisoners demonstrates what can be done in a time of national emergency and even of enmity between nations. At the time the United States entered the war, Pearl Harbor had been bombed and much of Europe was under fascist control. Despite these facts, as Reinhold Pabel stated in his book of the same name, "Enemies are human." The United States treated German prisoners with dignity and humanity. German POWs, arguably more than any other prisoners in any other war, were given opportunity and relative freedom in captivity to read, write, and play, and the United States and democracy certainly looked much better on a full stomach. During their stay, these men worked and learned, and while some may not have loved the United States, many, especially after the war ended and the alternatives were considered, came to respect it. So while hundreds eventually made the United States home, conclusions like Judith Gansberg's that "if there was any failure in the overall program, it was that the prisoners learned to like America too much" or Arnold Krammer's that the motives of the large number of former POWs who sought to return to the United States were due to not solely democratic ideals, but also to "poor conditions in Germany," are both narrowly cast.[9] The real value of the POW program is that it demonstrated that in a major world war with an especially brutal and vicious enemy, the United States, and any other nation, can treat a large number of enemy prisoners with humanity and dignity. This treatment gained the United States the respect of many of the prisoners. It may also have paid dividends through the treatment the roughly 94,000 captive Americans held in Germany received, especially considering that nation's ability to inflict reprisals upon them. Unfortunately, in the conflicts since World War II and especially in the current War on Terror, these standards seem to have been set aside.

Notes

Preface

1. Judith M. Gansberg, *Stalag: U.S.A. The Remarkable Story of German POWs in America* (New York: Thomas Y. Cromwell, 1977), 167.
2. Arnold Krammer, *Nazi Prisoners of War in America* (Chelsea, MI: Scarborough House, 1991), 263.
3. Lewis H. Carlson, *We Were Each Other's Prisoners: An Oral History of World War II American and German Prisoners of War* (New York: Basic Books, 1997), viii.
4. See James F. Tent, *Mission on the Rhine: Reeducation and Denazification in American-Occupied Germany* (Chicago: Univ. of Chicago Press, 1982).

1. Housing the Enemy

1. George Lewis and John Mewha, *History of Prisoner of War Utilization by the United States Army, 1776–1945*, DA Pamphlet 20-213 (Washington, DC: Department of the Army, June 24, 1955).
2. The "Historical Monograph," of the Prisoner of War Operations Division, Provost Marshal General's Office, states that "never before had the United States had prisoners of war in its own custody in such numbers. Never before in the history of modern warfare had prisoners been evacuated in such numbers and such distances by ocean and in some cases air transport to a country which was waging war on a foreign soil." See "Historical Monograph, Prisoner of War Operations Division, Provost Marshal General's Office," 3, in Office of the Provost Marshal General, RG 389, entry 439A: "Historical File, 1941–1958," box 36: "Prisoner of War Operations," vol. 1, folder: "Prisoners of War Operations," vol. 1 of 3, National Archives II, Modern Military Branch.
3. The Geneva Convention relative to the Treatment of Prisoners of War (Prisoner of War Convention) and the Geneva Convention for the Amelioration of the Wounded and Sick Armies in the Field (Red Cross Convention).
4. Lewis and Mewha, *History of Prisoner of War Utilization*, 67–70.
5. Ibid., 70–71.
6. Ibid., 74.
7. Ibid., 33.
8. Ibid, 38.
9. "Historical Monograph," 8.
10. Ibid., 40.
11. John D. Millet, *United States Army in World War II: The Organization and Role of the Army Service Forces* (Washington, DC: Office of the Chief of Military History, Department of the Army, 1954), 314–15.
12. "Historical Monograph," 9.
13. Lewis and Mewha, *History of Prisoner of War Utilization*, 80.
14. "Historical Monograph," 7–8.

15. U.S. War Department, Prisoner of War Circular No. 1 (Washington, DC: Government Printing Office [hereinafter abbreviated as GPO], Sept. 24, 1943), in Office of the Provost Marshal General, RG 389, entry 439A: "Historical File, 1941–1958," box 41: "Regulations Governing Prisoners of War," National Archives II, Modern Military Branch.
16. Ibid., 19–20.
17. Ibid., 22–23.
18. Ibid., 7.
19. Ibid.
20. The role of the State Department and the Internees Section is discussed briefly in the "Historical Monograph" but is covered in much more detail by Graham H. Stuart and John Brown Mason, who both served with the State Department. See Graham H. Stuart, "War Prisoners and Internees in the United States," *American Foreign Service Journal* 21 (Oct. 1944): 530–31, 568, 571–73; John Brown Mason, "German Prisoners of War in the United States," *American Journal of International Law* 34 (Apr. 1945): 198–215.
21. Stuart, "War Prisoners and Internees in the United States," 530.
22. Ibid., 531.
23. Ibid.
24. Ibid.
25. Mason, "German Prisoners of War in the United States," 202.
26. "Historical Monograph," 2.
27. This number has some variance. Secondary sources and Lewis and Mewha, in *History of Prisoner of War Utilization by the United States Army, 1776–1945*, list it as 150,000, but the PMGO records at the National Archives list the number in several places as 175,000.
28. Lewis and Mewha, *History of Prisoner of War Utilization*, 83–84.
29. This was an informal Joint Chiefs of Staff; the Joint Chiefs of Staff was not formally appointed until 1947.
30. Ibid., 78–79.
31. "Historical Monograph," 26.
32. Ibid., 26.
33. Ibid., 27.
34. "Historical Monograph," 10.
35. Office of the Provost Marshal General, *Historical Monograph: Prisoner of War Operations Division, Office of the Provost Marshal General: With appendices and supplement, 1945–1946*, 51–55, National Archives II, Modern Military Branch.
36. Lewis and Mewha, *History of Prisoner of War Utilization*, 86.
37. Office of the Provost Marshal General, *Historical Monograph*, 53.
38. Arthur M. Kruse, "Custody of Prisoners of War in the United States," *Military Engineer* 38, no. 244 (Feb. 1946): 70.
39. "Convention relative to the Treatment of Prisoners of War," *Multilateral, 1918–1930*, vol. 2 of *Treaties and Other International Agreements of the United States of America, 1776–1949*, ed. Charles I. Bevans (Washington, DC: Department of State, 1969), 940.
40. Ibid.
41. U.S. War Department, Prisoner of War Circular No. 1, 7.
42. Maxwell S. McKnight, "The Employment of Prisoners of War in the United States," *International Labour Review* 50 (July–Dec. 1944): 50.
43. Ibid., 50–51.
44. See Kruse, "Custody of Prisoners of War"; McKnight, "The Employment of Prisoners of War"; Krammer, *Nazi Prisoners of War in America;* and Lewis and Mewha, *History of Prisoner of War Utilization*.

45. Kruse, "Custody of Prisoners of War," 70.
46. Office of the Provost Marshal General, *Historical Monograph*, 53.
47. Ibid.
48. Krammer, *Nazi Prisoners of War in America*, 28.
49. Kruse, "Custody of Prisoners of War," 71.
50. U.S. War Department, Prisoner of War Circular No. 1.
51. Office of the Provost Marshal General, *Historical Monograph*, 53–56.
52. *Operation of an Eight Compound Enclosure*, in Office of the Provost Marshal General, RG 389, entry 439A: "Historical File, 1941–1958," box 29: "Nominal Roll of German Prisoners of War OPMO's Office, 1941–1932," folder: "POW Enclosure—Operation of An Eight Compound Prisoner of War Enclosure," National Archives II, Modern Military Branch.
53. Ibid.
54. Office of the Provost Marshal General, *Historical Monograph*, 60. Another source indicates that the numbers of American personnel were different—a commissioned officer commanded each company with assistance from three sergeants, one corporal, and up to two cooks. See U.S. War Department, Prisoner of War Circular No. 1, 19.
55. Office of the Provost Marshal General, *Historical Monograph*, 62.
56. William E. Kirwan, "German Prisoners of War," *Bulletin of the Bureau of Criminal Investigation*, Aug. 1944, 2.
57. U.S. War Department, Prisoner of War Circular No. 1, 19–20.
58. B. M. Bryan, Brigadier General, Assistant to The Provost Marshal General, "Memorandum for the Prisoner of War Division, Subject: Summary of a Report of Mr. Schneider, IRC Delegate," SPMGY, Sept. 2, 1944, in Office of the Provost Marshal General, RG 389, entry 457: "Subject Correspondence File, 1942–1946 (Subject Correspondence File Relating To The Construction of And Condition in Prisoner of War Camps, 1942–1946)," box 1424: "McCalester, Okla—Constr to Ogden, Utah—Constr," folder: "Memphis ASF Depot—Construction," National Archives II, Modern Military Branch.
59. Ibid.
60. Ibid.
61. Howard W. Smith Jr., Major, CMP, Chief, Camp Operations Branch, Prisoner of War Division, SPMM (24) 383.6, "Prisoner of War Camp, Memphis ASF Depot, Tennessee," Sept. 8, 1944, in same folder cited in n. 58.
62. Legation of Switzerland, "Memorandum to Special Division," Jan. 30, 1945, in same folder cited in n. 58.
63. Department of State, Washington, "In Reply to SWP 711/62114/1-3045," Feb. 12, 1945, in same folder cited in n. 58.
64. Stacy Knopf, Colonel, GSC, Director, Security & Intelligence Division, SPIIM 383.6, "To The Commanding General, Army Service Forces, Washington 25, DC, Attention: Prisoner of War Division, Office of The Provost Marshal General," Sept. 14, 1944, in Office of the Provost Marshal General, RG 389, entry 457: "Subject Correspondence File, 1942–1946 (Subject Correspondence File Relating To The Construction of And Condition in Prisoner of War Camps, 1942–1946)," box 1430: "Misc. Memphis ASF Depot, Tenn. To Misc. General," folder: "Memphis ASF Depot, Tenn.—Miscellaneous," National Archives II, Modern Military Branch.
65. Stephen M. Farrand, Major, CMP, Chief, Legal Branch, Prisoner of War Operations Division, SPMO (28) 383.6, Feb. 26, 1945, in same folder cited in n. 64.
66. "Cost Estimates Proposed Prisoner of War Camp, Fort Devens For 1200 Men," Oct. 23, 1943, and "Preliminary Estimate for the Construction of An Additional (1,000 Man) To The Existing Prisoner-Of-War Camp Fort Devens, Mass," Dec. 11, 1944, both in Office of the Provost Marshal General, RG 389, entry 457: "Subject Correspondence File, 1942–1946 (Subject Correspondence File Relating To The Construction of And Condition in Prisoner of War Camps, 1942–1946)," box

1421: "Cp. Crowder, Mo. Constr. to Florence, Ariz—Constr.," folder: "Fort Devens, Mass—Constr.," National Archives II, Modern Military Branch.

67. James R. Pollock, Lt. Colonel, Corps of Engineers, Executive Assistant, 620 Camp Grant, "Subject: Prisoner of War Camp—Camp Grant, Illinois," Dec. 9, 1942, and E. H. Marsden, Lt. Colonel, Corps of Engineers, Assistant, Operations Branch, Construction Division, CE 652, "Subject: Prisoner of War Camp," both in Office of the Provost Marshal General, RG 389, entry 457: "Subject Correspondence File, 1942–1946 (Subject Correspondence File Relating To The Construction of And Condition in Prisoner of War Camps, 1942–1946)," box 1429, folder: "Camp Grant, Illinois—Miscellaneous," National Archives II, Modern Military Branch.

68. C. Keller, Colonel, Corps of Engineers, District Engineer, ENG. 627 EET, "Subject: Site Plan, Prisoner-of-War Camp, Camp Grant, Illinois," Jan. 21, 1943, in same folder cited in n. 67.

69. Ibid.

70. R. G. Barrows, Colonel, Corps of Engineers, Division Engineer, 632 (J-a), "Subject: Hospitalization for Prisoner-of-War Camp, Camp Grant, Ill.," Apr. 21, 1943, in same folder cited in cited in n. 67.

71. A. L. Tynes, Lt. Colonel, Medical Corps, Assistant, 632.-1 C SPMCG, "Subject: Hospitalization for Prisoner-of-War Camp, Camp Grant, Ill.," Apr. 28, 1943, in same folder cited in n. 67.

72. B. M. Bryan, Brigadier General, Director, Aliens Division, "To Chief of Engineers, War Department, Washington, DC," SPMGA (24) 254, May 4, 1943, in same folder cited in n. 67.

2. Sprechen Sie Deutsch?

1. The transfer from Britain was estimated to consist of between 50,000 and 175,000 POWs. See chapter 1 for details on the agreement.

2. Omar Bartov, *Hitler's Army: Soldiers, Nazis, and War in the Third Reich* (New York: Oxford Univ. Press, 1991), 15.

3. J. Lee Ready, *The Forgotten Axis: Germany's Partners and Foreign Volunteers in World War II* (Jefferson, NC: McFarland, 1987), 34–36, 55–56, 67.

4. Ibid., 36–37, 67.

5. Ibid., 68.

6. Ibid., 69–70.

7. Ulrich Blennemann, "Hitler's Other Foreign Legions," *Command: Military History, Strategy & Analysis*, Nov. 1995, 66.

8. Peter R. Fecurka, "Se Hable Espanol Comrade? The Spanish Blue Division in Operation Barbarossa," *Command: Military History, Strategy & Analysis*, Mar.–Apr. 1994, 27.

9. Ismael Garcia Romero, letter of Jan. 27, 1942, World War II and Prisoner of War Documents, Kentucky Building, Western Kentucky Univ., Bowling Green.

10. Fecurka, "Se Hable Espanol Comrade?" 31.

11. Ready, *The Forgotten Axis*, 188–91.

12. Blennemann, "Hitler's Other Foreign Legions," 66.

13. Ibid., 107–12.

14. The historian Matthew Cooper explained that in the fall of 1943, "a new pattern for infantry divisions was introduced, with an establishment of 10,708 men (plus 2,005 Hiwis-Hilfswillige, former Soviet prisoners-of-war who had volunteered to help with non-combat duties)." See Cooper, *The German Army, 1933–1945* (Chelsea, MI: Scarborough House, 1991), 486.

15. Ready, *The Forgotten Axis*, 158.

16. These legions, including the Georgian Legion, Volga Tartar Legion, Azerbaijani Legion, North Caucasian Legion, and Turkestan Legion, molded recruits from throughout the Soviet Union into battalion-sized groups within the German armed forces.

17. Antonio J. Munoz, "Losing World War II: Nazi Racial and Recruitment Policies in the East," *Command: Military History, Strategy & Analysis*, Nov. 1995, 59.

18. Max Seydewitz, *Civil Life in Wartime Germany: The Story of the Home Front* (New York: Viking Press, 1945), 401–2.

19. Charles Burdick, "Prisoners as Soldiers: The German 999th Penal Division," *Army Quarterly and Defense Journal* 102 (Oct. 1971–July 1972): 67.

20. Ready, *The Forgotten Axis*, 29.

21. Ibid., 29–30.

22. Blennemann, "Hitler's Other Foreign Legions," 65; Ready, *The Forgotten Axis*, 190.

23. John Ellis, *Brute Force: Allied Strategy and Tactics in the Second World War* (New York: Viking-Penguin Books, 1990), 147.

24. Ibid., 3.

25. Carlson, *We Were Each Other's Prisoners*, 175.

26. Robin Neillands and Roderick De Normann, *D-day 1944: Voices from Normandy* (London: Cassell Military Paperbacks, 2001), 203–5.

27. Ellis, *Brute Force*, 354.

28. Ibid., 359.

29. Ibid.

30. Carlson, *We Were Each Other's Prisoners*, 19.

31. Elizabeth Anne Wheal, Stephen Pope, and James Taylor, *Encyclopedia of the Second World War* (Secaucus, NJ: Castle Books, 1989), 146; Gordon Wright, *The Ordeal of Total War, 1939–1945* (New York: Harper and Row, 1968), 38.

32. Fritz Schmidt, letter of May 25, 1944, World War II, Matthew Gore Collection, folder 7, Manuscripts, Kentucky Building, Western Kentucky Univ., Bowling Green.

33. Siegfried Knappe, *Soldat—Reflections of a German Soldier, 1936–1949*, ed. Ted Brusaw (New York: Dell, 1992), 309.

34. Hans von Luck, *Panzer Commander: The Memoirs of Colonel Hans von Luck* (New York: Dell, 1989), 264.

35. Bartov, *Hitler's Army*, 169.

36. Stephen G. Fritz, *Frontsoldaten: The German Soldier in World War II* (Lexington: Univ. of Kentucky Press, 1995), 215–16.

37. The forms involved in screening included either the WD-AGO Form No. 19-2 or WD-AGO Form No 19-3. Office of the Provost Marshal General, *Historical Monograph*, 49.

38. Carlson, *We Were Each Other's Prisoners*.

39. Jeffrey E. Geiger, *German Prisoners of War at Camp Cooke, California: Personal Accounts of 14 Soldiers, 1944–1946* (Jefferson, NC: McFarland, 1996), 7.

40. Friedrich Biallas, correspondence with Jerry Yocum and the Camp Algona POW Project Committee, Mar. 2002, oral history from the Wartime Memories Project.

41. Georg Gaertner, *Hitler's Last Soldier in America*, with Arnold Krammer (New York: Stein and Day, 1985), 54.

42. Ibid.

43. Reinhold Pabel, *Enemies Are Human* (Philadelphia: John C. Winston, 1955), 127.

44. Ibid., 122–33.

45. Ibid., 122–33, 143.

46. Office of the Provost Marshal General, *Historical Monograph*, 29–31.

47. Ibid.

48. Ibid.

49. Paul Mengelberg, interview by Antonio Thompson, Aug. 2005.

50. Yvonne E. Humphrey, "On Shipboard with German Prisoners," *American Journal of Nursing* 43, no. 9 (Sept. 1943): 821.

51. Carlson, *We Were Each Other's Prisoners*, 88.

52. Humphrey, "On Shipboard with German Prisoners," 822.

53. Ibid., 821.

54. Ibid., 822.

55. Jim Stiles, interview by Antonio Thompson, Aug. 2005.

56. Howard Tromp, interview by Antonio Thompson, Aug. 2005.

57. Office of the Provost Marshal General, *Historical Monograph*, 49.

58. Paul Lohmann, "Paul Lohmann's Story: Former Prisoner of War Incarcerated at the POW Camp at Fort Dix, New Jersey" (unpublished manuscript), 9.

59. Helmut Hörner, *A German Odyssey: The Journal of a German Prisoner of War*, trans. and ed. Allan Kent Powell (Golden, CO: Fulcrum, 1991), 94.

60. Carlson, *We Were Each Other's Prisoners*, 34.

61. Army Service Forces, ASF Circular No. 84 (Washington 25, DC: GPO, Sept. 21, 1945), 1, in Office of the Provost Marshal General, *Historical Monograph*.

62. Carlson, *We Were Each Other's Prisoners*, 44.

63. Office of the Provost Marshal General, *Historical Monograph*, 50.

64. Ibid.

65. *Clarksville (TN) Leaf-Chronicle*, Jan. 24, 1944.

66. Anton Richter, ed., "A German P.O.W. at Camp Grant: The Reminiscences of Heinz Richter," *Journal of the Illinois State Historical Society* 76, no. 1 (Spring 1983): 62.

67. Ibid., 63.

68. Unknown Unteroffizier, *And Still We Conquer! The Diary of a Nazi Unteroffizier in the German Africa Corps Who Was Captured by the United States Army, May 9, 1943 and Imprisoned at Camp Shelby, Mississippi*, ed. Stanley Hoole (University, AL: Confederate Publishing, 1968), 34–35.

69. Pabel, *Enemies Are Human*, 148.

70. Richter, "A German P.O.W. at Camp Grant," 64.

71. Howard Tromp, interview by Antonio Thompson, Aug. 2005.

72. Frederick J. Doyle, "German Prisoners of War in the Southwest United States during World War II: An Oral History" (PhD diss., Univ. of Denver, 1978), 66. The soldier is referred to only as Karl F.

73. Ibid., 116. He is referred to only as Peter W.

74. Lohmann, "Paul Lohmann's Story," 9.

75. Carlson, *We Were Each Other's Prisoners*, 35–36.

76. Ibid., 44.

77. Army Service Forces, ASF Circular No. 155 (Washington 25, DC: GPO, May 1, 1945), 4–5, in Office of the Provost Marshal General, *Historical Monograph*.

78. Ibid.

79. "Iron Crosses Are Dime-a-Dozen in New Prison Group," *Concordia (KS) Blade-Empire*, Aug. 7, 1943.

80. "News of Concordia Prisoner Camp," *Concordia (KS) Blade-Empire*, Aug. 4, 1943; "More Prisoners Arrive via 16-Car Special," *Concordia (KS) Blade-Empire*, Aug. 12, 1943; "More Nazi Prisoners Arrive for the Camp," *Concordia (KS) Blade-Empire*, Aug. 16, 1943; "Sunday Train of German Prisoners Brings Camp to Near-Capacity Point," *Concordia (KS) Blade-Empire*, Aug. 20, 1943; "News of Concordia Prisoner Camp," *Concordia (KS) Blade-Empire*, Sept. 29, 1943.

81 "Iron Crosses Are Dime-a-Dozen" (see n. 79).

82. "Trainload of Captured Germans Unloaded for Prisoner of War Camp," *Concordia (KS) Blade-Empire*, Aug. 26, 1943.

83. "Nazis in the U.S.," *Time*, May 1, 1944, 64.
84. Beverly Smith, "'The Afrika Korps Comes to America," *American*, Aug. 1943, 28.
85. Note that some of the "plunder" came from countries that the Nazis never occupied.
86. John A. Moroso III, "'Tough' German Officers Are Dudes and Crybabies," *Concordia (KS) Blade-Empire*, Aug. 7, 1943.
87. "Iron Crosses Are Dime-a-Dozen" (see n. 79).
88. John Pepin, *POW Camps in the U.P.* (Marquette, MI: Mining Journal, 2000), 5.
89. "'PW' Signs No Joke: Army Warns Pranksters against Inscriptions on Clothing," *New York Times*, Apr. 26, 1945.

3. Igniting the Powder Keg

1. "Holy Ghost" was a term commonly used by POWs to denote a guilty verdict at court-martials. These were conducted by midnight tribunals and typically resulted in a death sentence.
2. Herston Cooper, *Crossville* (Chicago: Adams Press, 1965), 40.
3. Ibid.
4. Ibid.
5. Richard S. Warner, "Barbed Wire and Nazilagers: PW Camps in Oklahoma," *Chronicles of Oklahoma* 64, no. 1 (Spring 1986): 40.
6. Krammer, *Nazi Prisoners of War in America*, 163.
7. Kathy Roe Coker, "World War II Prisoners of War in Georgia: German Memories of Camp Gordon, 1943–1945," *Georgia Historical Quarterly* 76, no. 4 (Winter 1992): 849.
8. Krammer, *Nazi Prisoners of War in America*, 163.
9. Hörner, *A German Odyssey*, 275.
10. Allen V. Koop, *Stark Decency: German Prisoners of War in a New England Village* (Hanover, NH: Univ. Press of New England, 1988), 45–46.
11. Robert D. Billinger Jr., *Hitler's Soldiers in the Sunshine State: German POWs in Florida* (Gainesville: Univ. Press of Florida, 2000), 55.
12. Four books are actually devoted to this topic. Wilma Parnell was the stenographer who accompanied army officials during the investigation, questioning, and trial. She wrote the first book on the topic, titled *The Killing of Corporal Kunze*, with Robert Taber (Secaucus, NJ: Lyle Stuart, 1981). Vincent Green's *Extreme Justice* (New York: Pocket Books, 1995), which promised to reveal "for the first time, the remarkable true story behind these events" (back cover), is also devoted to the topic. Neither Parnell nor Green used bibliographies or footnotes. Green, in addition, took the liberty to add what he felt the participants believed, thought, and said, based on his evidence. Leon Jaworski, the judge advocate during the proceedings, wrote *After Fifteen Years* (Houston: Gulf Publishing Co., 1961) and *Confession and Avoidance: A Memoir* (Garden City, NY: Anchor Press/Doubleday, 1975).
13. Parnell, *The Killing of Corporal Kunze*, 17; Green, *Extreme Justice*, 18. Green added that this was a common prayer among the Germans who had fought in North Africa.
14. Parnell, *The Killing of Corporal Kunze*, 36.
15. Ibid., 36–39.
16. The five men accused were Walter Beyer, Berthold Seidel, Hans Demme, Willi Scholz, and Hans Schomer. See also Richard Whittingham, *Martial Justice: The Last Mass Execution in the United States* (Chicago: Henry Regnery, 1971), 5.
17. Parnell, *The Killing of Corporal Kunze*, 60, 63.
18. Ibid., 173–75.
19. "Death and Treason," *Newsweek*, Feb. 5, 1945, 47–48.
20. Parnell, *The Killing of Corporal Kunze*, 95.

21. "Seven by the Rope," *Newsweek,* July 23, 1945, 27.

22. Berthold Seidel, a member of the Social Democratic Party of Germany, admitted his role in the attack along with the four Nazi attackers.

23. Both Hugo Hrubek, a Czeck, and his father, a Czech officer, were impressed into the Wehrmacht. Franz Krasinski, a Pole, feared the Nazis, who ridiculed him and prevented him from using his native language in letters home. Josef Heidutzek was also Polish and spoke only a little German. He too had been "forced" into the army and professed no loyalty to the "brutal" Germans. See Parnell, *The Killing of Corporal Kunze,* 47–49, 56.

24. Lowell A. May, *Camp Concordia: German POWs in the Midwest* (Manhattan, KS.: Sunflower Univ. Press, 1995), 31–32; Krammer, *Nazi Prisoners of War in America,* 170–71.

25. John Hammond Moore, "Nazi Troopers in South Carolina, 1944–1946," *South Carolina Historical Magazine* 81, no. 4 (Oct. 1980): 309; "Seven by the Rope," 27.

26. Michael R. Waters, *Lone Star Stalag: German Prisoners of War at Camp Hearne* (College Station: Texas A&M Univ. Press, 2004), 121.

27. Krammer, *Nazi Prisoners of War in America,* 171.

28. Waters, *Lone Star Stalag,* 124–29.

29. Ibid., 130.

30. Ibid.

31. Ibid., 134.

32. David Fiedler, *The Enemy among Us: POWs in Missouri during World War II* (Saint Louis: Missouri Historical Society Press, 2003), 43.

33. "Disciplinary and Control Measures Applicable to Prisoners of War," in Office of the Provost Marshal General, *Historical Monograph.*

34. "Check List for Records of Trial of Prisoners of War by General Court-Martial, as to Compliance with the Geneva Convention," in Office of the Provost Marshal General, *Historical Monograph.*

35. "General Courts-Martial of Prisoners of War," in Office of the Provost Marshal General, *Historical Monograph.*

36. Hans Rott, Free Austria Movement, "Response to Mr. Rudolf Tirk," Oct. 12, 1943, in Office of the Provost Marshal General, RG 389, entry 459A: "Decimal File, 1943–1946 (Special Projects Division, Administrative Branch Decimal File, 1943–1946)," box 1626: "Decimal File 312.1 to 315," folder 312.1, general, National Archives II, Modern Military Branch.

37. Allan Kent Powell, *Splinters of a Nation: German Prisoners of War in Utah* (Salt Lake City: Univ. of Utah Press, 1989), 142.

38. Ibid., 143.

39. Ibid.

40. Cooper, *Crossville,* 77.

41. Gansberg, *Stalag: U.S.A.,* 29.

42. John Hammond Moore, *The Faustball Tunnel: German POWs in America and Their Great Escape* (New York: Random House, 1978), 222–23.

43. See Gansberg, *Stalag: U.S.A.,* 17.

44. "Finds Pin-up Girls Decorating Walls of German Prison Camps," *Concordia (KS) Blade-Empire,* Oct. 23, 1943.

45. On August 9, 1943, Captain Gustav Dormann, having spent one week behind barbed wire at Concordia, hanged himself using a "bath robe cord." See "Inmate at Prison of War Compound Takes Own Life," *Concordia (KS) Blade-Empire,* Aug. 10, 1943. See also May, *Camp Concordia,* chap. 2; Patrick O'Brien, Thomas D. Isern, and R. Daniel Lumley, "Stalag Sunflower: German Prisoners of

War in Kansas," *Kansas History* 7, no. 3 (Autumn 1984): 182–98. Private Franz Kettner took his own life by slashing his wrists in January of 1944. Kettner, an Austrian and anti-Nazi, feared for his life after making defeatist comments and being threatened by his fellow POWs. U.S. officials agreed to segregate Kettner at his request, but apparently his fear overcame him and he took his own life. "Nazi Terrorism Specter behind Prison Camp Deaths," *Concordia (KS) Blade-Empire*, Jan. 13, 1944. For the murders of both Dormann and Kettner, see also "German Prisoners End Lives after Camp 'Court-Martials,'" *Los Angeles Times*, Jan. 13, 1944.

46. Corporal Adolf Huebner was the soccer player shot by the guards.
47. May, *Camp Concordia*, 30.
48. "Nazi Scorn in Kansas," *Kansas City (MO) Star*, Jan. 16, 1944.
49. May, *Camp Concordia*, 30.
50. Ibid. Casey Stangel was the American guard.
51. "456th Guard Company Returns to Prison Camp from Missouri Duty," *Concordia (KS) Blade-Empire*, Aug. 6, 1943.
52. "Berserk Captain Shoots Wife of Col. Sterling," *Concordia (KS) Blade-Empire*, Oct. 25, 1943. Mrs. Sterling later recovered. See "Town Talk: Condition of Mrs. John A. Sterling," *Concordia (KS) Blade-Empire*, Oct. 26, 1943.
53. "Accidentally Wounded," *Kansas*, Oct., 28, 1943, 1.
54. May, *Camp Concordia*, 33–34; O'Brien, Isern, and Lumley, "Stalag Sunflower," 184.
55. May, *Camp Concordia*, 33.
56. "Concordia Prison Camp Suicides Make Front Page of London Paper," *Concordia (KS) Blade-Empire*, Feb. 17, 1944.
57. See nn. 45 and 52.
58. Billinger, *Hitler's Soldiers in the Sunshine State*, 73–75.
59. "Another Lost Soul on Enemy Soil," *Palm Beach (FL) Post*, Dec. 28, 1994.
60. Ibid.
61. "Arrogant Nazis Still Laud Hitler," *Miami (FL) Daily News*, June 8, 1944. See also Billinger, *Hitler's Soldiers in the Sunshine State*, 74–75.
62. "Nazi War Prisoner Escapee Found Dead," *Palm Beach (FL) Post*, Jan. 2, 1945.
63. "Another Lost Soul on Enemy Soil" (see n. 59).
64. Billinger, *Hitler's Soldiers in the Sunshine State*, 76–86.
65. Most of the men accused of causing these problems were transferred from Crossville to Papago Park, Arizona, where they joined other "problem" POWs.
66. Moore, *The Faustball Tunnel*, 64–65.
67. Ibid., 60.
68. Ibid., 61.
69. Ibid.
70. Ibid., 66–67.
71. Cooper, *Crossville*, 123.
72. Much of this story comes from Cooper's book, but it is also related in *The Faustball Tunnel* by Moore and in various articles as noted. It is not made clear why Cooper did not act on the threat sooner.
73. This instance is described in greater detail in Herston Cooper's *Crossville*, but he failed to provide dates and referred to the participants only by rank and not name. John Hammond Moore also related this event and provides names and dates. The details of the event are fairly similar and it is assumed that they are the same event. Neither author provided footnotes that would allow the reader to double-check the validity of the tale.

74. Cooper, *Crossville*, 133.
75. It is not clear if Cooper was the stockade commanding officer referred to or the commanding officer over the entire camp.
76. Cooper, *Crossville*, 135.
77. Ibid., 136.
78. Ibid., 136–42.
79. Moore, *The Faustball Tunnel*, 67.
80. This number was difficult to maintain and it was reduced throughout 1944 and 1945, at times to only one guard to fifteen prisoners. See Krammer, *Nazi Prisoners of War in America*, 38–39.
81. See ibid., 39–41; Gansberg, *Stalag: U.S.A.*, 42–44; and Billinger, *Hitler's Soldiers in the Sunshine State*, 13.
82. Gansberg, *Stalag: U.S.A.*, 42–43.
83. Derek R. Mallett, "'They Were Just People Like We Were': World War II German and Italian Prisoners of War in Missouri" (MA thesis, Truman State Univ., 1997), 47–48. See also Fritz Ensslin, "A German Soldier Tells What It Is Like Visit Ft. Leonard Wood in 1943 as a POW," *Essayons*, June 27, 1991, 46.
84. Giuseppe Cerradini was the POW. See Richard P. Walker, *The Lone Star and the Swastika: Prisoners of War in Texas* (Austin, TX: Eakin Press, 2001), 83.
85. Mallett, "They Were Just People," 51–52. Investigations found these charges baseless. See also "Inspection Report, Camp Clark, May 8–9, 1945," PMG, in Office of the Provost Marshal General, RG 389, Box 1429, Entry 457, National Archives II, Modern Military Branch.
86. Powell, *Splinters of a Nation*, 139.
87. Ibid., 80.
88. Allen W. Paschal, "The Enemy in Colorado: German Prisoners of War, 1943–46," *Colorado* 56, no. 3-4 (Summer–Fall 1979): 125.
89. Gerhardt Lange and Heinz Rehner were the POWs. See Walker, *The Lone Star and the Swastika*, 82.
90. Herbert Barkhoff was the POW. See Powell, *Splinters of a Nation*, 80.
91. Major Paul A. Neuland, "Memorandum For Director, Prisoner of War Special Projects Divisions, 21 Apr. 1945; Field Service Report on Visit to Prisoner of War Camp, Camp Patrick Henry, 4 Apr. 1945, by Captain Herman W Graupner," 1, in Office of the Provost Marshal General, RG 389, entry 459A: "Decimal File, 1943–1946 (Special Projects Division, Administrative Branch Decimal File, 1943–1946)," box 1613: "Camp Edgewood to Fort Eustis," folder 255 (Ft. Eustis, VA), general, National Archives II, Modern Military Branch.
92. "Midnight Massacre," *Time*, July 23, 1945, 24.
93. Glenn Thompson, *Prisoners on the Plains: German POWs in America* (Holdrege, NE: Phelps County Historical Society, 1993), 113, 117, quoted from a secret document reported to Captain Alexander Lakes, March 15, 1945.
94. Ibid., 114.
95. James M. Alexander, "Special Projects Division, Prisoner of War Base Camp, Indiantown Gap Military Reservation, Pennsylvania, 1 May 1945," 10, in Office of the Provost Marshal General, RG 389, entry 459A: "Decimal File, 1943–1946 (Special Projects Division, Administrative Branch Decimal File, 1943–1946)," box 1616: "Camp Indianola to Fort Knox," folder 255 (Cp. Indiantown Gap Mil. Resv.), general, National Archives II, Modern Military Branch.
96. Clayton R. Koppes and Gregory D. Black, "Blacks, Loyalty, and Motion-Picture Propaganda in World War II," *Journal of American History* 73, no. 2 (Sept. 1986): 388.
97. Phillip McGuire, ed., *Taps for a Jim Crow Army: Letters from Black Soldiers in World War II* (Lexington: Univ. Press of Kentucky, 1993), 217. This letter was addressed to Mr. Prattis of the *Pittsburgh Courier*.

98. The soldier was Private James Pritchett. Ibid., 23.
99. Mary Penick Motley, ed., *The Invisible Soldier: The Experience of the Black Soldier, World War II* (Detroit, MI: Wayne State Univ. Press, 1975), 43.
100. Ibid., 162.
101. Ibid., 263.
102. Ibid., 266.
103. Ibid., 326.
104. *Atlanta Daily World,* Feb. 9, 1945. See also Gary R. Mormino, "G.I. Joe Meets Jim Crow: Racial Violence and Reform in World War II Florida," *Florida Historical Quarterly* 73, no. 1 (July 1994): 35.

4. Love Thy Enemy

1. The epigraph is drawn from Smith, "The Afrika Korps Comes to America," 85.
2. Italian and other ancestry also affected Americans' feelings and their treatment of the POWs.
3. Geiger, *German Prisoners of War at Camp Cooke,* 96.
4. Ibid., 94.
5. Ibid., 93.
6. Ibid., 94.
7. Ibid., 95.
8. Mallett, "They Were Just People," 53.
9. Ibid., 48. See also "A German Soldier," 51.
10. Mallett, "They Were Just People," 50.
11. Ibid., 49–50.
12. Ibid.
13. Penny Clark, "Farm Work and Friendship: The German Prisoner of War Camp at Lake Wabaunsee," *Emporia State Research Studies* 36, no. 3 (Winter 1988): 16.
14. Ibid., 18–19.
15. Ibid., 22.
16. Geiger, *German Prisoners of War at Camp Cooke,* 96.
17. Ibid., 92–93. See also "Admits Guilt in Relations with Nazi PW," *Santa Maria (CA) Daily Times,* June 9, 1945.
18. Moore, *The Faustball Tunnel,* 222.
19. Cooper, *Crossville,* 37.
20. Ibid., 38.
21. F. G. Alletson Cook, "Nazi Prisoners Are Nazis Still," *New York Times Magazine,* Nov. 21, 1943, 12, 38.
22. Ibid.
23. Ibid.
24. "Prison Camp Menus Criticized," *New York Times,* Dec. 24, 1943.
25. Carlson, *We Were Each Other's Prisoners,* 78.
26. Powell, *Splinters of a Nation,* 107.
27. Carlson, *We Were Each Other's Prisoners,* 72.
28. See George J. Davis, *The Hitler Diet: As Inflicted on American P.O.W.'s in World War II* (Los Angeles: Military Literary Guild, 1990).
29. "Stops 5 Meals a Day for Nazi Prisoners," *New York Times,* Apr. 12, 1945.
30. "Captives 'Coddled' in U.S., Russia Says," *New York Times,* May 26, 1944.
31. Robert Devore, "Our 'Pampered' War Prisoners," *Collier's,* Oct. 14, 1944, 14.

32. Ibid., 14, 144.

33. Mary K. Frederickson, ed., "Some Thoughts on Prisoners of War in Iowa, 1943 to 1946," *Palimpsest* 65, no. 2 (Mar.–Apr. 1984): 77. See also *Des Moines (MT) Register,* Apr. 8, 1945.

34. "What Would They Say?" *Huntington (WV) Herald-Dispatch,* Feb. 19, 1945, in Office of the Provost Marshal General, RG 389, entry 439A: "Historical File, 1941–1958," box 37: "Prisoner of War Operations," vols. 2–3, folder: "Prisoner of War Operations," vol. 3 of 3, National Archives II, Modern Military Branch.

35. "Treatment of Prisoners," *Wilmington (NC) Star,* Feb. 20, 1945, in same folder cited in n. 34.

36. "War Prisoner Probe," *Fort Worth (TX) Star-Telegram,* Feb. 21, 1945, in same folder cited in n. 34.

37. The writer likely meant "Kamerad"; this was probably a misspelling in the original newspaper article. "Complaints about Pampering Nazi Prisoners of War," *Montana Standard,* Feb. 21, 1945, in same folder cited in n. 34.

38. "Nazi Prisoners 'as Fat as Hogs' Are Reported at Arizona Camp," *New York Times,* Apr. 23, 1945.

39. Ibid.

40. Ibid.

41. "German Prisoners Get Cut in Menus," *New York Times,* Apr. 25, 1945.

42. Archer Lerch, "The Army Reports on Prisoners of War," *American Mercury,* May 1945, 537.

43. Ibid, 539.

44. "Coddling Prisons," *Lima (OH) News,* Apr. 29, 1945, in same folder cited in n. 34.

45. "Decency Shortens the War," *Grand Rapids (MI) Press,* Apr. 30, 1945, in same folder cited in n. 34.

46. "'Coddling' Vindicated," *Bayonne (NJ) Times,* June 6, 1945, and "Ninety-Nine Per Cent Saved," *Springfield (IL) Register,* June 6, 1945, both in same folder cited in n. 34.

47. "Food for War Prisoners," *Reno (NV) Gazette,* June 26, 1945, in same folder cited in n. 34.

48. Captain Elbert E. Foster, Director, Security and Intelligence Division, "Political Activities of Prisoners of War, Including Future Plans re Underground Organization upon Return to Germany, PW Camp, Camp Forrest, Tennessee," 1, in Office of the Provost Marshal General, RG 389, entry 459A: "Decimal File, 1943–1946 (Special Projects Division, Administrative Branch Decimal File, 1943–1946)," box 1614: "Camp Cambridge to Camp Clinton," folder 255 (Cp. Forrest), general, National Archives II, Modern Military Branch.

49. Edward F. Witsell, Brigadier General, Acting the Adjutant General, "Screening of German Prisoners of War," SPMGA (12) 383.6, Nov. 20, 1944, in Office of the Provost Marshal General, RG 389, entry 439A: "Historical File, 1941–1958," box 35, folder: "Prisoners of War, Letters and Directives," National Archives II, Modern Military Branch.

50. Lt. Colonel Earl L. Edwards, Assistant Director Prisoner of War Division, "Anti-Nazi German Prisoners of War, 22 April 1944," SPMGA (12) 383.6, in Office of the Provost Marshal General, RG 389, entry 457: "Subject Correspondence File, 1942–1946 (Subject Correspondence File Relating To The Construction of And Condition in Prisoner of War Camps, 1942–1946)," box 1428: "Camp McCloskey," folder: "Camp Campbell, Kentucky—Misc.," National Archives II, Modern Military Branch.

51. Lt. Colonel Carl B. Byrd, "Segregation of Anti-Nazi Prisoners of War, 20 March 1944," in same folder cited in n. 50.

52. "The German 'Anti-Nazis,' Deutschen Anti-Nazi Kriegsgefangenenlager Prisoner of War (Anti-Nazi) Camp, Camp Campbell, Kentucky, September 1944," in Office of the Provost Marshal General, RG 389, entry 459A: "Decimal File, 1943–1946 (Special Projects Division, Administrative Branch

Decimal File, 1943–1946),'' box 1611: "Camp Cambridge to Camp Clinton," folder 255 (Cp. Campbell), general, National Archives II, Modern Military Branch.

53. Ibid.
54. Ibid.
55. Ibid.
56. This statement negates the intent of the military to keep the Nazi and anti-Nazi compounds completely separate from each other.
57. 1st Lt. Walter Schoenstedt, Special Program Section, "Special Projects Branch, *SPMGA* (95), 24 November 1944," 1–4, in Office of the Provost Marshal General, RG 389, entry 459A: "Decimal File, 1943–1946 (Special Projects Division, Administrative Branch Decimal File, 1943–1946)," box 1611: "Camp Cambridge to Camp Clinton," folder 255 (Cp. Campbell), general, National Archives II, Modern Military Branch.
58. Krammer, *Nazi Prisoners of War in America*, 175.
59. Captain Herman W. Graupner for Major Paul A. Neuland, "Memorandum for Director, Prisoner of War Special Projects Division, Field Service Report on Visit to Prisoner of War Camp, Alva, Oklahoma, on 3–4 April 1945, by Captain Alexander Lakes, 25 April 1945," in Office of the Provost Marshal General, RG389, entry 459A: "Decimal File, 1943–1946 (Special Projects Division, Administrative Branch Decimal File, 1943–1946)," box 1613: "Camp Edgewood to Fort Eustis," folder 255 (Ft. Eustis, VA), general, National Archives II, Modern Military Branch.
60. See also Krammer, *Nazi Prisoners of War in America*, 177–81.
61. Major Paul A. Neuland, "Memorandum for Director, Prisoner of War Special Projects Division, Field Service Report on Visit to Prisoner of War Camp, Crossville, Tennessee, 10–11 Jan. 1945, by Captain William F. Raugust," 2, in Office of the Provost Marshal General, RG 389, entry 459A: "Decimal File, 1943–1946 (Special Projects Division, Administrative Branch Decimal File, 1943–1946)," box 1612: "POW Special Operations Division, Administrative Branch, Decimal File, 1943–1946," folder 255 (Crossville, TN), National Archives II, Modern Military Branch.
62. "Memorandum for the Director, Intelligence, A.S.F, 17 May 1944," SPMGA (58) 383.6, in Office of the Provost Marshal General, RG 389, entry 439A: "Historical File, 1941–1958," box 35, folder: "Prisoners of War, Letters and Directives," National Archives II, Modern Military Branch.
63. Edward F. Witsell, Brigadier General, Acting the Adjutant General, "Screening of German Prisoners of War of Polish, French, Czechoslovakian, Belgian, and Luxembourg Origin," SPMGA (58) 383.6, Nov. 28, 1944, in same folder cited in n. 62.
64. Lt. Colonel Earl L. Edwards, Assistant Director, Prisoner of War Division, SPMGA (19) 383.6, in Office of the Provost Marshal General, RG 389, entry 458: "Policy File, 1942–1945 (Policy and Procedural Records relating to the Supervision of Prisoners of War and Their Camps, 1942–1945)," box 1429: "Misc. Douglas, Wyo. To Ft. Meade, Maryland," folder: "Indiantown Military Gap Military Reservation—Misc.," National Archives II, Modern Military Branch.
65. Colonel E. J. Garr, Director, Security and Intelligence Division, "Screening of Soviet Citizens," May 9, 1945, in Office of the Provost Marshal General, RG 389, entry 439A: "Historical File, 1941–1958," box 35, folder: "Prisoners of War, Letters and Directives," National Archives II, Modern Military Branch.
66. Arieh J. Kochavi, *Confronting Captivity: Britain and the United States and Their POWs in Nazi Germany* (Chapel Hill: Univ. of North Carolina Press, 2005), 256–57.
67. Ibid., 265.
68. Ibid., 260.
69. See chapter 3.
70. Neuland, "Memorandum for Director," 2 (see n. 61).

71. Captain Marshall Hawks, Chief Prisoner of War Branch, "Letter to Major Ralph J. Schuetz, Special Projects Division, 21 February 1946," 1, in Office of the Provost Marshal General, RG 389, entry 459A: "Decimal File, 1943–1946 (Special Projects Division, Administrative Branch Decimal File, 1943–1946)," box 1612: "POW Special Operations Division, Administrative Branch, Decimal File, 1943–1946," folder 255 (Crossville, TN), National Archives II, Modern Military Branch.

72. Major J. A. Ulio, Adjutant General, "Prisoners of War—Violations of regulations, ASF Circular No. 39, 2 February 1945," 1, in "Historical Monograph."

73. Ibid. Many of these provisions concerning fraternization and proper treatment are contained in Section I, U.S. War Department, Prisoner of War Circular No. 3, (Washington, DC: GPO, 1944) in Office of the Provost Marshall General, RG 389, Entry 439A: "Historical File, 1941–1958," Box 41: "Regulations Governing Prisoners of War."

74. Ulio, "Prisoners of War," 1 (see n. 72).

75. Ibid.

76. Major General J. A. Ulio by the command of Lt. General Somervell, "Violations of Prisoner of War Regulations, 17 February 1944," in "Historical Monograph," vol. 2.

77. "Anger at Nazi Atrocities Is Rising, but U.S. Treats Prisoners Fairly," *Newsweek*, May 7, 1945, 58.

5. The Devil Is in the Details

1. Walter W. Wilcox, *The Farmer in the Second World War* (Ames: Iowa State College Press, 1947), 83.

2. Ibid., 87–89.

3. Only ten articles of the Geneva Convention discuss this; they are Articles 23 through 32.

4. "Convention relative to the Treatment of Prisoners of War," 944.

5. Ibid., 945 (Articles 31 and 32).

6. Ibid.

7. *Civilian Enemy Aliens and Prisoners of War*, Apr. 22, 1942, in Office of the Provost Marshal General, RG 389, entry 439A: "Historical File, 1941–1958," National Archives II, Modern Military Branch. See also chapter 1.

8. The Joint Chiefs of Staff, established by FDR during World War II, was not formally recognized as the Joint Chiefs of Staff until the National Security Act of 1947 was passed.

9. *Civilian Enemy Aliens and Prisoners of War*, 38 (see n. 7).

10. Lewis and Mewha, *History of Prisoner of War Utilization*, 78–79.

11. "Development of the Employment Program—August 1942 to January 1943," III-9, in Office of the Provost Marshal General, RG 389, entry 439A: "Historical File, 1941–1958," box 19: "Internal Security Program (Volume IV)—International Red Cross Team in Korea," folder: "Utilization of P/O; Section Labor," National Archives II, Modern Military Branch.

12. Ibid.

13. Ibid., III-11.

14. Ibid., III-12,

15. Lewis and Mewha, *History of Prisoner of War Utilization*, 89.

16. Ibid.

17. George Catlett Marshall, "Memorandum for General Somervell," in *The Right Man to Do the Job*, vol. 3 of *The Papers of George Catlett Marshall*, ed. Larry I. Bland (Baltimore: Johns Hopkins Univ. Press, 1991), 497.

18. Ibid., 498.

19. *War Department Policy with Respect to Labor of Prisoners of War*, AG 383.6 (10-30-42), OB-S-PMGO-M (Jan. 10, 1943), in Office of the Provost Marshal General, *Historical Monograph*.

20. Ibid, 2.
21. The IPD was also a branch of the ASF.
22. "Development of the Employment Program," III-18 (see n. 11).
23. "The Manpower Situation Worsens: The Employment Situation, Spring 1943," IV-6, in Office of the Provost Marshal General, RG 389, entry 439A: "Historical File, 1941–1958," box 19: "Internal Security Program (Volume IV)—International Red Cross + Red Cross Team in Korea," folder: "Utilization of P/O; Section Labor," National Archives II, Modern Military Branch.
24. Ibid., IV-1.
25. Ibid., IV-4 through IV-5.
26. Major General J. A. Ulio, The Adjutant General, *Labor of Prisoners of War,* AG 383.6 (Aug. 12, 1943), OB-S-A-M, War Department, Adjutant General's Office, Washington, Aug. 14, 1943, 1–2, in *Historical Monograph,* Office of the Provost Marshal General.
27. Major General J. A. Ulio, The Adjutant General, *Employment of Prisoners of War off Reservations,* AG 383.6 (Aug. 23, 1943), OB-S-A-M, War Department, Adjutant General's Office, Washington, Aug. 4, 1943, in *Historical Monograph,* Office of the Provost Marshal General.
28. Many of these noncommissioned officers, however, proved uncooperative. A large volume of correspondence demonstrates that some of these men were directly responsible for work slow-down or stoppages. See also chapter 3. Other accounts demonstrate that at times considerable difficulty in translation occurred even when the POW noncom could speak fluent English.
29. Ulio, *Employment of Prisoners of War,* 1–4 (see n. 27).
30. U.S. War Department, Prisoner of War Circular No. 1.
31. See Office of the Provost Marshal General, Prisoner of War Operations Division, "Population Lists, June 1942 thru June 1944, Weekly Report on Prisoners of War," microfilm compilation, Library of Congress; "The Manpower Situation Worsens" (see n. 23).
32. Lewis and Mewha, *History of Prisoner of War Utilization,* 121–22.
33. Walter Rundell Jr., "Paying the POW in World War II," *Military Affairs* 22, no. 3 (Autumn 1958): 122. See also U.S. War Department, *Enemy Prisoners of War,* TM 19-500 (Washington, DC: GPO, Jan. 15, 1945), chap. 4; U.S. War Department, Prisoner of War Circular No. 10.
34. U.S. War Department, Prisoner of War Circular No. 1. See also Rundell, "Paying the POW in World War II," 122–24.
35. Hörner, *A German Odyssey,* 277–78.
36. Ulio, *Labor of Prisoners of War,* 3 (see n. 26).
37. Ibid., 1–2.
38. Lewis and Mewha, *History of Prisoner of War Utilization,* 110, 115–16.
39. Ibid., 118.
40. Captain William D. Home, Commanding, Headquarters, Camp Sidnaw, Michigan, "Physical Condition of Certain PW's," Mar. 21, 1944, in Office of the Provost Marshal General, RG 389, entry 457: "Subject Correspondence File, 1942–1946 (Subject Correspondence File Relating To The Construction of And Condition in Prisoner of War Camps, 1942–1946)," box 1422: "Cp. Forrest, Tenn—Const. to Cp Hood, Texas—Constr.," folder: "Camp Grant, Illinois," National Archive II, Modern Military Branch.
41. A. M. Tollefson, Colonel, CMP, Assistant Director, Prisoner of War Division, SPMGA (75) 383.6, Headquarters, ASF, PMGO, Washington 25, DC, Apr. 10, 1944, in same folder cited in n. 40.
42. Earl L. Edwards, Lt. Colonel, CMP, Assistant Director, Prisoner of War Division, SPMGA (19) 383.6, ASF, PMGO, Washington 25, DC, Apr. 12, 1944, in same folder cited in n. 40.
43. George H. Lobdell, "A Tale of Two Christmases at the Algona Prisoner-of-War Camp," *Palimpsest* 73, no. 4 (Winter 1997): 178.

44. Lewis and Mewha, *History of Prisoner of War Utilization*, 128–29.

45. See Army Service Forces, *Safe Work Practices for Prisoners of War (German)*, Army Service Forces Manual M-805 (Washington, DC: GPO, Sept. 22, 1944).

46. See U.S. War Department, *Handbook for the Director of Civilian Training* (Washington, DC: GPO, Aug. 1943).

47. See Army Service Forces, *Handbook for Work Supervisors of Prisoner of War Labor*, Army Service Forces Manual M-811 (Washington, DC: GPO, July 1945), 4.

48. Ibid., 6.

49. Ibid.

50. Ibid.

51. "Priorities in Allocation of Services of Prisoners of War," *Monthly Labor Review*, June 1944, 1189; "Policies for Employment of Prisoners of War," *Monthly Labor Review*, July 1944, 93.

52. John K. Collins, Director, Bureau of Placement to Regional Manpower Director, Region II, *War Department Technical Manual on Enemy Prisoners of War*, in Records of the War Manpower Commission, RG 211, entry 175, box 1, folder: "Region II," National Archive II, Modern Military Branch.

53. Lewis and Mewha, *History of Prisoner of War Utilization*, 157.

54. Ibid., 144–46.

55. B. M. Bryan, Brigadier General, Assistant to The Provost Marshal General, "Memorandum for the Prisoner of War Division, Subject: Summary of a Report of Mr. Schneider, IRC Delegate," SPMGY, Sept. 2, 1944, in Office of the Provost Marshal General, RG 389, entry 457: "Subject Correspondence File, 1942–1946 (Subject Correspondence File Relating To The Construction of And Condition in Prisoner of War Camps, 1942–1946)," box 1424: "McCalester, Okla—Constr to Ogden, Utah—Constr," folder: "Memphis ASF Depot—Construction," National Archives II, Modern Military Branch.

56. Ibid.

57. Lewis and Mewha, *History of Prisoner of War Utilization*, 148.

58. Unknown Unteroffizier, *And Still We Conquer!* 48.

59. Lohmann, "Paul Lohmann's Story," 5.

60. Richter, "A German P.O.W. at Camp Grant," 64.

61. "War Prisoners at Work," *New York Times*, Sept. 17, 1943.

62. "Sugar Cane Crop Being Harvested," *Palm Beach (FL) Post*, Nov. 2, 1944; Cowley, *Stalag Wisconsin*, 180–82.

63. Pabel, *Enemies Are Human*, 153.

64. Clark, "Farm Work and Friendship," 19.

65. Ibid., 20.

66. Ibid., 21.

67. Lowell A. Bangerter, *German Prisoners of War in Wyoming* (Laramie: Wyoming Council for the Humanities, 1979), 38.

68. Lohmann, "Paul Lohmann's Story," 5.

69. Geiger, *German Prisoners of War at Camp Cooke*, 89.

70. Lohmann, "Paul Lohmann's Story," 5.

71. Geiger, *German Prisoners of War at Camp Cooke*, 89.

72. Wesley Harris, *Fish out of Water: Nazi Submariners as Prisoners in North Louisiana during World War II* (Ruston, LA: RoughEdge, 2004), 22. See also Hans Goebeler, *Steel Boats, Iron Hearts: A U-Boat Crewman's Life aboard U-505*, with John Vanzo (London: Chatham, 2008).

73. "War Prisoners Working on Southwest Farms," *New York Times*, Oct. 10, 1943.

74. "Captives Aiding Farmers," *New York Times*, Aug. 8, 1943.

75. Waters, *Lone Star Stalag*, 53–54.
76. Robert Warren Tissing, "Stalag-Texas, 1943–1945: The Detention and Use of Prisoners of War in Texas during World War II," *Military History of Texas and the Southwest* 13 (Fall 1976): 26.
77. Waters, *Lone Star Stalag*, 55.
78. "Ask Ample Pulp Supply," *New York Times*, June 26, 1943.
79. "Wants Paper Field Classed Essential," *New York Times*, Aug. 13, 1943.
80. Lewis and Mewha, *History of Prisoner of War Utilization*, 132.
81. Koop, *Stark Decency*, 78.
82. Bangerter, *German Prisoners of War in Wyoming*, 39.
83. Lobdell, "A Tale of Two Christmases," 178.
84. Lewis and Mewha, *History of Prisoner of War Utilization*, 132–35.
85. See Kenneth S. Record, "WWI and WWII Axis Burials in the Continental United States and Canada," 1998, unpublished manuscript, CS403 R42X, Manuscripts, Kentucky Building, Western Kentucky Univ., Bowling Green.
86. Pepin, *POW Camps in the U.P.*, 3–4.
87. Ibid., 5.
88. James E. Fickle and Donald W. Ellis, "POWs in the Piney Woods: German Prisoners of War in the Southern Lumber Industry, 1943–1945," *Journal of Southern History* 56, no. 4 (1990): 709.
89. Merrill R. Pritchet and William L. Shea, "The Afrika Korps in Arkansas, 1943–1946," *Arkansas Historical Quarterly* 37, no. 1 (Spring 1978): 19.
90. "Dewey Asks Use of Prisoner-Labor," *New York Times*, Sept. 10, 1943.
91. "Italian War Prisoners to Work in Canneries," *New York Times*, Sept. 27, 1943, 2.
92. "Nazi Prisoners Make Jam," *New York Times*, Oct. 5, 1943.
93. Brigadier General Robert H. Dunlop, Acting the Adjutant General, "Utilization of Prisoners of War in Food Processing Plants," SPX 383.6 (Feb. 24, 1945), B-S-SPUG-SPMGV (Mar. 13, 1945), in *Historical Monograph*, Office of the Provost Marshal General.
94. Claude E. Cook, "The German Prisoner of War Camp at Austin, Indiana, and its connection with Campbellsburg, Indiana, during World War II," unpublished manuscript, Fort Knox (KY) Historical Preservation Office, 3.
95. Betty Cowley, *Stalag Wisconsin: Inside WWII Prisoner-of-War Camps* (Oregon, WI: Badger Books, 2002), 97.
96. Ibid.
97. Cook, "The German Prisoner of War Camp at Austin, Indiana," 3 (see n. 94).
98. Lewis and Mewha, *History of Prisoner of War Utilization*, 136.
99. F. W. Hunter, "Field Trip—Regions V, VI, and IX, Nov. 12, 1943, 2–3, in Office of the Provost Marshal General, RG 211, entry 175, box 1, folder: "POWs Region V," National Archives II, Modern Military Branch.
100. Billinger, *Hitler's Soldiers in the Sunshine State*, 68.
101. Koop, *Stark Decency*, 78.
102. Unknown Unteroffizier, *And Still We Conquer!* 44, 45.
103. Hörner, *A German Odyssey*, 289.
104. Clark, "Farm Work and Friendship," 21.
105. Lobdell, "A Tale of Two Christmases," 178.
106. Devore, "Our 'Pampered' War Prisoners," 14.
107. Lewis and Mewha, *History of Prisoner of War Utilization*, 150–51.
108. Unknown Unteroffizier, *And Still We Conquer!* 47.
109. Bangerter, *German Prisoners of War in Wyoming*, 39.

110. See "Convention relative to the Treatment of Prisoners of War."

111. Major General J. A. Ulio, The Adjutant General, *Administrative and Disciplinary Measures*, AG 383.6 (Oct. 13, 1943), OB-S-A-M, War Department, Washington, DC, Oct. 27, 1943, in "Historical Monograph."

112. Ibid., 2. Lewis and Mewha suggest that this restricted diet could be continued, at the discretion of the camp commander, until the POWs agreed to work as long as medical inspections approved of the restricted diet: "Thus, the PW could be given a full meal or a day's ration or more and then placed again on the restricted diet, provided the conditions which warranted its imposition continued to exist" (*History of Prisoner of War Utilization*, 151).

113. "German Prisoners Strike," *New York Times*, July 7, 1944.

114. "Punish Nazi Captives for Strike on Hours," *New York Times*, Aug. 11, 1944.

115. "Nazis in Idaho Punished," *New York Times*, Apr. 22, 1945, 11; "Striking Prisoners' Diet Curbed," *New York Times*, Mar. 2, 1945; and "Nazis Push Camp 'Strike,'" *New York Times*, Mar. 3, 1945.

116. "Punish Nazi Captives for Strike on Hours" (see n. 114); "German Prisoners Strike" and "Nazis in Idaho Punished" (see n. 115).

117. "Bible Hint Quells Nazi War Captives," *New York Times*, July 16, 1944.

118. Cowley, *Stalag Wisconsin*, 94.

119. Ibid., 98.

120. Major General J. A. Ulio, The Adjutant General, *Prisoner of War Labor*, AG 383.6 (Sept. 23, 1943), War Department, Washington, DC (Nov. 16, 1943), 1, in Office of the Provost Marshal General, *Historical Monograph*.

121. War Manpower Commission, Regional Operations Bulletin No. 82, Revision No. 1, "Utilization of Prisoner-of-War Labor," June 30, 1944, 5, in Records of the War Manpower Commission, RG 211: "Records of the War Manpower Commission," entry 175, box 1, folder: "POWs Region V," National Archives II, Modern Military Branch.

122. Alex Legault, Pres. UAW CIO, to John B. Bennett, Congressman, "Protest," in same folder cited in n. 121.

123. John B. Bennett, MC, Congress of the United States, House of Representatives, Washington, DC, Jan. 7, 1944, to Mr. F. W. Hunter, War Manpower Commission, in same folder cited in n. 121.

124. Harold E. Arnold, Acting President, Timber & Sawmill Workers Union to Robert Goodwin, Regional Director, WMC, and Paul V. McNutt, Director, WMC, Jan. 7, 1944, in same folder cited in n. 121.

125. Arnold to Goodwin and McNutt, in same folder cited in n. 121.

126. Swan Aserson, President, Midwest District Council No. 12, International Woodworkers of America, in same folder cited in n. 121.

127. R. L. Shaw, Acting Chief, Division of Placement, "Protest of Timber and Sawmill Workers Union CIO Local 15 to Use Prisoners-of-War in the Upper Peninsula," Jan. 17, 1944, 1–2, in same folder cited in n. 121.

128. Clifford S. Urwiller, Colonel, CE, Assistant Director, Prisoner of War Division, Oct. 5, 1944, 1–2. SPMGA 253.5 (55), Headquarters Army Service Forces, RG 211, entry 175, box 1, folder: "Region II," National Archives II, Modern Military Branch.

129. Ibid.

130. "Seen as Army-Union Problem," *New York Times*, Feb. 12, 1944.

131. Ibid.

132. "War Prisoner Pay Is Held Inviolate," *New York Times*, Feb. 12, 1944.

133. Unknown Unteroffizier, *And Still We Conquer!* 46.

134. Lewis and Mewha, *History of Prisoner of War Utilization*, 172.

135. "Provost Marshal Progress Report," Jan. 31, 1946, 25, in Office of the Provost Marshal General, RG 389, entry 439A: "Historical File, 1941–1958," box 43: "Progress Reports (1946)—Provost Marshal General," folder: "Progress Reports," National Archives II, Modern Military Branch.

6. Idle Hands

1. See chapter 3.
2. "Convention relative to the Treatment of Prisoners of War," 942.
3. John Brown Mason, "German Prisoners of War in the United States," *American Journal of International Law* 34 (Apr. 1945): 201. The epigraph to this chapter is drawn from Mason's "Prisoners from the Master Race," *Infantry Journal*, no. 53 (Dec. 1943): 41–42, based on his speech delivered shipboard during the invasion of Sicily.
4. "Historical Monograph," 90.
5. Paul A. Neuland, Major (QMC), CMP, Chief, Field Service Branch, "Field Service Report on Visit to Prisoner of War Camp, Memphis, ASF Depot, Memphis Tennessee, 14–16 Jan. 1945, by Captain William F. Raugust," in Office of the Provost Marshal General, RG 389, entry 459A: "Decimal File, 1943–1946," box 1618: "Camp McCloskey to Camp Orlando," folder 255 (Cp. Memphis ASF Depot), general, National Archives II, Modern Military Branch.
6. Maxwell S. McKnight, Major, CMP, Acting Director, Prisoner of War Special Projects Division, "Removal of Prisoner of War Clergyman," SSPMGX (2) Feb. 17, 1945, in same folder cited in n. 5.
7. "Historical Monograph," 91.
8. Ibid., 89.
9. Gansberg, *Stalag: U.S.A.*, 111.
10. Krammer, *Nazi Prisoners of War in America*, 163.
11. Geiger, *German Prisoners of War at Camp Cooke*, 122.
12. "Spiritual Aid for War Prisoners," *New York Times*, Jan. 1, 1944.
13. Steven V. Dahms, "World War II Prisoners of War and the Missouri Synod," *Concordia Historical Institute Quarterly* 68, no. 3 (Fall 1995): 123.
14. P. E. Kretzmann, "The Lutheran Commission for Prisoners of War," *Lutheran Witness*, Dec. 1943, 421.
15. Ibid.
16. Dahms, "World War II Prisoners of War," 120–31.
17. Melissa Weldon, "Restoring the Light: Ministry to German Prisoners of War in America during the Second World War" (MA thesis, Univ. of Richmond, 1993), 30–34.
18. "Inspection Report, Special Projects Division, Prisoner of War Base Camp, Indiantown Gap Military Reservation, Pennsylvania, May 1, 1945," 5, in Office of the Provost Marshal General, RG 389, entry 459A: "Decimal File, 1943–1946 (Special Projects Division, Administrative Branch Decimal File, 1943–1946)," box 161: "Camp Indianola to Fort Knox," folder 255 (Cp. Indiantown Gap Mil. Resv.), general, National Archives II, Modern Military Branch.
19. Karl Gustaf Almquist, "Report of Visit to Prisoner of War Camp, Memphis ASF Depot, Tennessee, Nov. 16, 1945, in Office of the Provost Marshal General, RG 389, entry 459A: "Decimal File, 1943–1946," box 1618: "Camp McCloskey to Camp Orlando," folder 255 (Cp. Memphis ASF Depot), general, National Archives II, Modern Military Branch.
20. Olle Axberg "Report of visit to Prisoner of War Camp, Camp Shelby, Mississippi, February 28 and March 3 and 4, 1946," in Office of the Provost Marshal General, RG 389, entry 459A: folder 255: "Camp Rupert to Fort Sheridan," National Archives II, Modern Military Branch.
21. Pabel, *Enemies Are Human*, 157.

22. *The Echo: By the Hospital—for the Hospital,* Dec. 1945, 27.
23. Axberg, "Report of visit to Prisoner of War Camp, Camp Shelby, Mississippi" (see n. 20).
24. Axberg, "Report of Visit to Prisoner of War Camp, Shanks, New York, Dec. 4, 1945, in Office of the Provost Marshal General, RG 389, entry 459A: "Decimal File, 1943–1946 (Special Projects Division, Administrative Branch Decimal File, 1943–1946)," box 1621: "Camp Rupert to Fort Sheridan," folder 255 (Cp. Shanks, N.Y.), general, National Archives II.
25. B. Frank Stoltzfun, "Report on Visit to Prisoner of War Camp Memphis A.S.F. Depot, Tennessee, Mar. 17, 1945," in Office of the Provost Marshal General, RG 389, "Decimal File, 1943–1946," entry 459A: "Decimal File, 1943–1946," box 1618: "Camp McCloskey to Camp Orlando," folder 255 (Cp. Memphis ASF Depot), general, National Archives II, Modern Military Branch.
26. *The Echo: By the Hospital—for the Hospital,* Dec. 1945, 18.
27. *The Echo: By the Hospital—for the Hospital,* Jan. 1, 1946, 19.
28. "Inspection Report, Special Projects Division, Prisoner of War Base Camp, Indiantown Gap Military Reservation," (see n. 18).
29. Memorandum for the Fiscal Director, Army Service Forces (Attention: Major J. K. Cranmer, Fiscal Control Branch), in Office of the Provost Marshal General, RG 389, entry 461: "POW Information Bureau, Reporting Branch, Subject File, 1942–1946," box 2468: "Activities to Athletic and Recreational Equip.," folder: "Athletic and Recreational Equipment," National Archives II, Modern Military Branch.
30. Ibid.
31. Several folders in RG 389 of the Office of the Provost Marshal General, at the National Archives II, Modern Military Branch, are full of simple requisition orders for kits, affirmative responses from the Prisoner of War Operations Division, and acknowledgments of receipt of the kits.
32. Howard W. Smith Jr., Major, CMP, Chief, Camp Operations Branch, Prisoner of War Operations Division, SPMGO (12) 400, in Office of the Provost Marshal General, RG 389, entry 461: "POW Information Bureau Reporting Branch, Subject File, 1942–1946," box 2468: "Activities to Athletics and Recreational Equipment," no folder, National Archives II, Modern Military Branch.
33. Allen W. Guillion, Major General, USA, The Provost Marshal General, "Recreational Funds for Internment Camps," May 21, 1942, in same folder cited in n. 32.
34. Alfred L. Cardinaux, Assistant to the Delegate, International Red Cross Committee, to Brigadier General B. M. Bryan, Chief, Aliens Division, REF: C/53, Oct. 12, 1943, in same folder cited in n. 32.
35. Earl L. Edwards, Major, CMP, Assistant Director, Prisoner of War Division to Alfred L. Cardinaux, Assistant to the Delegate, International Red Cross Committee, SPMGA (24) 400, Oct. 14, 1943, and "Athletic and Recreational Equipment," both in same folder cited in n. 32.
36. "Historical Monograph," 144.
37. Andre Vulliet, *Preliminary Report of the War Prisoners Aid, Young Men's Christian Associations during World War II* (Geneva, Switzerland: International Committee of the Young Men's Christian Association, 1946), 26–27.
38. Chip Walker, "German Creative Activities in Camp Aliceville, 1943–1946," *Alabama Review* 38, no. 1 (Jan. 1985): 24–29.
39. Olle Axberg, "Report of Visit to Prisoner of War Camp, Memphis ASF Depot, Tennessee, June 10–12, 1945," in Office of the Provost Marshal General, RG 389, entry 459A: "Decimal File, 1943–1946," box 1618: "Camp McCloskey to Camp Orlando," folder 255 (Cp. Memphis ASF Depot), general, National Archives II, Modern Military Branch.
40. James M. Alexander, "Visit to Indiantown Gap Military Reservation, Pennsylvania, May 1, 1945," 8–10, in Office of the Provost Marshal General, RG 389, entry 459A: "Decimal File, 1943–1946

(Special Projects Division, Administrative Branch Decimal File, 1943–1946)," box 1616: "Camp Indianola to Fort Knox," folder 255 (Cp. Indiantown Gap Mil. Resv.), general, National Archives II, Modern Military Branch.

41. James M. Alexander, 1st Lt., Cavalry, Assistant Executive Officer, "Visit to Camp Sharpe, Gettysburg, March 1, 1945," 4–6, in Office of the Provost Marshal General, RG 389, entry 459A: "Decimal File, 1943–1946 (Special Projects Division, Administrative Branch Decimal File, 1943–1946)," box 1618: "Camp McCloskey to Camp Orlando," folder 255 (Cp. Memphis ASF Depot), general, National Archives II, Modern Military Branch.

42. "Historical Monograph," 144.

43. "Index—German Synopses," in Office of the Provost Marshal General, RG 389, entry 439A: "Historical File, 1941–1958," box 40: "PW Polish-Prisoners of War Reorientation," folder: "Movies Shown to German Prisoners," National Archives II, Modern Military Branch.

44. "By the order of the secretary of war," approved by G. C. Marshall, Chief of Staff, and by J. A. Ulio, Major General, The Adjutant General, U.S. War Department, Prisoner of War Circular No. 4 (Washington 25, DC: GPO, Jan. 23, 1945), 1–2, in Office of the Provost Marshal General, RG 389, entry 439A: "Historical File, 1941–1958," box 38: "PW Policies Not Covered in Regulations Book 1," folder: "PW Circulars," National Archives II, Modern Military Branch. See also "Books for Prisoners of War," *Publishers Weekly*, May 22, 1943, 1970.

45. "Historical Monograph," 144.

46. Calvin N. Jones, "Views of America and Views of Germany in German POW Newspapers of World War II," *Yearbook of German American Studies* 17 (1982): 63–65; John Arndt, ed., *Microfilm Guide and Index to the Library of Congress Collection of German Prisoner of War Newspapers Published in the United States from 1943–1946* (Worcester, MA: Clark Univ., 1965).

47. Arndt, *Microfilm Guide and Index*.

48. Ibid., 57.

49. William B. Gemmill, "German P/W Camp Newspapers," in Office of the Provost Marshal General, RG 389, entry 459A, box 1616: "Prisoner of War Operations Division, Operations Branch," folder: "Factory Fort Kearney, R.I.," National Archives II, Modern Military Branch.

50. Gemmill, "German P/W Camp Newspapers," in same folder cited in n. 49.

51. Numerous groups aided POWs of all nations in acquiring books. These include the Universal Christian Commission for Aid for Prisoners of War, the European Student Aid Fund, and the World's Student Christian Federation. See A. C. Breycha-Vauthier, "Reading for Prisoners of War as Seen from Geneva," *Library Quarterly* 11 (1941): 442–47.

52. U.S. War Department, Prisoner of War Circular No. 1.

53. "Books for Prisoners of War." See also U.S. War Department, Prisoner of War Circular No. 1, 55.

54. B. M. Bryan, Brigadier General, Director, Aliens Division, "Newspapers and Magazines for Prisoners of War," SPMGA (10) 311.7, Mar. 23, 1943, in Office of the Provost Marshal General, RG 389, entry 439A: "Historical File, 1941–1958," box 38: "PW Policies Not Covered in Regulations Book 1," folder: "PW Circulars," National Archives II, Modern Military Branch. See also "Books for Prisoners of War."

55. "Books for Prisoners of War."

56. "Chicago Library Compiles Book List for Prisoners of War," *Publishers Weekly*, July 22, 1944, 241.

57. Vulliet, *Preliminary Report*, 20.

58. Lawrence B. Meyer, "A Plea for Prison Camp Literature," *Lutheran Witness*, Sept. 14, 1943, 311.

59. "Summary of Camp Report, Camp Cooke, California, Visited by Mr. Schneider on June 9 and 10, 1945, in Office of the Provost Marshal General, RG 389, entry 459A: "Decimal File, 1943–1946

(Special Projects Division, Administrative Branch Decimal File, 1943–1946)," box 1608: "250.1 to Camp Ashby," folder 255, general, National Archives II, Modern Military Branch.

60. Olle Axberg, "Report of Visit to Prisoner of War Camp, Camp Shelby, Mississippi" (see n. 20).

61. Vulliet, *Preliminary Report*, 20.

62. Olle Axberg, "Report of Visit to Prisoner of War Camp, Shanks, New York," (see n. 24).

63. Ralph Pierson, "The Barbed-Wire Universities," *School and Society*, Sept. 8, 1945, 157.

64. U.S. War Department, Prisoner of War Circular No. 52 (Washington 25, DC: GPO, Nov. 29, 1944, in Office of the Provost Marshal General, RG 389, entry 439A: "Historical File, 1941–1958," box 38: "PW Policies Not Covered in Regulations Book 1," folder: "PW Circulars," National Archives II, Modern Military Branch.

65. *The Echo: By the Hospital—for the Hospital*, Dec. 1945, 10.

66. Ibid.

67. "The YMCA War Prisoners' Aid Offers Educational Assistance," *School and Society*, May 6, 1944, 325.

68. "Studies and Sports in German Prison Camps," *Prisoners of War Bulletin*, Sept. 1943, 1.

69. Vulliet, *Preliminary Report*, 25.

70. Walter Schmid, *A German POW in New Mexico*, trans. Richard Rundell, ed. Wolfgang T. Schlauch (Albuquerque: Univ. of New Mexico Press, 2005), 29.

71. Ibid., 30.

72. *The Echo: By the Hospital—for the Hospital*, Dec. 45–No. 8/9: 17.

73. Axberg, "Report of Visit to Prisoner of War Camp, Memphis ASF Depot" (see n. 39).

74. Axberg, "Report of Visit to Prisoner of War Camp, Shanks, New York, Dec. 4, 1945" (see n. 24).

75. Richard Sieger, PhD, Director of Camp Studies, PW Camp Indiantown, "Schedule for the month of March 1945," in Office of the Provost Marshal General, RG 389, entry 459A: "Decimal File, 1943–1946 (Special Projects Division, Administrative Branch Decimal File, 1943–1946)," box 1616: "Camp Indianola to Fort Knox," folder 255 (Cp. Indiantown Gap Mil. Resv.), general, National Archives II, Modern Military Branch.

76. Vulliet, *Preliminary Report*, 25.

7. Exorcising the Beast

1. Ron Robin, *The Barbed-Wire College: Reeducating German POWs in the United States during World War II* (Princeton, NJ: Princeton Univ. Press, 1995), 3–13. See also Prisoner of War Operations Division, Provost Marshal General's Office, "Historical Monograph—Reeducation program at Kearney, Wetherill, and Eustis," in Office of the Provost Marshal General, RG 389, entry 439A: "Historical File, 1941–1958," box 36: "Prisoner of War Operations," National Archives II, Modern Military Branch.

2. Henry C. Cassidy, "What to Do with German Prisoners: The Russian Solution," *Atlantic Monthly*, Nov. 1944, 43–45.

3. "Reactions to Buecherreihe Neue Welt," in Office of the Provost Marshal General, RG 389, entry 439A: "Historical File, 1941–1958," box 40: "PW Polish-Prisoners of War Reorientation," folder: "PW Education Program," 1–5, National Archives II, Modern Military Branch.

4. Ibid.

5. Ibid., 5.

6. Ibid., 6.

7. Krammer, *Nazi Prisoners of War in America*, 202–3; Robin, *The Barbed-Wire College*, 62–66.

8. Robin, *The Barbed-Wire College*, 120–21; Krammer, *Nazi Prisoners of War in America*, 210.

9. Geiger, *German Prisoners of War at Camp Cooke*, 113–16.
10. Krammer, *Nazi Prisoners of War in America*, 210.
11. Walter H. Rapp, Capt. (Cav), CMP, "Fort Phillip Kearney, Rhode Island, 10 Jan. 1945," in Office of the Provost Marshal General, RG 389, entry 459A: "Decimal File, 1943–1946 (Special Projects Division, Administrative Branch Decimal File, 1943–1946)," box 1616: "Camp McCloskey to Camp Orlando," folder 255 (Ft. Kearney), general, National Archives II, Modern Military Branch.
12. Otto Johnson, "Establishment of Prisoner of War Camp, For Philip Kearney, Rhode Island, 27 Feb. 1945," in same folder cited in n. 11.
13. "Report on the Experimental Administrative School for Selected German Prisoners of War established at Fort Kearney, Rhode Island, May 7 to July 7," 1945, 1–3, in Office of the Provost Marshal General, RG 389, entry 439A: "Historical File, 1941–1958," box 40: "PW Polish-Prisoners of War Reorientation," folder: "Reeducation of Enemy PW Projects II and III," National Archives II, Modern Military Branch.
14. These men wrote many of the articles published about various aspects of the POW program appearing in journals and magazines.
15. Walter Schoenstedt, Capt. (CAC), CMP, "Kearney Activities and Check List," SPMGX (4), in Office of the Provost Marshal General, RG 389, entry 459A: "Decimal File, 1943–1946 (Special Projects Division, Administrative Branch Decimal File, 1943–1946)," box 1616: "Camp McCloskey to Camp Orlando," folder 255 (Ft. Kearney), general, National Archives II, Modern Military Branch.
16. "Report on the Experimental Administrative School" (see n. 13).
17. Krammer, *Nazi Prisoners of War in America*, 200–202; Robin, *The Barbed-Wire College*, 50–68.
18. Robin, *The Barbed-Wire College*, 2–6.
19. Ibid., 6.
20. Ibid., 7–9.
21. E. Targum, Capt., AGD, Commanding, "Special Training Course," SPMGX (4), May 11, 1945, in Office of the Provost Marshal General, RG 389, entry 459A: "Decimal File, 1943–1946 (Special Projects Division, Administrative Branch Decimal File, 1943–1946)," box 1616: "Camp McCloskey to Camp Orlando," folder 255 (Ft. Kearney), general, National Archives II, Modern Military Branch.
22. F. L. B., "Annex to Report of Visit to Fort Kearney PW Camp, same date, 14 April 1945," in Office of the Provost Marshal General, RG 389, entry 459A: "Decimal File, 1943–1946 (Special Projects Division, Administrative Branch Decimal File, 1943–1946)," box 1616, folder: "Factory, Fort Kearney, R.I.," National Archives II, Modern Military Branch.
23. Ibid.
24. Memorandum for Director, Prisoner of War Special Projects Division, "Transfer of Kearney Project Program #1, 13 Aug. 1945," in same folder cited in n. 22.
25. "Memorandum," Maxwell S. McKnight, Major, CMP, Acting Director, Prisoner of War Special Projects Division, Provost Marshal General's Office, SPMX (19), June 7, 1945, in Office of the Provost Marshal General, RG 389, entry 439A: "Historical File, 1941–1958," box 40: "PW Polish-Prisoners of War Reorientation," folder: "Fort Getty Project," National Archives II, Modern Military Branch.
26. F. G. Alletson Cook, "Democratic ABC's for Nazi PW's," *New York Times Magazine*, Nov. 11, 1945.
27. See Henry W. Ehrmann, "An Experiment in Political Education: The Prisoner of War Schools in the United States," *Social Research* 14 (Sept. 1947): 304–20. Figures come from page 304 of the article.
28. "Historical Monograph of the Re-education of Enemy Prisoners of War, Eustis Project," Apr. 4, 1946, 2–5, in Office of the Provost Marshal General, RG 389, entry 457: "Subject Correspondence File, 1942–1946 (Subject Correspondence File Relating To The Construction of And Condition in

Prisoner of War Camps, 1942–1946)," box 41: "Prisoners of War Re-orientation—Progress Reports, Section II, 1943," no folder, National Archives II, Modern Military Branch.

29. Ibid., 1.
30. Ibid., 7.
31. Ibid., 11–19.
32. Ibid., 20–22.
33. Ehrmann, "An Experiment in Political Education," 304.
34. Ibid., 305.
35. "Historical Monograph of the Re-education" (see n. 28).
36. Robin, *The Barbed-Wire College*, 4–5.
37. Ibid., 5.
38. Ibid., 9.

8. Leaving a Place Called Amerika

1. *Washington Post*, Apr. 24, 1945.
2. "'Last' of 430,353 PW's to Leave the U.S.; Only Ones Remaining Are 'Escapees' or Ill," *New York Times*, Aug. 8, 1947.
3. Record, "WWI and WWII Axis Burials."
4. This included members of the Spanish Blue Division.
5. Hörner, *A German Odyssey*, 375.
6. Schmid, *A German POW in New Mexico*, 82.
7. Heino R. Erichsen, *The Reluctant Warrior: Former German POW Finds Peace in Texas*, as told to Jean Nelson-Erichsen (Austin, TX: Eakin Press, 2001).
8. Pabel, *Enemies Are Human*, 247.
9. Gansberg, *Stalag: U.S.A.*, 167; Krammer, *Nazi Prisoners of War in America*, 263.

Bibliography

Books

Arndt, John, ed. *Microfilm Guide and Index to the Library of Congress Collection of German Prisoner of War Newspapers Published in the United States from 1943–1946.* Worcester, MA: Clark University, 1965.
Bailey, Ronald H. *Prisoners of War.* Chicago: Time-Life Books, 1981.
Bangerter, Lowell A. *German Prisoners of War in Wyoming.* Laramie: Wyoming Council for the Humanities, 1979.
Bartov, Omar. *Hitler's Army: Soldiers, Nazis, and War in the Third Reich.* New York: Oxford University Press, 1991.
Billinger, Robert D., Jr. *Hitler's Soldiers in the Sunshine State: German POWs in Florida.* Gainesville: University Press of Florida, 2000.
———. *Nazi POWs in the Tar Heel State.* Gainesville: University Press of Florida, 2008.
Bosworth, Allan R. *America's Concentration Camps.* New York: W. W. Norton, 1967.
Buck, Anita. *Behind Barbed Wire: German Prisoner of War Camps in Minnesota.* St. Cloud, MN: North Star Press, 1998.
Carlson, Lewis H. *We Were Each Other's Prisoners: An Oral History of World War II American and German Prisoners of War.* New York: Basic Books, 1997.
Clausewitz, Carl von. *On War.* Princeton, NJ: Princeton University Press, 1989.
Cooper, Herston. *Crossville.* Chicago: Adams Press, 1965.
Cooper, Matthew. *The German Army, 1933–1945.* Chelsea, MI: Scarborough House, 1991.
Cowley, Betty. *Stalag Wisconsin: Inside WWII Prisoner-of-War Camps.* Oregon, WI: Badger Books, 2002.
Davis, Calvin DeArmond. *The United States and the Second Hague Peace Conference: American Diplomacy and International Organization, 1899–1914.* Durham, NC: Duke University Press, 1975.
Davis, George J. *The Hitler Diet: As Inflicted on American P.O.W.'s in World War II.* Los Angeles: Military Literary Guild, 1990.
Demos, John. "The Deerfield Massacre." In *To 1877.* Vol. 1 of *Portrait of America.* Edited by Stephen B. Oates and Charles J. Errico, 47–54. New York: Houghton Mifflin, 2003.
Dennett, Carl. *Prisoners of the Great War.* Boston: Houghton Mifflin, 1919.
Doyle, Michael W. *Ways of War and Peace: Realism, Liberalism, and Socialism.* New York: W. W. Norton, 1997.
Eisenhower, John S. D. *So Far from God: The U.S. War with Mexico, 1846–1848.* Norman: University of Oklahoma Press, 2000.
Ellis, John. *Brute Force: Allied Strategy and Tactics in the Second World War.* New York: Viking-Penguin Books, 1990.
Erichsen, Heino R. *The Reluctant Warrior: Former German POW Finds Peace in Texas.* As told to Jean Nelson-Erichsen. Austin, TX: Eakin Press, 2001.
Fiedler, David. *The Enemy among Us: POWs in Missouri during World War II.* Saint Louis: Missouri Historical Society Press, 2003.

Flory, William E. S. *Prisoners of War: A Study in the Development of International Law*. Washington, DC: American Council on Public Affairs, 1942.
Foy, David A. *For You the War Is Over: American Prisoners of War in Nazi Germany*. New York: Stein and Day, 1984.
Freidel, Frank. *The Splendid Little War*. Boston: Little, Brown, 1958.
Fritz, Stephen G. *Frontsoldaten: The German Soldier in World War II*. Lexington: University of Kentucky Press, 1995.
Gaertner, Georg. *Hitler's Last Soldier in America*. With Arnold Krammer. New York: Stein and Day, 1985.
Gansberg, Judith M. *Stalag: U.S.A. The Remarkable Story of German POWs in America*. New York: Thomas Y. Cromwell, 1977.
Geiger, Jeffrey E. *German Prisoners of War at Camp Cooke, California: Personal Accounts of 14 Soldiers, 1944–1946*. Jefferson, NC: McFarland, 1996.
Gimmeson, Johanna K. *German POW Camp in Deaver, Wyoming, 1944–1945*. Powell, WY: Polecat Printery, 2001.
Goebeler, Hans. *Steel Boats, Iron Hearts: A U-Boat Crewman's Life aboard U-505*. With John Vanzo. London: Chatham. 2008.
Green, Vincent S. *Extreme Justice*. New York: Pocket Books, 1995.
Gussmann, Hans, with Nancy Hite and Hilga Gussman McKee. *Prisoner of Peace: The Journal of a German Soldier's Captivity after World War II*. Bloomington, IN: Xlibris, 2003.
Handel, Michael I. *Masters of War: Classical Strategic Thought*. Portland, OR: Frank Cass, 2001.
Harris, Wesley. *Fish out of Water: Nazi Submariners as Prisoners in North Louisiana during World War II*. Ruston, LA: RoughEdge, 2004.
Hickey, Donald R. *The War of 1812: A Forgotten Conflict*. Urbana: University of Illinois Press, 1989.
Holloway, A., and J. W. Buell, eds. *Hero Tales of the American Soldier and Sailor as Told by the Heroes Themselves and Their Comrades*. A. Holloway, 1899.
Hörner, Helmut. *A German Odyssey: The Journal of a German Prisoner of War*. Translated and edited by Allan Kent Powell. Golden, CO: Fulcrum, 1991.
Hull, William I. *The Two Hague Conferences and Their Contributions to International Law*. New York: Garland, 1972.
Jackson, Robert. *The Prisoners, 1914–18*. New York: Routledge, Kegan & Paul, 1989.
Jaworski, Leon. *After Fifteen Years*. Houston: Gulf Publishing Co., 1961.
———. *Confession and Avoidance: A Memoir*. Garden City, NY: Anchor Press/Doubleday, 1975.
Johnson, Clarence. *Prisoners of War*. Los Angeles: University of Southern California Press, 1941.
Knappe, Siegfried. *Soldat—Reflections of a German Soldier, 1936–1949*. Edited by Ted Brusaw. New York: Dell, 1992.
Kochavi, Arieh J. *Confronting Captivity: Britain and the United States and Their POWs in Nazi Germany*. Chapel Hill: University of North Carolina Press, 2005.
Koller, Berneda. *An Ironic Point of Light: The Story of a German from Russia Who Survived an American World War II Prisoner of War Camp*. Freeman, SD: Pine Hill Press, 1994.
Koop, Allen V. *Stark Decency: German Prisoners of War in a New England Village*. Hanover, NH: University Press of New England, 1988.
Krammer, Arnold. *Nazi Prisoners of War in America*. New York: Scarborough House, 1996.
Leckie, Robert. *"A Few Acres of Snow": The Saga of the French and Indian Wars*. New York: John Wiley & Sons, 1999.
Luck, Hans von. *Panzer Commander: The Memoirs of Colonel Hans von Luck*. New York: Praeger, 1989.
Machiavelli, Niccolo. *The Prince and Other Writings*. Edited and translated by Wayne Rebhorn. New York: Barnes and Noble Classics, 2003.
Marshall, George Catlett. *The Right Man to Do the Job*. Vol. 3 of *The Papers of George Catlett Marshall*. Edited by Larry I. Bland. Baltimore: Johns Hopkins University Press, 1991.

May, Lowell A. *Camp Concordia: German POWs in the Midwest*. Manhattan, KS: Sunflower University Press, 1995.
McGuire, Phillip, ed. *Taps for a Jim Crow Army: Letters from Black Soldiers in World War II*. Lexington: University Press of Kentucky, 1993.
Metzger, Charles H. *The Prisoner in the American Revolution*. Chicago: Loyola University Press, 1971.
Moore, Bob, and Kent Fedorowich. *The British Empire and Its Italian Prisoners of War, 1940–1947*. New York: Palgrave, 2002.
———. *Prisoners of War and Their Captors in World War II*. Oxford: Berg, 1996.
Moore, John Hammond. *The Faustball Tunnel: German POWs in America and Their Great Escape*. New York: Random House, 1978.
Motley, Mary Penick, ed. *The Invisible Soldier: The Experience of the Black Soldier, World War II*. Detroit, MI: Wayne State University Press, 1975.
Neillands, Robin, and Roderick De Normann. *D-day 1944: Voices from Normandy*. London: Cassell Military Paperbacks, 2001.
Pabel, Reinhold. *Enemies Are Human*. Philadelphia: John C. Winston, 1955.
Paret, Peter, and Gordon A. Craig, eds. *Makers of Modern Strategy from Machiavelli to the Nuclear Age*. Princeton, NJ: Princeton University Press, 1986.
Parnell, Wilma. *The Killing of Corporal Kunze*. With Robert Taber. Secaucus, NJ: Lyle Stuart, 1981.
Petit, Ira. *The Diary of a Dead Man, 1862–1864*. Compiled by J. P. Ray. New York: Publishing Center for Cultural Resources, 1976.
Pictet, Jean. *Development and Principles of International Humanitarian Law*. Leiden, the Netherlands: Martinus Nijhoff, 1985.
Powell, Allan Kent. *Splinters of a Nation: German Prisoners of War in Utah*. Salt Lake City: University of Utah Press, 1989.
Ready, J. Lee. *The Forgotten Axis: Germany's Partners and Foreign Volunteers in World War II*. Jefferson, NC: McFarland, 1987.
Reid, Major Pat, and Maurice Michael. *Prisoner of War*. New York: Beaufort Books, 1984.
Riconda, Harry P. *Prisoners of War in American Conflicts*. Lanham, MD: Scarecrow Press, 2003.
Roberts, Jeff. "POW Camps in World War II." In *The Tennessee Encyclopedia of History and Culture*. Edited by Carroll Van West, 746–47. Nashville: Tennessee Historical Society, 1998.
Robin, Ron. *The Barbed-Wire College: Reeducating German POWs in the United States during World War II*. Princeton, NJ: Princeton University Press, 1995.
Schmid, Walter. *A German POW in New Mexico*. Translated Richard Rundell. Edited by Wolfgang T. Schlauch. Albuquerque: University of New Mexico Press, 2005.
Schmidt, Wolfgang D. *The Education and Reeducation of POW 31G-23742357*. Bloomington, IN: Xlibris, 2001.
Schott, Matthew J., and Rosalind Foley. *Bayou Stalags: German Prisoners of War in Louisiana*. Lafayette: University of Southwestern Louisiana, 1981.
Seydewitz, Max. *Civil Life in Wartime Germany: The Story of the Home Front*. New York: Viking Press, 1945.
Smith, Arthur L., Jr. *The War for the German Mind: Re-educating Hitler's Soldiers*. Providence, RI: Berghahn Books, 1996.
Speer, Lonnie R. *Portals to Hell: The Military Prisons of the Civil War*. Mechanicsburg, PA: Stackpole Books, 1997.
Steinhilper, Ulrich, and Peter Osborne. *Ten Minutes to Buffalo: The Story of Germany's Great Escaper*. Independent Books, 1991.
Strasser, Steven, ed. *The Abu Ghraib Investigations: The Official Reports of the Independent Panel and the Pentagon on the Shocking Prisoner Abuse in Iraq*. New York: Public Affairs, 2004.

Sun-Tzu. *The Art of War*. Edited and translated by Samuel B. Griffith. New York: Oxford University Press, 1963.
Tacitus. *The Annals of Imperial Rome*. Translated by Michael Grant. New York: Barnes and Noble Books, 1971.
Tent, James F. *Mission on the Rhine: Reeducation and Denazification in American-Occupied Germany*. Chicago: University of Chicago Press, 1982.
Thompson, Antonio. *German Jackboots on Kentucky Bluegrass: Housing German Prisoners of War in Kentucky, 1942–1946*. Clarksville, TN: Diversion Press, 2008.
Thompson, Glenn. *Prisoners on the Plains: German POWs in America*. Holdrege, NE: Phelps County Historical Society, 1993.
Towle, Philip, Margaret Kosuge, and Yoichi Kibata, eds. *Japanese Prisoners of War*. London: Hambledon and London, 2000.
Treaties and Alliances of the World: An International Survey covering Treaties in Force and Communities of State. New York: Charles Scribner's Sons, 1968.
Unknown Unteroffizier. *And Still We Conquer! The Diary of a Nazi Unteroffizier in the German Africa Corps Who Was Captured by the United States Army, May 9, 1943 and Imprisoned at Camp Shelby, Mississippi*. Edited by Stanley Hoole. University, AL: Confederate Publishing, 1968.
Vance, Jonathan F., ed. *Encyclopedia of Prisoners of War and Internment*. Santa Barbara, CA: ABC-CLIO, 2000.
Vulliet, Andre. *Preliminary Report of the War Prisoners Aid, Young Men's Christian Associations during World War II*. Geneva, Switzerland: International Committee of the Young Men's Christian Association, 1946.
Walker, Richard P. *The Lone Star and the Swastika: Prisoners of War in Texas*. Austin, TX: Eakin Press, 2001.
Wall, Randy. *Inside the Wire: Aliceville and the Afrika Korps*. South Carolina State Museum, Heritage. December 7, 1991.
Washington, George. *September–December 1775*. Vol. 2 of *The Papers of George Washington: Revolutionary War Series*. Edited by W. W. Abbot. Charlottesville: University Press of Virginia, 1987.
Waters, Michael R. *Lone Star Stalag: German Prisoners of War at Camp Hearne*. College Station: Texas A&M University Press, 2004.
Wheal, Elizabeth Anne, Stephen Pope, and James Taylor. *Encyclopedia of the Second World War*. Secaucus, N.J.: Castle Books, 1989.
Wheaton, Henry. *History of the Law of Nations in Europe and America from the Earliest Times to the Treaty of Washington, 1842*. Albany, N.Y.: Gould, 1845.
Whittingham, Richard. *Martial Justice: The Last Mass Execution in the United States*. Chicago: Henry Regnery, 1971.
Wilcox, Walter W. *The Farmer in the Second World War*. Ames: Iowa State College Press, 1947.
Wright, Gordon. *The Ordeal of Total War, 1939–1945*. New York: Harper and Row, 1968.
Zellers, Larry. *In Enemy Hands: A Prisoner in North Korea*. Lexington: University Press of Kentucky, 1991.
Zollo, Burt. *Prisoners*. Chicago: Academy Chicago, 2003.

Unpublished Material

Albertson, Hans-Albert Smolinski. "My Memories of the Prisoner of War Camp in Crossville, Tennessee." Unpublished manuscript, March 8, 1993. University of Tennessee Special Collections.

Bibliography

Blank, Bruce J. "Camp Plauche POWS: Germans under the Huey P. Long Bridge, 1944–1946." MA thesis, University of New Orleans, 1991.
Corbett, Edward C. "Interned for the Duration: Axis Prisoners of War in Oklahoma, 1942–1946." BA thesis, Oklahoma City University, 1965.
Dahms, Steven Victor. "The Work of the Lutheran Church—Missouri Synod and Its Pastors and Congregations among German Prisoners of War in the United States during World War II." MA thesis, University of Wisconsin–Oshkosh, 1989.
Doyle, Frederick J. "German Prisoners of War in the Southwest United States during World War II: An Oral History." PhD diss., University of Denver, 1978.
Emerson, Tamsen. "An Experiment in Agricultural Labor: The German Prisoner of War Camp in Council Grove, Kansas." MA thesis, Emporia State University, 1988.
Jonas, Clyde Larry. "Camp Campbell, Kentucky: A History of Construction and Occupation during World War II." MA thesis, Austin Peay State University, 1973.
Kupsky, Gregory. "Making the Most of a Bad Situation: Coddling, Fraternization, and Total War in Camp Crossville, Tennessee." MA thesis, University of Tennessee, Knoxville, 2004.
Lohmann, Paul. "Paul Lohmann's Story: Former Prisoner of War Incarcerated at the POW Camp at Fort Dix, New Jersey." Unpublished manuscript. 1998. Authors possession.
Mallett, Derek R. "'They Were Just People Like We Were': World War II German and Italian Prisoners of War in Missouri." MA thesis, Truman State University, 1997.
Muskiet, Charles Michael, II. "Educating the Afrika Korps: The Political Reeducation of German POWs in America during the Second World War." MA thesis, Baylor University, 1995.
Neidt, Charles O. "Swastikas on Aspen Trees: Prisoners of War in America during World War II." Paper presented to the Fort Collins Westerners, Fort Collins, Colo., November 14, 1994.
Pluth, Edward J. "The Administration and Operation of German Prisoner of War Camps in the United States during World War II." PhD diss., Ball State University, 1970.
Proud, Philip J. "A Study of the Reeducation of German Prisoners of War at Fort Custer, Michigan, 1945–1946." MA thesis. University of Michigan, 1949.
Ragsdale, James Howton. "A Study of the Use of Axis Prisoners of War in the United States during World War II." MA thesis, Ohio State University, 1948.
Speakman, Cummins E., Jr. "Re-education of German Prisoners of War in the United States during World War II." MA thesis, University of Virginia, 1948.
Springer, Paul Joseph. "German Prisoners of War in America during World War II." MA thesis, University of Northern Iowa, 1998.
Thompson, Antonio. "Colonel George Chescheir and the Operation of Axis POW Camps in the American South." Paper presented at the Ohio Valley History Conference, Johnson City, TN, October 2006.
———. "Entertaining the Afrika Korps in America: German POW Camp Life in Kentucky." Paper presented at the Ohio Valley History Conference, Murray, KY, October 2005.
———. "German POWs in the United States during World War II with a Focus on Kentucky and Tennessee." MA thesis, Western Kentucky University, 2001.
———. "Men in German Uniform: German Prisoners of War Held in the United States during World War II." PhD diss., University of Kentucky, 2006.
———. "Working for the Enemy? German POW Labor in Kentucky and Tennessee during World War II." Paper presented at the Ohio Valley Conference, Cookeville, TN, October 2004.
Tissing, Robert Warren, Jr. "Utilization of Prisoners of War in the United States during World War II: Texas: A Case Study." MA thesis, Baylor University, 1973.
Weldon, Melissa. "Restoring the Light: Ministry to German Prisoners of War in America during the Second World War." MA thesis, University of Richmond, 1993.

Williams, J. Barrie. "Re-education of German Prisoners of War in the United States during World War II." MA thesis, College of William and Mary, 1993.

Wyatt, Judy Ledford. "United States Policy toward German Prisoners of War and Its Application in South Carolina." MA thesis, University of South Carolina, 1985.

Government Documents

"Amelioration of the Condition of the Wounded and the Sick of Armies in the Field (Red Cross Convention)." Convention between the United States of America and Other Powers, Treaty Series No. 847. Washington, D.C.: United States Government Printing Office. 1–47.

"Amelioration of the Condition of the Wounded and the Sick of Armies in the Field (Red Cross Convention)." In *Multilateral, 1918–1930*. Vol. 2 of *Treaties and Other International Agreements of the United States of America, 1776–1949*. Edited by Charles I. Bevans, 965–82. Washington, D.C.: Department of State, 1969.

Army Service Forces. *Army Service Forces Organization*. Army Service Forces Manual M-301. Washington, D.C.: United States Government Printing Office, August 15, 1944.

———. *Handbook for Work Supervisors of Prisoner of War Labor*. Army Service Forces Manual M-811. Washington, D.C.: U.S. Government Printing Office, July 1945.

———. *Safe Work Practices for Prisoners of War (German)*. Army Service Forces Manual M-805. Washington, D.C.: U.S. Government Printing Office, September 22, 1944.

———. *Wartime Supervision*. Washington, D.C.: U.S. Government Printing Office, June 14, 1948.

"Convention Relative to the Treatment of Prisoners of War." *Multilateral, 1918–1930*. Vol. 2 of *Treaties and Other International Agreements of the United States of America, 1776–1949*. Edited by Charles I. Bevans, 932–64. Washington, D.C.: Department of State, 1969.

Defense Advisory Committee on Prisoners of War. *POW, the Fight Continues after the Battle; the Report of the Secretary of Defense's Advisory Committee on Prisoners of War*. Washington, D.C.: Government Printing Office, August 1955.

Doyle, Robert C. "Making Experience Count." The Harmon Memorial Lectures in Military History, United States Air Force Academy No. 43. Washington, D.C.: U.S. Government Printing Office, 2002.

"Escape of Officers and Men from German Ships Interned in the United States." *American Journal of International Law* 10, no. 4 (1916): 433–44.

Federal Bureau of Investigations. "Famous Cases: George Dasch and the Nazi Saboteurs." http://www.fbi.gov; 6 p. Accessed November 2007.

General Board, United States Forces, European Theater. *The Military Police Activities in Connection with the Evacuation and Detention of Prisoners of War, Civilian Internees, and Military Personnel Recovered from the Enemy*. Provost Marshal Section 11, Study No. 103.

Lee, Ulysses. *The Employment of Negro Troops*. United States Army in World War II: Special Studies. Washington, D.C.: Office of the Chief of Military History, United States Army, 1966.

Lewis, George, and John Mewha. *History of Prisoner of War Utilization by the United States Army, 1776–1945*. DA Pamphlet 20-213. Washington, D.C.: Department of the Army, June 24, 1955.

Millet, John D. *United States Army in World War II: The Organization and Role of the Army Service Forces*. Washington, D.C.: Office of the Chief of Military History, Department of the Army, 1954.

Office of the Provost Marshal General, Prisoner of War Operations Division. "Weekly Reports on Prisoners of War." Prisoner of War Population Lists June 1942 to June 1944. Washington, D.C.: U.S. Government Printing Office.

U.S. War Department. *Enemy Prisoners of War.* TM 19-500. Washington, D.C.: U.S. Government Printing Office, January 15, 1945.
———. *Handbook for the Director of Civilian Training.* Washington, D.C.: U.S. Government Printing Office, August 1943.

Special Collections / Archival Materials

Fort Campbell, Kentucky

Don F. Pratt Museum. "The History of the 101st Airborne Division (Air Assault) and Fort Campbell, Kentucky." Installation. History Department. Government Printing Office. Photographs. Various documents. German POWs at Fort Campbell. Fort Campbell Archives. Folder 1.

Fort Knox, Kentucky

Cook, Claude E. "The German Prisoner of War Camp at Austin, Indiana, and Its Connection with Campbellsburg, Indiana, during World War II," 8 pages, unpublished manuscript. Cultural Resources Center.
Hessenthaler, Egon, Memoirs (manuscript). German copy. Cultural Resources Center.
Photographs. Cultural Resources Center.
Photographs. Patton Museum Archives.
POW sketchbook. Cultural Resources Center.
POW sketchbook. Patton Museum Archives.
Various documents. Cultural Resources Center.
Various documents. German POWs at Fort Knox. File 3, 91-142-01, Box 49-2. Patton Museum Archives.
Various documents. POW Daily Time Records. File 2, Box 54-2. Patton Museum Archives.

Kentucky Historical Society, Frankfort

Chescheir, George, Collection. Special Collections.
Heady, Peyton. *History of Camp Breckinridge, KY.* Hites Imperial Printing, 1987. Library and Book Room.
Oral History Collection. Special Collections.
Various documents. World War II, General Files of Kentucky History. Library and Book Room.

Military History Institute, Carlisle, Pennsylvania

Broyles, Watkins A., Papers.
Carvolth, Joseph R., Papers.
Fort Sheridan Papers, History 1940s to 1980s.
"Nationality and Age of German Armed Forces, Prisoners Captured in Northern France, Early August to 10 September 1944."
OCHM Personal Papers A–Z.
Ruchti, James R., Papers.

National Archives II, Modern Military Branch, College Park, Maryland

"Descriptive Lists of Monthly Progress Reports of Headquarters Army Service Forces, September 1942–May 1946." National Archives Library.

"Historical Monograph, Prisoner of War Operations Division, Provost Marshal General's Office." In Office of the Provost Marshal General. RG 389. Entry 439A: "Historical File, 1941–1958." Box 36: "Prisoner of War Operations." Vol. 1. Folder: "Prisoner of War Operations." Vol. 1 of 3.

"A Letter from Home." Preston, County West Virginia, 1944–1945. Series of Letters sponsored by the Veterans of Foreign Wars, Post 1588.

Office of the Provost Marshal General. RG 389. Entry 439A: "Historical File, 1941–1958." Boxes 1–53.

———. RG 389. Entry 457: "Subject Correspondence File, 1942–1946 (Subject Correspondence File relating to the Construction of and Condition in Prisoner of War Camps, 1942–1946)." Boxes 1419–40.

———. RG 389. Entry 458: "Policy File, 1942–1945 (Policy and Procedural Records relating to the Supervision of Prisoners of War and Their Camps, 1942–1945)." Boxes 1429, 1441–48.

———. RG 389. Entry 459A: "Decimal File, 1943–1946 (Special Projects Division, Administrative Branch Decimal File, 1943–1946)." Boxes 1593–655.

———. *Historical Monograph: Prisoner of War Operations Division, Office of the Provost Marshal General: With appendices and supplement, 1945–1946.*

Records of the War Manpower Commission. RG 211. Entry 114: "Records of the Reports and Analysis Service, Records of the Foreign Labor Market Section, Manpower Reports 1940–1944." Boxes 1–4.

———. RG 211. Entry 175: "I–IV."

U.S. War Department. Prisoner of War Circular No. 1. Washington, D.C.: Government Printing Office, September 24, 1943. In Office of the Provost Marshal General. RG 389. Entry 439A: "Historical File, 1941–1958." Box 41: "Regulations Governing Prisoners of War."

———. Prisoner of War Circular No. 3. Washington, D.C.: Government Printing Office, 1944. In Office of the Provost Marshal General. RG 389. Entry 439A: "Historical File, 1941–1958." Box 41: "Bulletin Governing Prisoners of War."

Personal Collections

Dickson, Calvin, Collection. Cookeville, TN
Ellis, Patricia, Collection. Fayette County, KY
Mathis, Walter, Collection. Christian and Madison Counties, KY
Smith, E. T. "Hammer," Collection. Henry County, KY
Smith Broadbent Family Collection, Trigg County, KY

Western Kentucky University, Bowling Green

Record, Kenneth S. "WWI and WWII Axis Burials in the Continental United States and Canada," 1998, unpublished manuscript. CS403 R42X, Manuscripts, Kentucky Building.

Romero, Ismael Garcia. Letter of January 27, 1942. World War II and Prisoner of War Documents. Kentucky Building.

Schmidt, Fritz. Letter of May 25, 1944. World War II, Matthew Gore Collection, folder 7, Manuscripts, Kentucky Building.

Various letters. World War II and Prisoner of War Documents, Manuscripts and Folklife Archives, Kentucky Building.

Articles

Journals

Anderson, Chandler P. "Agreement between the United States and Germany concerning Prisoners of War." *American Journal of International Law* 13, no. 1 (1919): 97–101.

Ansbacher, H. L. "Attitudes of German Prisoners of War: A Study of the Dynamics of National-Socialistic Followership." *Applied Psychological Monographs: General and Applied* 62, no. 1 (1948): 1–42.

Balsamo, Larry T. "Germany's Armed Forces in the Second World War: Manpower, Armaments, and Supply." *History Teacher* 24, no. 3 (1991): 263–77.

Billinger, Robert D., Jr. "Behind the Wire: German Prisoners of War at Camp Sutton, 1944–1946." *North Carolina Historical Review* 61, no. 4 (October 1984): 481–509.

Billinger, Robert D., Jr. "The Other Side of Now: What Blanding Prisoners of War Told the Wehrmacht." *Florida Historical Quarterly* 73, no. 1 (July 1994): 62–78.

Billinger, Robert D., Jr. "With the Wehrmacht in Florida: The German POW Facility at Camp Blanding, 1942–1946." *Florida Historical Quarterly* 58, no. 2 (October 1979): 160–73.

Bondy, Curt. "Observation and Reeducation of German Prisoners of War." *Harvard Educational Review* 14 (January–December 1944): 12–19.

Breycha-Vauthier, A. C. "Reading for Prisoners of War as Seen from Geneva." *Library Quarterly* 11 (1941): 442–47.

Burdick, Charles. "Prisoners as Soldiers: The German 999th Penal Division." *Army Quarterly and Defense Journal* 102 (October 1971–July 1972): 65–69.

Butler, Joseph T., Jr. "Prisoner of War Labor in the Sugar Cane Fields of Lafourche Parish, Louisiana: 1943–1944." *Louisiana History* 14 (Summer 1973): 283–96.

Casady, Edwin. "The Reorientation Program for POWs at Fort Eustis, Virginia." *American Oxonian* (July 1947): 146–54.

Clark, Penny. "Farm Work and Friendship: The German Prisoner of War Camp at Lake Wabaunsee." *Emporia State Research Studies* 36, no. 3 (Winter 1988): 43.

Coker, Kathy Roe. "World War II Prisoners of War in Georgia: German Memories of Camp Gordon, 1943–1945." *Georgia Historical Quarterly* 76, no. 4 (Winter 1992): 837–61.

Coles, David J. "Hell-by-the Sea': Florida's Camp Gordon Johnston in World War II." *Florida Historical Quarterly* 73, no. 1 (July 1994): 1–22.

Curt, Bondy. "Problems of Internment Camps." *Journal of Abnormal and Social Psychology* 38 (1943): 453–75.

Davis, Geo B. "The Prisoner of War." *American Journal of International Law* 7, no. 3 (1913): 521–45.

Davis, Gerald H. "Prisoners of War in Twentieth-Century War Economies." *Journal of Contemporary History* 12, no. 4 (October 1977): 623–34.

Dahms, Steven V. "World War II Prisoners of War and the Missouri Synod." *Concordia Historical Institute Quarterly* 68, no. 3 (Fall 1995): 120–32.

Dickinson, Calvin. "Camp Crossville, 1942–1945." *Journal of East Tennessee History* no. 68, (1996): 31–40.

Ehrmann, Henry W. "An Experiment in Political Education: The Prisoner of War Schools in the United States." *Social Research* 14 (September 1947): 304–20.

Ensslin, Fritz. "A German Soldier Tells What It Is Like to Visit Ft. Leonard Wood in 1943 as a POW." *Essayons* (June 1991): 46.
Fay, Sidney B. "German Prisoners of War." *Current History* 8, no. 43 (March 1945): 193–200.
Fickle, James E., and Donald W. Ellis. "POWs in the Piney Woods: German Prisoners of War in the Southern Lumber Industry, 1943–1945." *Journal of Southern History* 56, no. 4 (November 1990): 695–724.
Fisher, Paul. "Repatriation Labor: A Preliminary Analysis." *Quarterly Journal of Economics* 60, no. 3 (May 1946): 313–39.
Flynn, Eleanor C. "The Geneva Convention on Treatment of Prisoners of War." *George Washington Law Review* (June 1943): 505–20.
Frederickson, Mary K., ed. "Some Thoughts on Prisoners of War in Iowa, 1943 to 1946." *Palimpsest* 65, no. 2 (March–April 1984): 68–80.
Haase, Norbert. "Anti-Nazi Prisoners of War in American Prison Camps: The Example of Fort Devens, Massachusetts." http://www.traces.org/2002conference.nhaase.html. Accessed November 1, 2008.
Hiscocks, C. R. "The Development of Democracy in Western Germany since the Second World War." *Canadian Journal of Economics and Political Science* 20, no. 4 (Nov 1954): 493–503.
Holl, Richard E. "Swastikas in the Bluegrass State: Axis Prisoners of War in Kentucky, 1942–46." *Register of the Kentucky Historical Society* 100, no. 2 (Spring 2002): 139–65.
Hoover, J. Edgar. "Alien Enemy Control." *Iowa Law Review* 29 (March 1944): 396–408.
Humphrey, Yvonne E. "On Shipboard with German Prisoners." *American Journal of Nursing* 43, no. 9 (September 1943): 821–22.
Hyde, Charles Cheney. "Concerning Prisoners of War." *American Journal of International Law* 10 (1916): 600–603.
Jepson, Daniel A. "Camp Carson, Colorado: European Prisoners of War in the American West during World War II." *Midwest Review,* 2nd ser., 13 (1991): 32–53.
Jones, Calvin N. "Views of America and Views of Germany in German POW Newspapers of World War II." *Yearbook of German American Studies* 17 (1982): 63–70.
Kirwan, William E. "German Prisoners of War." *Bulletin of the Bureau of Criminal Investigation*, August 1944, 1–6.
Koppes, Clayton R., and Gregory D. Black. "Blacks, Loyalty, and Motion-Picture Propaganda in World War II." *Journal of American History* 73, no. 2 (September 1986): 383–406.
Krammer, Arnold. "American Treatment of German Generals during World War II." *Journal of Military History* 54, no. 1 (January 1990): 27–46.
———. "German Prisoners of War in the United States." *Military Affairs* 40, no. 2 (April 1976): 68–73.
———. "Hitler's Legions in America: POWs on the home front." *American History* 18, no. 4 (June 1983): 54–64.
———. "Japanese Prisoners of War in America." *Pacific Historical Review* 52 (February 1983): 67–91.
Kruse, Arthur M. "Custody of Prisoners of War in the United States." *Military Engineer* 38, no. 244 (February 1946): 70–74
Levie, Howard S. "The Employment of Prisoners of War." *American Journal of International Law* 57, no. 2 (April 1963): 318–53.
Levie, Howard S. "Penal Sanctions for Maltreatment of Prisoners of War." *American Journal of International Law* 56, no. 2 (April 1962): 433–68.
Levy, David M. "The German Anti-Nazi: A Case Study." *American Journal of Orthopsychiatry* 16 (1946): 507–15.
Lobdell, George H. "A Tale of Two Christmases at the Algona Prisoner-of-War Camp." *Palimpsest* 73, no. 4 (Winter 1997): 170–83.

Bibliography

Lunden, Walter A. "Captivity Psychosis among Prisoners of War." *Journal of Criminal Law and Criminology* 39, no. 6 (March–April 1949): 721–33.

MacKenzie, S. P. "The Treatment of Prisoners of War in World War II." *Journal of Modern History* 66, no. 3 (September 1944): 487–520.

Marguiles, Newton L. "Proper Treatment of War Prisoners." *Vital Speeches of the Day* no. 15 (May 15, 1945): 477–80.

Mason, John Brown. "German Prisoners of War in the United States." *American Journal of International Law* 34 (April 1945): 198–215.

Mason, John Brown. "Prisoners from the Master Race." *Infantry Journal* no. 53 (December 1943): 39–42.

Mazuzan, George T., and Nancy Walker. "Restricted Areas: German Prisoner of War Camps in Western New York, 1944–1946." *New York History* 59, no. 1 (January 1978): 54–72.

McCormack, Richard Blaine. "The San Patricio Deserters in the Mexican War." *Americas* 8, no. 2 (October 1951): 131–42.

McKnight, Maxwell S. "The Employment of Prisoners of War in the United States." *International Labour Review* 50 (July–December 1944): 47–64.

Moore, John Hammond. "Hitler's Afrika Korps . . . in New England." *Yankee*, June 1976, 82–88, 116.

Moore, John Hammond. "Hitler's Wehrmacht in Virginia, 1943–1946." *Virginia Magazine of History and Biography* 85, no. 3 (1977): 260–73.

Moore, John Hammond. "Italian POWs in America: War Is Not Always Hell." *Prologue: The Journal of the National Archives* 8 (Fall 1976): 141–51.

———. "Nazi Troopers in South Carolina, 1944–1946." *South Carolina Historical Magazine* 81, no. 4 (October 1980): 306–15.

Mormino, Gary R. "G.I. Joe Meets Jim Crow: Racial Violence and Reform in World War II Florida." *Florida Historical Quarterly* 73, no. 1 (July 1994): 23–42.

Moulton, William G. "Our Profession in Reverse: Teaching English to German Prisoners of War." *Modern Language Journal* 32, no. 6 (October 1948): 421–30.

O'Brien, Patrick, Thomas D. Isern, and R. Daniel Lumley. "Stalag Sunflower: German Prisoners of War in Kansas." *Kansas History* 7, no. 3 (Autumn 1984): 182–98.

Paschal, Allen W. "The Enemy in Colorado: German Prisoners of War, 1943–46." *Colorado* 56, no. 3–4 (Summer–Fall 1979): 119–42.

Peak, Helen. "Some Psychological Problems in the Re-education of Germans." *Journal of Social Issues* 2, no. 3 (August 1946): 26–39.

Pepin, John. *POW Camps in the U.P.* Marquette, Mich.: Mining Journal, 2000.

Pluth, Edward J. "Prisoner of War Employment in Minnesota during World War II." *Minnesota History* (Winter 1975): 290–303.

Pritchett, Merrill R., and William L. Shea. "The Afrika Korps in Arkansas, 1943–1946." *Arkansas Historical Quarterly* 37 no. 1 (Spring 1978): 3–22.

———. "Axis Prisoner-of-War Camps." *Journal of the West* 18, no. 2 (April 1979): 30–34.

———. "The Enemy in Mississippi 1943–1946." *Journal of Mississippi History* 41, no. 4 (1979): 351–71.

Radford, R. A. "The Economic Organization of A P.O.W. Camp." *Economica* 11 (November 1945): 189–201.

Reiss, Matthias. "Bronzed Bodies behind Barbed Wire: Masculinity and the Treatment of German Prisoners of War in the United States during World War II." *Journal of Military History* 69 (April 2005): 475–504.

Richter, Anton, ed. "A German P.O.W. at Camp Grant: The Reminiscences of Heinz Richter." *Journal of the Illinois State Historical Society* 76, no. 1 (Spring 1983): 61–70.

Root, Elihu. "Francis Lieber." *American Journal of International Law* 7, no. 3 (July 1913): 453–69.

Rosen, Stephen Peter. "Military Effectiveness: Why Society Matters." *International Security* 19, no. 4 (Spring 1995): 5–31.
Rundell, Walter, Jr. "Paying the POW in World War II." *Military Affairs* 22, no. 3 (Autumn 1958): 121–34.
Shea, William L., and Merrill R. Pritchett. "The Wehrmacht in Louisiana." *Louisiana History* 23, no. 1 (Winter 1982): 5–19.
Spencer, Ralph. "Prisoners of War in Cheyenne County, 1943–1946." *Nebraska State Historical Society* 63, no. 3 (Fall 1982): 438–49.
Spidle, Jake W. "Axis Invasion of the American West: POWs in New Mexico, 1942–1946." *New Mexico Historical Review* 49, no. 2 (April 1974): 92–122.
———. "Axis Prisoners of War in the United States, 1942–1946: A Bibliographical Essay." *Military Affairs* 39, no. 2 (April 1975): 61–66.
Stone, Raymond. "The American-German Conference on Prisoners of War." *American Journal of International Law* 13, no. 3 (July 1919): 406–49.
Stuart, Graham H. "War Prisoners and Internees in the United States." *American Foreign Service Journal* 21 (October 1944): 530–31, 568, 571–73.
Thompson, Antonio. "Winning the War behind the Lines: Colonel George Chescheir and the Axis POWs at Fort Benning, Georgia." *Register of the Kentucky Historical Society* 105, no. 3 (2007): 417–60.
Tissing, Robert Warren. "Stalag-Texas, 1943–1945: The Detention and Use of Prisoners of War in Texas during World War II." *Military History of Texas and the Southwest* 13 (Fall 1976): 23–34.
Tureen, Louis L., and James O. Palmer. "Some Group Differences in Personal Values between American Soldiers and German Prisoners of War." *Journal of Social Psychology* 42, (1955): 305–13.
Vance, Jonathan F. "Men in Manacles: The Shackling of Prisoners of War, 1942–1943." *Journal of Military History* 59, no. 3 (July 1995): 483–505.
Wages, Hazel. "Memphis Armed Service Forces Depot Prisoner of War Camp: 1944–1946." *Tennessee Historical Quarterly* 52 (Spring 1993): 19–32.
Walker, Chip. "German Creative Activities in Camp Aliceville, 1943–1946." *Alabama Review* 38, no. 1 (January 1985): 19–37.
Walker, Richard P. "The Swastika and the Lone Star: Nazi Activity in Texas POW Camps." *Military History of the Southwest* 19 (Spring 1989): 39–70.
Walzer, Michael. "Prisoners of War: Does the Fight Continue After the Battle?" *American Political Science Review* 63, no. 3 (September 1969): 777–86.
Warner, Richard S. "Barbed Wire and Nazilagers: PW Camps in Oklahoma." *Chronicles of Oklahoma* 64, no. 1 (Spring 1986): 37–67.
Wilson, Robert R. "Escaped Prisoners of War in Neutral Jurisdiction." *American Journal of International Law* 35, no. 3 (July 1941): 519–23.
Zimmerman, Harold. "Harvesting Peaches with German Prisoners of War." *Journal of the Western Slope* 2, no. 1 (Winter 1987): 18–21.

Magazines

"Anger at Nazi Atrocities Is Rising, but U.S. Treats Prisoners Fairly." *Newsweek*, May 7, 1945, 58.
Anonymous Sergeant. "Brave, Brave, Warriors." *Commonweal*, June 29, 1945, 261–62.
"Behind the Wire." *Time*, June 21, 1943, 67.
Blennemann, Ulrich. "Hitler's Other Foreign Legions." *Command: Military History, Strategy & Analysis*, November 1995, 65–67.
"Books for Prisoners of War." *Publishers Weekly*, May 22, 1943, 1970.

"Boss of 200,000 Enemies." *American,* January 1944–June 1944, 131.
Byrd, Martha H. "Captured by the Americans." *American History Illustrated,* February 1977, 24–35.
"The Captive Enemy." *Newsweek,* March 29, 1945, 32, 34.
Cassidy, Henry C. "What to Do with German Prisoners: The Russian Solution." *Atlantic Monthly,* November 1944, 43–45.
"Chicago Library Compiles Book List for Prisoners of War." *Publishers Weekly,* July 22, 1944, 241.
"Conditions of Employment of Prisoners of War." *Monthly Labor Review,* May 1943, 891–95.
Cook, Dave. "Fort Robinson Prisoner of War Camp Revisited." *Crawford Clipper's Northwest Nebraska Post,* September 1987, 2–5.
Cook, F. G. Alletson. "Democratic ABC's for Nazi PW's." *New York Times Magazine,* November 11, 1945, 8, 32.
———. "Nazi Prisoners Are Nazis Still." *New York Times Magazine,* November 21, 1943, 12, 38.
Davis, Jerome. "Millions Behind Barbed Wire." *Survey Graphic,* August 1942, 345–47.
"Death and Treason." *Newsweek,* February 5, 1945, 47–48.
Deutsch, Albert. "German PWs Living Better Than Our War Workers." *PM,* May 15, 1945, 6.
Devore, Robert. "Our 'Pampered' War Prisoners." *Collier's,* October 14, 1944, 14, 144.
"Escape in Arizona." *Time,* January 8, 1945, 16.
Fecurka, Peter R. "Se Hable Espanol Comrade? The Spanish Blue Division in Operation Barbarossa." *Command: Military History, Strategy & Analysis,* March–April 1994,
Frost, Meigs O. "Afrika Korps Veteran Flays Nazism, Tells of Torture." *Times-Picayune Sunday Magazine,* September 23, 1945, 2.
———. "New Orleans Test Tube for German Democracy." *Times-Picayune Sunday Magazine,* September 15, 1945, 1–2.
"German Atrocities Raise Questions: Are Nazi POWs 'Coddled' Here?" *Newsweek,* May 7, 1945, 60–61.
"German Prisoners." *Army and Navy Register,* April 28, 1945, 20.
"German Propaganda." *Army and Navy Register,* April 14, 1945, 8.
Hoover, J. Edgar. "Enemies at Large." *American,* April 1944, 17, 97–99.
Howes, Cecil. "Prisoners at Work." *Kansas,* 1944, 57–62.
Janta, Alexander. "The German Ego in Defeat." *Plain Talk,* April 1947, 10–13.
Kretzmann, P. E. "The Lutheran Commission for Prisoners of War." *Lutheran Witness,* December 1943, 421–26.
"The Kriegsmarine Escape." *Newsweek,* January 8, 1945, 33–34.
Kunzig, Robert Lowe. "360,000 PW's—the Hope of Germany." *American,* November 1946, 23, 132–37.
"Last of the Supermen." *Newsweek,* April 5, 1946, 20.
Lerch, Archer. "The Army Reports on Prisoners of War." *American Mercury,* May 1945, 536–47.
Lerch, Archer. "Handling German Prisoners in the United States." *Prisoners of War Bulletin,* May 1945, 4–5.
Lerner, Max. "The Chances Are Dark for a Democratic Germany." *PM,* March 26, 1945, 2–3.
"Life in a German Prison Camp." *Prisoners of War Bulletin,* February 1944, 4–5.
"Manpower Boost." *Business Week,* May 29, 1943, 20–22.
"Masquerader." *Time,* March 23, 1953, 25.
Meyer, Lawrence B. "A Plea for Prison Camp Literature." *Lutheran Witness,* September 14, 1943, 311.
"Midnight Massacre." *Time,* July 23, 1945, 24.
Mooth, Verla. "Memories of Christmas, 1944." *Good Old Days,* February 2001, 58–59.
Munoz, Antonio J. "Losing World War II: Nazi Racial and Recruitment Policies in the East." *Command: Military History, Strategy & Analysis,* November 1995, 58–67.
"The Nation: Enough Nazis." *Newsweek,* May 21, 1945, 38.

"Nazis in the U.S." *Time,* May 1, 1944, 64–65.
"No Converts?" *Time,* December 11, 1944, 24.
Pabel, Reinhold. "It's Easy to Bluff Americans." *Collier's,* May 16, 1953, 20–21.
Pierson, Ralph. "The Barbed-Wire Universities." *School and Society,* September 8, 1945, 156–58.
"Points System in Prison Camps." *Prisoners of War Bulletin,* August 1943, 9.
"Policies for Employment of Prisoners of War." *Monthly Labor Review,* July 1944, 93.
"Postwar Policies regarding Foreign Workers and Prisoners of War." *Monthly Labor Review,* November 1945, 910–12.
Powers, James H. "What to Do with German Prisoners: The American Muddle." *Atlantic Monthly,* November 1944, 46–50.
"POWs Outbound." *Newsweek,* May 28, 1945, 34.
"Priorities in Allocation of Services of Prisoners of War." *Monthly Labor Review,* June 1944, 1189.
"Prisoner of War Labor." *American City,* March 1944, 87.
"Prisoners' Dues?" *Business Week,* February 19, 1944, 94.
"Prisoners of War: Non-Germans Want to Go Back and Fight." *Military Police Training Bulletin,* January 1945, 33.
"P.W. Camp 168." *New Statesman and Nation,* July 21, 1945, 4.
"Re-educating the Nazis." *America,* August 26, 1944, 515.
"Reorienting the Supermen." *Newsweek,* January 10, 1944, 78.
"Repatriates Arrive Home from Germany." *Prisoners of War Bulletin,* December 19, 1943, 7.
Roberts, Tim. "POWs Spend Duration of War in Missouri." *Bearfacts,* February 1999.
Rutherford, John. "The Birthplace of Route 66: Lands O'Reilly General Army Hospital." *Show Me Route 66,* Spring 2002, 16–17.
"Set These Slaves Free." *Christian Century,* July 31, 1946, 933–34.
"Seven by the Rope." *Newsweek,* July 23, 1945, 27.
Shafer, Jack. "... And Here's How We Treat Captives." *PM,* May 1, 1945, 9.
Shays, Eugene. "German Prisoners of War in the U.S.: Observations of a Soldier." *Fourth International,* December 1945, 366–71.
Smith, Beverly. "The Afrika Korps Comes to America." *American,* August 1943, 28–29, 83–84.
———. "Nazi Supermen Hit the Dirt." *American,* July 1945, 45, 82
Smith, T. V. "Behind Barbed Wire." *Saturday Review of Literature,* May 4, 1946, 5–7, 43–44.
Stenbuck, Jack. "German War Prisoner for Democratic Leadership." *Magazine Digest,* December 1945, 66–72.
Stevens, Leland. "Thoroughly American." *Lutheran Witness,* May 1997, 14–16.
Strong, Tracy. "Prisoners under the Law." *Christian Century,* April 14, 1943, 455–57.
"Studies and Sports in German Prison Camps." *Prisoners of War Bulletin,* September 1943, 1, 5.
"Swastika over Arizona." *Newsweek,* February 26, 1945, 58.
"Treatment of War Prisoners." *Army and Navy Register,* May 5, 1945, 8.
"Uncle Sam in the Slave Trade." *Christian Century,* June 12, 1946, 24.
"Utilize Prisoners of War." *Army and Navy Journal,* May 13, 1944, 96.
"War over Prisoners." *Newsweek,* November 2, 1942, 24.
"War Prisoners Opposed." *Business Week,* January 15, 1944, 96.
Worall, Janet E. "Prisoners on the Home Front: Community Reactions to German and Italian POWS in Northern Colorado, 1943–1946." *Colorado Heritage,* 1990: 32–47.
"The YMCA War Prisoners' Aid Offers Educational Assistance." *School and Society,* May 6, 1944, 325.
Yochum, H. L. "I Went to a POW Camp." *Lutheran Outlook,* March 1946, 72.

Interviews and Oral Histories

Biallas, Friedrich. Correspondence with Jerry Yocum and the Camp Algona POW Project Committee, February and March 2002. Oral history from the Wartime Memories Project.
Blumenberg, Horst. Interview by Antonio Thompson, Spring and Summer 2007.
Columbia, Bill. Interview by Antonio Thompson, 2005.
Ellis, Patricia. Interview by Antonio Thompson, Summer 2005.
Erichsen, Heino R. Interview by Antonio Thompson, Summer 2005.
Gardner, Paul. Interview by Antonio Thompson, 1999.
James, Barbara. Interview by Antonio Thompson, March 2007.
Lilly, Mary Ellen. Interview by Antonio Thompson, 2006.
Mathis, Walter. Interview by Antonio Thompson, Summer 2005.
Mathis, Junior. Interview by Antonio Thompson, Fall 2005.
McCullough, Jim. Interview by Antonio Thompson, 2006
McGhee, Monroe. Interview by Antonio Thompson, 2006.
Mengelberg, Paul. Interview by Antonio Thompson, August 2005.
Pool, Myron. Interview by Antonio Thompson, May 2000.
Radford, Ed. Interview by Antonio Thompson, May 11, 2000.
Rudd, Margaret. Interview by Antonio Thompson, 2005.
Stiles, Jim. Interview by Antonio Thompson, August, 2005.
Tromp, Howard. Interview by Antonio Thompson, May 2006 and August 2005.

Newspapers

Atlanta Daily World
Cadiz (KY) Record
Cambria (WI) News
Clarksville (TN) Leaf-Chronicle
Concordia (KS) Blade-Empire
Cudahy (WI) Reminder
Des Moines (MI) Register
Kansan
Kansas (MO) City Star
Kentucky New Era
Los Angeles Times
Louisville (KY) Courier-Journal
Manitowoc (WI) Herald Times
Miami (FL) Daily News
Milwaukee (WI) Journal
New Orleans (LA) Times-Picayune
New York Times
Owensboro (KY) Messenger
Palm Beach (FL) Post
Park City (Bowling Green, KY) Daily News
Portland Press Herald / Maine Sunday Telegram
Santa Maria (CA) Daily Times.
Tennessean
Union County (KY) Advocate

Index

Afrika Korps, 21, 25, 32, 34–35, 37, 39, 41, 47
Agriculture, 86–87, 89, 114, 115; U.S. Department of, 81–83
Aiken, SC, Camp, 41
Algona, ID, Camp, 86, 93, 96, 139n40, 149n43
Aliceville, AL, Camp, 11, 47, 109, 154n38
Alva, OK, Camp, 67–68, 104, 126, 147n59
American Free Corps, 20
Anti Bolshevik Legion, 17
Anti Nazi, 15, 20, 37–39, 41, 43, 46, 64–68, 118–19, 121–23, 126, 132, 143n45, 146–47nn50–56
Army Service Forces (ASF), 2–3, 6–8, 11, 29, 70, 77–78, 87, 94, 103–4, 106, 109, 115, 119, 125, 135n11, 137n64, 140n61, 140n77, 150n45, 150n47
Atlanta, NE, Camp, 52
Atterbury, IN, Camp, 88
Austria, 16–17, 43–44, 142n36
Austrian, 17, 32, 43–44, 46, 65, 143n45
AuTrain, MI, Camp, 36, 94

Barkeley, TX, Camp, 51
Barrows, Col. R. G., 13, 138n70
Bavarian, 34
Behrens, Karl, 48
Belgium, 68, 131
Bertucci, Clarence, 51
Beyer, Walter, 37, 40–41, 141n16
Biallas, Friedrich, 25, 139n40
Blanding, FL, Camp, 39, 68
books (for POWs), 66, 105, 112–15, 118–19
Breckinridge, KY, Camp, 111
British Free Corps, 20
Bryan, Gen. Blackshear M., Assistant PMGO, 4, 11, 14, 67, 82, 88–89, 108–9, 137n58, 138n72, 150n55, 154n34, 155n54
bread and water, 97
boxing, 107

Butner, NC, Camp, 68, 111, 119
Byrd, Lt. Col. Carl, 65, 146n51

Campbell, KY, Camp, 65–68, 111, 146n50, 146n52, 163, 165
canneries, 95, 151n91
canteen, 12, 49, 74, 76, 84, 97, 107, 109–10, 114, 118–19
Carson, CO, Camp, 32, 51
Casablanca, Morocco, 21, 27
Chescheir, Col. George, 72
Claiborne, LA, Camp, 53
Clarinda, IA, Camp, 61
Clark, MO, Camp, 51, 144n85
Clewiston, FL, Camp, 45, 47–48, 90
College, POWs, 45, 114
Communists, 19, 37–38
Concordia, KS, Camp, 34, 41, 45–47, 60–61, 96, 140n80, 140n82, 141n86, 142n24, 142n45, 143n52
Cooke, CA, Camp, 57, 58, 105, 113, 139n39, 155n59, 160
concentration camps, 19, 120
Crossville, TN, Camp, 35, 38, 44–45, 48–50, 58, 68–69, 111, 143n65, 143n73, 147n61
Czechoslovakia, 18, 35, 68, 130

Death's Head, 18
Denmark, 17
Dermott, AR, Camp, 94
Der Ruf, 117–20
DuPont, DE, Fort, 38, 105

Eastern Legion, 19
Ehrenburg, Ilya, 23
Ehrmann, Henry, 120, 123, 126, 157n27

Eisenhower, Dwight D., 80
Erichsen, Heino, POW, 76, 131, 158n7
escapes, 48, 55, 58, 109

Farrand, Maj. Stephen M., 12, 137n65
Federal Bureau of Investigations (FBI), 4, 54
Finland, 19
Flanders Legion, 17
Florence, AZ, Camp, 58, 137–38n66
Forrest, TN, Camp, 106–7, 115, 146n48, 149n40
Fort Benning, GA, 72, 74, 76
Fort Bliss, TX, 52
Fort Devens, ME, 12–13, 65, 67–68, 137–38n66
Fort Dix, NJ, 52, 91, 140n58
Fort Eustis, VA, 117, 122–26, 144n91, 147n59
Fort Getty, RI, 117, 122–23, 157n24
Fort Gordon, GA, 38, 53
Fort Knox, KY, 73, 76, 131, 151n94, 153n18, 154–55n40, 156n75
Fort Leavenworth, KS, 41, 43, 64
Fort McClellan, AL, 34
Fort Meade, MD, 30
Fort Oglethorpe, GA, 108
Fort Patrick, VA, 51
Fort Warren, WY, 111
Fort Wetherill, RI, 117, 122–23
France, 16, 22, 30, 33, 38–39, 68, 77, 80, 118, 123, 130
Franco, Francisco, 18
Frikorps, Danish, 17

Gaertner, Georg, POW, 25–26, 139n41
Gauss, Erich, 41
Geneva Convention, ix–x, xii–xiii, 1–2, 4, 6–8, 10–11, 23, 27, 43, 48, 50, 56, 58–59, 61–63, 66, 69–70, 77–79, 85, 88–89, 93–95. 97, 102–4, 108, 114, 116–17, 125, 127, 129–30, 132–34, 135n3, 142n34, 148n3
Glasgow, Scotland, 28
Goebeler, Hans, POW, 91–92, 150n72
Grant, IL, Camp, 12–13, 31, 86, 131, 138n67–71, 140n66
Gruber, OK, Camp, 37, 39, 114
guards, 8–10, 25, 27, 31, 34–35, 37, 39–40, 42–44, 46–58, 60, 62, 64, 66, 69–70, 74, 77, 85, 87,
90–91, 93–95, 97–98, 105, 107, 121–22, 129, 133–34
Guillion, Allen, Provost Marshal General, 2, 5, 79, 80, 82, 108, 154n33
Guillion, Edmund, Head of Internees Section, 5
Günther, Horst, 41

Hackbarth, Karl-Heinz, 22
Halifax, Canada, 29
Halloran General Hospital, NY, 118
Harless, Richard, 62–63
Hearne, TX, Camp, 42, 92, 142
Hellfritsch, Wolfgang Hermann, 48
Hilfswillige (Hiwi's), 19, 138n14
Hitler, Adolph, 17–20, 22, 24, 35, 44, 53, 60, 64, 103, 106, 122, 132
Holy Ghost, 37, 42, 45
Hörner, Helmut, 29, 38, 84, 96, 129–31, 140n59
Humphrey, Yvonne, 27, 28, 140n50
Hungarian, 19
Hungary, 19

Indian(s), 20; Legion, 20
Indiantown Gap Military Reservation, PA, 52, 106, 107, 109, 115, 144n95, 147n64, 153n18, 154n28, 154–55n40, 156n75
Internees Section, 5, 104, 136n20
Irish, 20; Legion, 20
Italian(s), 5, 15–17, 21, 25, 30, 35, 44–45, 51, 58–59, 84, 89, 93–94, 130, 132–33; Service Units (ISU), 45, 53
Italy, ix, 16, 19, 21–22, 26, 32, 45

Japanese, ix, xiii, 5, 16–17, 30, 59, 69, 84, 130

Kohlhaas, Radbert, 38
Knappe, Siegfried, 23, 139n33
Krauss, Hugo, 42
Kriegsmarine, 21, 37
Kunze, Johannes, 37, 39–41, 57, 141n12, 142n23
Kunzig, Robert, 120

Labor Union, 9, 78, 82–83, 98–101, 118, 129–31
Ladwig, Eberhard, 25, 28
Lerch, Archer, PMGO, 63, 64, 104, 146n42
Livingston, LA, Camp, 52
Lohmann, Paul, POW, 29, 33, 89, 91, 140n58
Leonard Wood, MO, 50, 144n83
Lodi, WI, Camp, 90
Luck, Col. Hans von, 24, 139n34
Luftwaffe, 25, 37
Lutheran Commission, 4, 11, 105, 113, 153n14

Marshall, George C., 2, 6, 80, 81
Maxey, TX, Camp, 92
McAlester, OK, Camp, 38
McCain, MS, Camp, 39, 65, 68
McKnight, Maj. Maxwell, 50, 104, 122–23, 136n42, 153n6, 157n25
McLean, TX, 26
Memphis, ASF Depot, TN, 11–12, 104, 106, 109, 115, 137n58, 150n55, 153n5, 154n25, 154n39
Mengelberg, Paul, POW, 27
Military Police Corps (MPC), 1–2, 4, 6, 10
Mongolian, xiiii
Moulton, William, 120
Mussolini, Benito, 35

Nazi(s), ix, x, 9, 11, 14–18, 20–21, 25–26, 29, 32–47, 49, 53–55, 59, 61–68, 71, 87, 97, 104–6, 111, 117–19, 121–23, 126, 132–33
Neuland, Maj. Paul, 52, 144n91, 147n59, 153n5
New Orleans, point of embarkation, 129
Non-Germans, 15–18, 32, 37, 41, 43, 65–66, 68
Nordwest, Regiment, 17

Oran, Algeria, North Africa holding camp, 21, 25–26, 28
Opp, Frederick, 40
orchestra, 109

Pabel, Reinhold, POW, 26, 27, 31, 90, 106, 131, 134, 139n43
Papago Park, AZ, Camp, 58, 68, 143n65
Penal Division (999th), 20–22, 41, 139n19

Peary, VA, Camp, 69
Perry, OH, Camp, 97
Petsch, Lt. Col. Alfred C., 40
ping pong, 56, 106, 107
plays, 109, 113
Provost Marshal General's Office (PMGO), 1–3, 6–7, 12, 30, 39, 42–43, 61–62, 77–78, 82, 103–5, 108, 112, 114, 119–23, 125
Prussian, 20

Red Cross (International Red Cross, IRC), ix, xiii, 4, 6, 11–12, 47, 60, 63, 85, 108–9, 112–13
Richmond ASF Depot, 119
Richter, Heinz, 30–31, 89, 140n66
Robinson, AR, Camp, 52, 94
Romania, 19
Roosevelt, Franklin D., 42, 92
Rupert, LA, Camp, 97, 153n20, 154n24
Rupprecht, George, 66
Russian, 23–24, 69, 118
Ruston, LA, Camp, 73, 75, 91, 150

Sakamaki, Kazuo, 5
Schmidt, Fritz, 23, 139n32
Schoenstedt, Walter, 66, 120, 147n57, 157n15
Seydewitz, Max, 19, 139n18
Shanks, NY, Camp, 29, 107, 113, 115, 129, 131, 154n24, 156n62
Sharpe, Camp, 109
Shelby, MS, Camp, 31, 89, 95, 96, 101, 106–7, 113, 140n68, 153n20, 154n24, 156n60
Shulz, Erwin, 21
Smith, Maj. Henry, 120
Smith, Maj. Howard, 12
Smith, Col. Leonard, 52
Smith, Col. T. V., 120
soccer, 44, 46, 106, 107
Socialist, 16, 19, 37–38, 60
Solbücher, 29, 84
Somervell, Maj. Gen. Brehon B., 2, 70, 79–81, 85, 14872n
Soviet Union, ix, xiii, 16–20, 23–24, 42, 69, 118, 130
Spanish Blue Division (DEV), 18, 138n8, 158n4
Special Projects Division, 50, 69–70, 104, 117, 119, 122, 142n36, 144n91

Stark, NH, Camp, 39, 93, 141n10
State Department, 4-6, 12, 69
Stimson, Henry L., Secretary of War, 2, 6, 69
Stockton, CA, Camp, 97
Straub, Rudolf, 41
suicide, among POWS, 33, 39, 41, 43, 45-46, 48, 143n56
Swiss Legation, 4, 12, 39

Tromp, Howard, POW, 28-29, 32
Tropschuh, Felix, POW, 41, 46
Tonkawa, OK, Camp, 39
Tynes, Lt. Col. A. L., 13-14, 138n71

Ulio, Maj. Gen. J. A., 70, 148n72, 149n26, 152n111, 155n44

Veltin, Franz, 38
Vienna, 44
Viking Division, 18

Waffen SS, 17
Walter Reed Hospital, 80
Walther, Berndt von, 39
War Food Administration, 4, 77
War Manpower Commission (WMC), 4, 77, 81-83, 88, 90, 98-101, 150n51, 152n121
War Production Board, 92
Wattenberg, Jürgen, POW, 48
Wehrmacht, xiii, 15-16, 18-20, 23-24, 32, 37-38, 42, 45, 104, 132, 142n23
Westland, Regiment, 17

Young Men's Christian Association (YMCA), 4, 11, 109-10, 112-15